STRAIGHT TALK FOR MONDAY MORNING

"Allan Cox demonstrates yet again in *Straight Talk* that he is one of the very few people who understands how the behavioral aspects of management are embedded in executive hierarchical organization. This is rich material."

Elliott Jaques, M.D., Ph.D.
Author, *Requisite Organization*

"Cox's latest is a book of big ideas, with chatty anecdotes as metaphors for change. Simply put but not simplistic, it will energize readers to aim for higher *quality* in their work. This is a book ripe for the manager of the '90s and many will adapt his 20 chapters into fresh-thinking, new management training programs."

Madelyn Jennings
Senior Vice President
Gannett Company

"Cox always is easy-to-read. In *Straight Talk* he brings us face-to-face with basic truths we neglect. Then he offers surprising insights on the challenges we all encounter. This is a timely book that works; it's for managers committed to making teamwork real in their organizations."

George V. Grune
Chairman and CEO
The Reader's Digest Association, Inc.

"Teamwork is demanded of us if our businesses are to succeed in a fast-changing world. That's why you must read Allan Cox's *Straight Talk*. Cox is clear and practical on the subject; a right-thinking enabler for the modern manager."

Richard G. Capen
Vice Chairman
Knight-Ridder Newspapers, Inc.

"In *Straight Talk for Monday Morning*, Allan Cox translates group relations theory into essential, practical applications for those who manage organizations. Refreshingly, this book aims to maximize team effectiveness while emphasizing that the team consists of individuals whose unique qualities need not be—dare not be—sacrificed for the myth of 'the greater good.' "

> Robert F. Baxter, M.D.
> President
> A. K. Rice Institute
> Director, Child Psychiatric Services
> School of Medicine
> University of Louisville

"In *Straight Talk* Allan Cox lays out uncanny insights on how employees and managements alike are able to thrive in teams. The payoff is obvious. Organizations that follow his advice will find themselves pulling together, not apart."

> Kenneth Blanchard
> Co-author, *The One-Minute Manager*

"What a rarity is this confusing world. Here is a powerful book, filled with business wisdom and strategies that anyone can apply for greater success and yet it is so well written that it was a joy to read! Wow!"

> Og Mandino
> Author/Speaker

"As you read this book, you quickly begin to understand that it's not just what you don't know about teamwork that hurts you, it's what you do know about it that's simply not true.

"Allan Cox articulates well the 'Big Idea' for the '90s—empowered employees working together in teams whose caring for and sharing with each other in open, truthful relationships changes the game from simply making this month's numbers to unleashing the power of the corporation's human resources, thus creating a new dimension of competitive advantage in the marketplace.

"Cox makes it easily understood that the future belongs to those corporations which best understand and execute the principle which says the individual wins when the team wins."

> Louis A. Pritchett
> Vice President–Sales (retired)
> Procter & Gamble Company

"*Straight Talk for Monday Morning* is described as a book about teamwork. But most of us will recognize that it is really a book about *leadership*, the most treasured quality in any organization. With penetrating, action-oriented, real-life insights, Allan Cox tells us more about harnessing the power of an organization than most managers will learn in a lifetime."

> Robert H. Beeby
> President & CEO
> Frito-Lay, Inc.

"Cox lays it out for us. His ideas are clear, to the point, supported by action plans, and in tune with today's performance issues and work force. *Straight Talk* adds brilliant pieces to the management mosaic."

> Robert A. Montgomery
> Vice President–U.S. Grocery Products
> Human Resources
> The Quaker Oats Company

"There's never been a time when Americans in business have been so tested by competition. Allan Cox has been giving us insight and encouragement for years. His latest book serves well those who want to stand up and be counted."

> John G. Breen
> Chairman and CEO
> The Sherwin-Williams Company

"As with his past work, Cox has done an outstanding job of distilling a complex range of ideas into a crisp, concise set of basic elements. This time his subjects are authenticity and teamwork. Want to learn how the relationship of these two critical factors has a powerful impact on corporate performance? Then read this book."

> Sid Burkett
> Vice President, Organization
>   Development
> Cargill, Incorporated

"Cox makes being an effective member or leader of a team an intensely personal business. He clarifies that such effectiveness on the team is much more a matter of what you do than what others do. Here is a book that skillfully charts the larger significance of the team while showing sensitivity to the detail of high-performance teamwork—sensitivity that is provocative and stimulating."

Roger W. Heyns
President
The William and Flora Hewlett
    Foundation
Former Chancellor
University of California at Berkeley

"This book states complex management philosophies in 'plain talk.' It makes for very enjoyable reading."

Ronald P. Carzoli
Vice President–Human Resources
Joseph E. Seagram & Sons, Inc.

"The pace and competitiveness of the '90s will make the collaboration of efficiency and effectiveness imperative for the successful enterprise. That's why Allan Cox's 'straight talk' about unleashing the energy and leverage of the team is so timely and right on the mark!"

Kendrick B. Melrose
Chairman and CEO
The Toro Company

"The unique ingredient to competitiveness in any organization can only be produced through people. Companies can be bought and sold, products can come and go, but nothing rivals a dedicated team of people. GE's Jack Welch says it's the single most important advantage America has, yet how many of us make use of it? If Allan Cox's *Straight Talk* can push this to the top of CEOs' agendas, it will perform a national service greater than *In Search of Excellence*."

J. P. Donlon
Editor
Chief Executive Magazine

"Allan Cox's sensitive and thoughtful work provides gentle but telling nudges—real learning—not glib pronouncements. Here are pleasantly revealing observations of behavior designed to quicken the response and increase the effectiveness of any size organization."

Preston Townley
President and CEO
The Conference Board

"*Straight Talk* is most always welcome, even on Monday morning, especially when it comes from Allan Cox. In his entertaining, no-nonsense style, Cox gives us both the principles and practical examples for empowering teams through different stages. This is a full-course meal, with plenty of meat, but it's presented in light style in bite-size sections. I come away with a value-based, vitamin-packed formula for becoming a more authentic team member and leader."

Ken Shelton
Editor
Executive Excellence Magazine

"Allan Cox has tossed off all the teamwork clichés and added many new insights to how to bring teams alive! Don't read this book alone: Have your own team read it, discuss it, debate it, apply it—and become a better team for having done so."

Tom Brown
Management Columnist
Industry Week

"Allan Cox can always be counted on to get managers thinking. In *Straight Talk* he confronts *the* issue for the '90s and beyond, how to build, motivate, and empower the team with solid advice, wit, and clarity."

Marilyn Moats Kennedy
Author, *Office Politics*
Job Strategies Editor, *Glamour*

"Straight Talk for Monday Morning is among the best of the breed. Allan Cox attends to the heart and soul of the matter while providing specific prescriptions for action. This book neatly and crisply covers the key issues which challange today's managers. His development of such crucial concepts as 'empowerment' reflects keen analysis strengthened by broad and deep organizational experience. With a lively, spirited text that both encourages and coaches, *Straight Talk* deserves a spot on the short list of knowledgeable, readable, helpful contemporary treatises on leadership and management."

> Walter F. Ulmer, Jr.
> President
> Center for Creative Leadership

"Empowered teams, with 'full voices' making 'superior choices.' *Leadership* charged with putting 'red blood back into blue-blooded management.' With intelligence and an almost palpable authenticity, Allan Cox sensitizes us to the source of our power as individuals and teams.

"Break open this book and discover a straightforward, actionable agenda. This is reading for every leader who intends to do more than dream about sustained competitive advantage."

> Mary Anne Williams
> Director, Corporate Education
> Eastman Kodak Company

"No manager would dare call teamwork a cliché after reading Cox's results-oriented, action-driven primer on how to get the best from people. He makes is clear why *team catalyst* may be the most important job description for survival in the '90s. *Straight Talk* will change the way you start Monday mornings."

> Darryl Hartley-Leonard
> President
> Hyatt Hotels Corporation

"Allan Cox's new book provides extraordinary insights and ideas that can turn a collection of individual managers into a high-performance team."

Myron Kandel
On-Air Host
CNN's "Inside Business"

"If you're one of those people who thinks authenticity has its place at work, you'll find much to encourage you in Allan Cox's latest book. Clean and direct as always, he provokes thought and action with his analysis of tcam-oriented behavior on the job."

Patricia Galagan
Editor
Training & Development Journal

"Allan Cox does a great job of integrating the 'I' and the 'we' and showing the enormous leverage of an empowered team—an imperative for organizations to be competitive in the '90s and beyond."

Robert H. Murphy
Senior Vice President
Organization & Human Resources
Rockwell International

"Allan Cox has always been a contrarian with insight and style—his observations about consensual decisionmaking hit home at what every senior manager intuitively feels but can't articulate."

Dana G. Mead
Executive Vice President
International Paper Company

"Provocative, insightful, practical—outstanding! *Straight Talk* is an absolute must for individuals who see themselves as team leaders."

Bruce R. Rismiller
Executive Vice President
Northwest Airlines

"Allan Cox distills essential principles of behavior, uniting them meaningfully and intelligently with first-rate management standards and old fashioned common sense. The end result is a tremendously useful book for all executives and leaders."

Henry B. Betts, M.D.
President and CEO
Rehabilitation Institute of Chicago

"Almost as good as having Allan Cox in person!"

Thomas J. Keller
Vice President
Corporate Communications
Siemens Corporation

ALSO BY ALLAN COX

Confessions of a Corporate Headhunter

Work, Love and Friendship: Reflections on Executive Lifestyle

Inside Corporate America

The Making of the Achiever

The Achiever's Profile

STRAIGHT TALK FOR MONDAY MORNING

STRAIGHT TALK FOR MONDAY MORNING

Creating Values, Vision, and Vitality at Work

Allan Cox

JOHN WILEY & SONS, INC.

New York • Chichester • Brisbane • Toronto • Singapore

For Carla, Deb, Doug, Gary, Joe, John, Kathy, Nancy,
Rick and Russ—who rallied round.

The article in appendix B is reprinted with permission from *Chief Executive* (March/April 1989). Copyright, Chief Executive Publishing, 233 Park Avenue South, New York, NY 10003. All rights reserved.

The publisher wishes to thank the editor of *Training and Development Journal* for permission to reprint "Maintaining Maximum Impact" that appears in appendix C. This article, with minor changes, was published in the September 1988 issue.

Recognizing the importance of preserving what is written, it is a policy of John Wiley & Sons., Inc., to have books of enduring value published in the United States printed on acid-free paper, and we exert our best efforts to that end.

Library of Congress Cataloging in Publication Data

Cox, Allan, 1937–
  Straight talk for monday morning / by Allan Cox.
    p.   cm.
  ISBN 0-471-52888-9
  1. Work groups. 2. Leadership. I. Title.
HD66.C59 1990
658.4—dc20

90-35356
CIP

Printed in the United States of America

90 91 10 9 8 7 6 5 4 3 2

DISCLAIMERS AND PROCLAMATIONS

God blesses still the generous thought,
And still the fitting word He speeds,
And Truth, at His requiring taught,
He quickens into deeds.

JOHN GREENLEAF WHITTIER

Straight Talk for Monday Morning, as its central purpose, shows you how to lay claim to your personal *authenticity* at work. Yet it does so by demonstrating the power that authenticity can have not only on you but also on the people with whom you work, the members of your team. It unites the concerns of the "I" and the "we" through short essays and fast takes on the essential lessons these essays teach us. Here's a glimpse of what follows:

Getting Smarter with Dumb Questions: how to admit that you don't know something and still come out ahead.

Diving Over the Dummies and *With Wings of Eagles*: how to chip away at the barnacles of your neglected strengths.

Saying No to Intimidation: the fine art of choosing your fights.

Inappropriate Intensity: why the world belongs to enthusiasts who keep cool.

Sacred Cows and the Truly Sacred: why you need to count the deadlines and commitments you've agreed to as a sacred trust.

The vitality and directness implicit in the book's title is indirectly inspired by definitions from the dictionary for *quicken*, the word that best captures my intent for your declaration of self in this undertaking, and is essentially another shading on authenticity itself. These definitions include "to make more rapid," but also "to give or restore vigor," "to animate or revive, restore life to," and "to become alive, receive life." Your empowered *team*, moreover, is one that has been quickened by, and in turn quickens, its members. It's faster, deeper, more vigorous. It's enriched.

An empowered team is a team of wholeness.

Other threads are woven into this book's fabric as well. For example, on the issue of speed alone, a growing body of literature in management underscores that fast responses in its initiatives validate a corporation's health and foreshadow its future viability. In the December 4, 1989 issue of *Industry Week*, Intel CEO Andrew Grove honors such speed by saying his company has to be faster: "Faster in responding to market opportunities, faster in responding to customer needs, and more cost-oriented. We have to understand our business better so that we can provide complete, ready-to-use building blocks rather than pieces that will require the customer a year to put together."

An empowered team is fast and resourceful.

Further, the emphasis in this book on *collaboration without consensus*—time-wasting, action-impeding, energy-sapping, mediocrity-inducing consensus—stands in support of quickened performance to meet the needs of those who count on us.

An empowered team is a decisive one that delivers the goods.

Then, too, the very format of the book itself is a quickened response. It's a fast-take, in-and-out, thematic treatment of 100 short subjects, each of which is designed to coach you to claim your authenticity and thereby empower your team. But relax; I won't wear you out with unnecessary references to an "empowered" team. You know already, I'll bet, that I'm just laying the groundwork, and that when I refer to "team," I'll be thinking of a functioning unit that is, in a word, empowered. By that I mean whole, resourceful, decisive, and dependable.

It's important that you not be led astray as you begin reading. Please know up front that this isn't a team-building manual. First of all, as you'll soon read in the introduction, I have an aversion to the term *team-building* itself. Second, and more important, there already are numerous such manuals on the market, and I don't believe the world of management is clamoring for another one from me. The works that I cite in "A Closing Word" on page 338 are among the very best offerings in this field. I enthusiastically point you to them.

Rather, what I want to do here is cast a small net to catch the attention of that executive or professional (you?) who recoils from touchy-feely methods and jargon, yet knows vigorous teamwork is imperative in today's complex climate for the sake of competitive advantage. This executive doubts that all the "team talk" of late is reflective of the genuine article and knows for sure he or she is not part of a true team effort, but wants to be.

Ultimately, as the opening paragraphs above hint, this is a book of values. Authenticity demands that you grab hold of your most deeply held values, take them out of hiding, shake them loose, and vigorously put them in place on the job. As documentation to my point that this is a book of values, note that chapter XI, "Exploring Values: Organizational Savvy and Reaping the Human Harvest," is the longest one. Yet the values I espouse are apparent on virtually every page of this volume. They declare the authentic state of humanity is union . . . collaboration . . . belonging . . . shared competence. I believe this is how man is at his best, at home with himself, and the optimal contributor to the human community.

That's the lofty view, to be sure, but you won't be short-changed on the nitty-gritty underside either. You'll be given directions—more than you'll sometimes want—on how your authenticity unavoidably translates to actions that make team a vital part of your work life. If you take the lessons of these pages to heart, you'll become known and appreciated for your team style. You truly can become the catalyst for ensuring that you and your associates enjoy the competitive advantage of teamwork. And this without selling out your own uniqueness.

This book is equally concerned with team effectiveness, but for many people may be a better starting point. This is because it rejects consensus seeking as a positive influence in team efforts, whereas the typical manual pays homage to it. In addition, as you've begun to sense by now, this book is aimed at the *individual* executive who wants to understand what it takes to stake a claim to his or her authenticity and be a team catalyst. It answers two questions: What's involved? and How do I get up to speed?

Summing up, seven major themes permeate this book. They are all shafts of light that illuminate various facets of human authenticity and their role in team effectiveness. I have touched on six of them already:

1. *Today's management style of necessity is one of quickened response.* This is accomplished best through the power of the team. A quickened team is an enabling one that makes its members perform faster, smarter, and better. Given our need for competitive advantage, we do well to remember the Biblical distinction between the quick and the dead!

2. *The need to belong is a powerful human force that finds expression in teamwork.* A person wants to feel his or her work is bigger than his or her job.

3. *Consensus seeking is a time-wasting, leveling influence that impedes distinctive performance.* It is a false ideal that must be rejected.

4. *The authentic state of humanity is union, and, ironically, this state enhances one's uniqueness.*

5. *Belief in men and women as social beings is a lofty one and is best authenticated with down-to-earth performance.* This book spins simple parables and follows them up with nitty-gritty action steps.

6. *A team catalyst is an individual who takes upon himself or herself the responsibility for modeling actions and attitudes that support shared competence.* This book is designed for that catalytic executive. That catalytic executive can be you!

The remaining theme is:

7. *Exercising vision is developing an understanding of where you are and where you're headed—both as an individual and as an organization.*

Each of the 20 chapters of *Straight Talk* begins with a brief description of how one or more of these themes is pertinent to the subject of that chapter.

Allan Cox
Chicago, Illinois

CONTENTS

—————————— REACHING ——————————

DELIVERING

INTRODUCTION

To find new things, take the path you took yesterday.

JOHN BURROUGHS

Personally, I'm bidding a thankful farewell to the 1980s. Generalizations are usually unfair but the last decade leaned too far in my opinion in the direction of greed and a "competition without scruples." Almost anything seemed to be acceptable in the quest for success. But excess at some point usually begins to tilt in the other direction and I think that we're beginning to see that now. Many feel that they've enjoyed career success at the expense of family, leisure time, and an ability to appreciate other things in life.

But, you say, you still need a successful career not only for material concerns but because it's also an important cornerstone in life. I couldn't agree more. And what I'm trying to do in *Straight Talk* is provide the ideas and values for a new success ethic. What follows are small but powerful moves you can start using today: the power of an authentic smile . . . telling someone that they're in trouble . . . why consensus doesn't work . . . letting others know when you're not getting what you need . . . sharing yourself . . . becoming the authentic you.

1

Fine, you say. But how do these "mom and apple pie" sentiments fit in with the hard nosed corporate world. To make my case I offer David Luther, a quality czar at Corning, Inc., as an example. Talk with him as I did recently about the outstanding quality program that he and his associates launched and you'll find that he knows his stuff. This company now defines quality at their plants as no more than five defective parts per million. You can see they aren't fooling around.

When the program began, Luther and his colleagues placed their emphasis in technical areas like statistics and problem-solving techniques. Get these big moves right, they reasoned, and we'll have the quality that we need.

But within a year they found that something was missing—the small day-to-day moves that help people feel that they're an important part of the big picture, that they belong, that they don't leave their authenticity at the door when they report to work, that they are part of a team. "Despite rigorous planning and the best intentions, we found that we were running into a brick wall," says Luther. "Today, the course where we teach everyone in the corporation from the executive suite to the shop floor how to make these so-called small moves has made the difference between success and failure."

This core component anchors Corning's efforts, because they learned that teamwork won't happen by chance and that without teamwork, quality can't go forward. Luther puts it this way: "The energy source for quality is the team. After all these years, we're still stunned at the ideas that emerge from our teams. Managing quality is largely knowing when to get out of the way."

From the plant floor to the CEO's office at corporate headquarters, from a local sales office to interregional and multifunctional networks halfway around the world, teamwork is igniting superior performance in American industry. It has turned up the heat for the 1990s and will fuel our formidable efforts at regaining lost ground here at home and around the globe.

This book quietly but intensely feeds the fire. These introductory pages are a primer on the building blocks of team effectiveness. The heart of the book—its 20 chapters—is made up of 100 short essays written between early 1988 and early 1990. Each essay was inspired by a question that prompts a point of view supporting personal authenticity and team effort. For optimal learning, I recommend that you mark your answers to all 100 questions (compiled in appendix A) before reading the essays. The question number corresponds to the number of the essay that it prompted.

Each essay concludes with two "take action" steps that set new directions so you can improve your performance as a team-style executive. As you'll see, I draw heavily on my own experience to probe the subjects of the essays. Further, each chapter is devoted to a behavioral dimension of authenticity required for team effectiveness and concludes with the essential lessons, called "fast takes," drawn from the essays of that chapter. Finally, you can tally your own "team-style profile" based on your answers to the 100 questions.

On this final feature, I'm the first to admit that taking stock of yourself in this way hardly meets the canons of rigorous science. After all, I made up the questions and arbitrarily judged the correct answers. Nonetheless, such an exercise offers the eager learner food for thought and some loose measure of your team-style competence. If your team-style profile results in a rotten score, you'd be ill advised to lay too much blame on poor science.

I had an even more sobering thought while drafting the questions for each chapter: It's one thing for me to answer them, but how would my associates respond if they were asked these questions about me? I'm certain I'm easier on myself than they would be. But, of course, they'd be right, not I!

The Fear of the Familiar

A cautionary note is in order. And I sound it because of the early, stumbling experience of Luther and Corning when they omitted basic training in group processes from their quality program. As you dig into this introduction, it's possible you'll say to yourself, "There's nothing new here. I already know this stuff—if not literally, then intuitively." Let me be blunt. If you accommodate this reaction, you'll be preempting yourself from a very important learning experience. What follows is ground-level advice on what's necessary for a group of people to be successful as a team. I describe what marks that group as exceptional. If you and your associates fully understood what's being asked for here, you'd already be doing it, but most likely you're not. And while you may *call* yourselves a team, it wasn't mere idleness that led you to pick up this book.

The information is basic, yes, but who actually puts it to work? In 25 years of consulting with top managements, I've heard ample talk about teams, but have seen very few teams in action. Now times have changed, and the talk must be converted into results we can see. How do we proceed? Some executives are fond of the term "team building." I'm not. It leads people to think that by assembling a group of executives they've formed a team. Nothing could be further from the truth.

I know that when executives are fortunate enough to be part of a team, a real team, not just an aggregate that pays lip service with the cliché, they thrive on their work and turn in strongly improved performances. And they continue to do so over time.

I know as well from the lessons at Corning and other places that teams aren't formed by accident. Teams get to be teams by *learning* to be teams. Training in teamwork is required. Study of the human animal is required. Interpersonal competence is required. People linked together by task also are required to be bonded in mind—not for reasons of group-think, but on the contrary, to debate with sensitivity the merits of various ideas and options. Finally, what's required is becoming expert in the group processes that assure full expression of the diversity and *authenticity* of you and all your teammates. None of this is easy, though to be sure it's quite apparent.

Any number of forces, factors, and attitudes can splinter a would-be team in no time at all. Cohesion and individual authenticity is a precious mixture that calls for deep insights and practice, practice, practice. Even if you and your associates "know" what's ahead on the next few pages, do you work at it? Do you practice what you know? Do you know that consensus is counterproductive? For many, the answer is no.

Great athletes, musicians, actors, scientists, or executives become what they are by mastering basics. They do so through concentration and practice. This "taming of the beast" indicates the commitment to subdue what I call the fear of the familiar. We avoid many familiar tasks because they frighten us. Failure always looms, and we sense this down deep. For example, we all grew up watching jugglers on television and at the circus. We've seen them time after time all our lives. It looks simple. Yet try keeping just two balls in the air in a staggered fashion. Sophistication is found not in the knowledge, but in the execution. It's easier to dream up a new idea than carry out an old one.

So when it comes to the prescriptions of this introduction, you may have heard them repeatedly. You may even have had flashes of them in actual experience. More importantly, you'll want to own them by mastering them the way actress Meryl Streep does when she takes command of a role, or basketball star Michael Jordan does when he dazzles us with his hang-time and scores in the clutch, or Placido Domingo does when he hits a high note, or some nameless, disciplined neurosurgeon at the Mayo Clinic does when she lays back someone's scalp and saves a life.

Forewarned is forearmed. Be prepared for the familiar and face your fear about it. Over the next few months, practice and begin to master what's prescribed herein and you won't find time to be scornful over what you already know. Before too long, if you and your associates will commit yourselves to competence in the everyday components of teamwork, you'll celebrate together over what you've become and what you've accomplished. Your confidence in managing with the team style will soar.

In describing team effectiveness, let's look at three critical questions: 1. What are the vital elements of a team? 2. How do I lead a team? 3. Where does the individual fit in?

1. *What are the vital elements of a team?*

There are four preconditions for team effectiveness. I'll treat each briefly.

- **Mutual need.** People have to acknowledge that they need each other. Even so-called individual contributors take on tasks spawned by collaborations they're a part of. We take our first step toward effective teamwork when we say, "Hey folks, we need each other."

- **Joint commitment.** Not only do we have to acknowledge that we need each other, which some people do with a sense of resignation, but we enliven our work with a proactive, affirmative linking of hands with those around us.
- **Declaration of purpose.** This is the statement of the group's reason for being. This can be a set of objectives, the itemization of critical success factors, a mission statement, or some other articulation of its charter. Regardless of the form chosen, a group requires knowing why it has been assembled.
- **Accountability.** There is a risk in group efforts that everyone is seen as responsible for a given task with the result that no one is. Avoid this by making sure that before a meeting is adjourned, one person is given a "what-by-when" assignment for each decision. This doesn't mean that one person is responsible for all the work on the project, but that he or she will assure its completion by a set date.

My comments on the preconditions for a team lead to the following conclusions:

- All teams are groups; but not all groups are teams.
- You have to give up something to be a member of a team. It may be a phony role you've assigned to yourself, such as the guy who talks too much, the woman who remains silent, the know-it-all, the know-nothing, the hoarder of talented subordinates, the non-sharer of some resource such as management information systems (MIS), or whatever. You give up something, to be sure, such as some petty corner of privilege, but gain authenticity in return. The team, moreover, doesn't quash individual accomplishment; rather, it empowers personal contributions. More on that later.
- For team action to take place, it has to be rewarded. Despite ample rhetoric in support of team play, the latter won't be in evidence in a company without an appraisal and reward (psychic and monetary) system in place that supports it.

6

What we measure, we do. What we don't measure, we don't do.

By way of summation, then, I offer the following mnemonic device to highlight the elements of good teams:

I	nclusiveness
D	irectness
E	ngagement
E	xperimentation
A	ccountability
S	ensitivity

First of all, notice that directness must be tempered with sensitivity. There is no room for bullies on the team. Then keep in mind that the purpose of teamwork is to produce superior ideas. A results-getting team is a *thinking* team. Teams aren't born to give us the warm-and-fuzzies. They are the means by which we advance our businesses. They are never the end.

In the January–February 1989 issue of the *Harvard Business Review*, revered banker Walter Wriston bluntly stated the most valid of all reasons for making our teams work: "The person who figures out how to harness the collective genius of the people in his or her organization is going to blow the competition away."

2. *How do I lead a team?*

In the last two decades, many researchers and experts in organizational behavior have become increasingly vocal in predicting the demise of the corporate pyramid. Hierarchy, they say, is D.O.A. By the year 2000, our organizations will be as flat as pancakes and managers will be supervising 70, 80, 100, or more people. I turn a gimlet eye on these pronouncements. So do others. Elliott Jaques, to my mind the most fertile organizational thinker of our time, notes that the pyramid, invented by the Chinese more than 3,000 years ago, has persisted as the dominant way we organize people and tasks on a large, complex scale. It remains the skeletal system of every single corporation I know, whatever their rhetoric to the contrary. Put 100 strangers into a room and they will cluster and rank themselves around such issues as competence, experience, values, status, and knowledge.

Hierarchy's ultimate longevity is beside the point, actually. Whether the predictions of these experts ever come to pass, hierarchy is very much a part of our lives and will remain so for some time. It offers you an inevitable opportunity for developing team effectiveness. If you are a manager of any kind, people who report to you form a function or department. A typical span of control for such a job is five to nine people. Right there at your level in the hierarchy, you can become an exemplary team leader.

Your boss is one level up in the hierarchy. You and the four to eight peers who report to him or her form another department. There you have the possibility of becoming a contributing team member. Putting team-management techniques into place will obliterate many of the ills of hierarchy that we pejoratively call "bureaucracy."

On the other hand, I have no quarrel with the view that we have become overly layered—in effect, organizationally obese. Nor do I do anything but applaud the fact that rigid, chain-of-command, order-giving styles have given way to people roaming wherever they choose to get the information they need to do their jobs.

But it's important to keep in mind that such moves aren't in conflict with hierarchy. Rather, the issue of consequence is that we have advanced our view of the human animal and enhanced the way we work, think, and talk with each other. Moreover, as I've just shown, nothing in the traditional pyramid prevents the creation of day-by-day departments where collaboration is the norm. The same is true of task forces, any number of interteam linkages, and multifunctional or interregional groups. Such alliances minimize the parochialism of fiefdoms and promote speedy, imaginative responses to unanticipated problems and special customer needs. They also keep nasty little fragments from falling between the organizational cracks.

Hierarchy remains, then, a part of corporate architecture for numerous good reasons, including the flexibility to design as flat an organization as most want and anyone can handle. In contrast, attitudes of what we expect in the workplace and the valuing of authentic gifts have undergone more dramatic changes. This is the good news of the modern age of management.

So given the current climate, let us ask again what you need to do to lead a team. Recalling that the purpose of a team is to generate superior ideas, the main thing is that you have to learn how to run meetings. I say this because the best ideas come out of well-managed collaborations. To manage such collaborations, you'll have to develop a firm grasp of the following:

1. The team leader's responsibilities
2. The team's task functions
3. The team's maintenance functions

Team Leader's Responsibilities

- *Set the agenda.* The agenda makes clear that you have already given thought to what is going to be covered. It also underscores that "homework" is required of all participants, that they aren't merely to show up and waste valuable time by talking off the tops of their heads. Itemize the time and date of the meeting, the time of the meeting's conclusion, who should attend, subjects to be covered in order, who has been asked to think about what, and what procedures will be used to facilitate the meeting. Send the agenda out as far in advance as is practicable.

  Don't use meetings slavishly to have people make routine reports. That can put everyone to sleep. Use them to *think.* Realize that your group will function truly as a task force when it can meet to pool its minds to solve problems rather than approve or reject recommendations or absorb mandates from on high. Take advantage of the talented people and bright minds with whom you're sharing time and space.

9

- *Set the attendees.* Not everybody has to attend every meeting. Not everybody has to attend the entire meeting. Make this standard operating procedure (S.O.P.), and rather than feeling left out, people will be grateful that their time has been given value and will know that their attendance is purposeful.
- *Set the "belonging" exercise.* Begin *every* meeting (no exceptions!) by making the rounds. Have *every* person belong to the enterprise of the hour by offering a one- to two-minute opinion on some question you pose that's related to the agenda. Those who have a tendency to talk too much are held in check. Those who are timid get used to the sound of their own voices. They have the ice broken. This assures that the meeting at least begins with everyone on equal footing and that all attendees have equal opportunity for influence.
- *Set the procedures.* Give thought to what you're going to do to facilitate discussion and quality thinking. The "belonging" exercise is an example. Are you going to break the group into pairs? Are you going to have them do any writing? Are you going to have the team "brainstorm"? Think this out beforehand. Some leaders even prefer to itemize such procedures in the agenda.
- *Set the record.* A quality meeting can be spoiled without a record of what was agreed to, relevant issues and problems yet unresolved, further study needed, and who's going to do what by when. Flip charts are a user-friendly way of keeping such a record. Have the sheets typed up and distributed to all concerned. This is an alternative to more formal "minutes," though in some cases isn't a wholly suitable substitute.
- *Set the spirit!* By doing all the above, you'll demonstrate your enthusiasm for the process of doing quality thinking together. Use every means to convey your desire for expressions of authenticity by the people with whom you work. Make people want to share their ideas and know that their ideas are sought and appreciated. Be alive, hopeful, optimistic. Animate your associates with your energy.

The Team's Task Functions

One of the team leader's jobs is to make sure *all* members of the team realize these tasks are *their* responsibilities. They are shared. Different people take them on at different times, depending on circumstances.

- *Getting started.* Somebody has to push the sled off the top of the hill with a question or statement or set of intentions.
- *Giving information.* All members owe each other information. Information is knowledge, beliefs, opinions, biases, cares, fears, hopes, questions, fantasies, facts as they are seen, and so on. Some people think knowledge is power and keep it to themselves. How wrong they are. Knowledge is power only when it's shared.
- *Getting information.* All team members need to get what they need to know to advance team thinking. If a statement isn't clear to a member, he or she will ask for it to be stated differently. The experienced ones will be expected to shed light on areas unknown to their associates. The team will pool their ignorance to identify items that need further investigation. All team members will feel free to inquire about the basis of any assumption put forth.
- *Clarifying.* Related to getting information, team members will work at gaining clarity of ideas. Testing ideas by subjecting them to use in a hypothetical situation is common. Or somebody might say, "George, I don't get it. Could you give me another example of how that would work?" Asking absurd questions is desirable, too, to try to gain new perspective: "What if water ran uphill? How would that change the way we do things?"
- *Elaborating.* An example of elaboration is a team member in a food company asking, "If we move into desserts, will the consumer think we're moving out of our frozen entree business?" One banker might say to another, "If we keep promoting only commercial loan officers, it seems to me we won't be able to get any of the best and brightest to go into trust services." This function is to understand conse-

11

quences—the possible fallout from adopted thoughts and actions. No idea can come of age and be practicable unless its consequences are debated.

- *Summarizing.* A team needs to know how far it has come, where it is, and whether it needs to go back over a cold trail, start over, or consider a big new leap. It needs to know when it's time to quit, speed up, or acknowledge that it is confused and lost. All members will be called on at various times to stick a flag into the ground to mark its whereabouts.

- *Decision reaching.* Notice I do not write decision *making.* Team thinking is done to produce the very best options—many of them competing—from which one is chosen that is likely to lead to distinctive results. One of the seven themes of authenticity in this book is that consensus thinking comes about by finding the lowest common denominator—something everyone can agree on—and most often leads to mediocrity. (See essays 40, 41, 55, and 95.) The result of consensus is likely to be a three-legged duck that can't walk or fly. Let the team wrangle and think and generate options. *Then let the person at the head of the table say yea or nay to this option or that.* Then let the team close ranks and move forward by getting behind that decision and onto other challenges. It's wiser to win collaborator buy-in on the decision-reaching *system* than seek it for every decision. Let's be grown-up!

The Team's Maintenance Functions[1]

As with the task functions, these also fall to all team members at various times.

- *Gatekeeping.* Members will work at noticing who is participating and who is not. They'll notice if someone has "gone away" and isn't contributing. Someone will say, "Craig, we haven't heard from you on this. Tell us what you think."

[1]The terminology and classification of task and maintenance functions was first presented by K. Benne and P. Sheets in a 1948 article in the *Journal of Social Issues*, 2: 42–47.

Someone else will see that Christine is fidgety but silent. He might say, "Chris, this seems to be boring you. Am I wrong? Do you think we're somehow missing the point?" Someone else will notice Carl is talking too much and repeating himself; others will be invited to give their views as well. Gatekeeping, then, is awareness of the level of engagement of fellow members in the discussion.

- *Harmonizing/confronting.* If people are enthusiastic about their work, believe in what they do, and advance their ideas in a team with a verve that is rewarded, then they are going to have strong feelings and a stake in events. As a result, high emotions are going to be an integral part of team processes.

  Clashes will occur over competing options. This is not only inevitable; it is desirable. Yet it creates problems that must be managed well if conflict is to be kept from being destructive. The team needs to negotiate a harmony whereby people can be truthful with each other when they think their fellow team members are letting their feelings overpower their better business judgment. This harmony is never easy to achieve, but the best teams find a way to get past these sensitive times with a minimum of disturbance and hard feelings. A little forgiveness when certain boundaries have been exceeded never hurts either.

- *Fostering an equal-influence opportunity climate.* Think of when you've joined a small group of strangers. All of you were thrown together for the first time. Remember the glances you all stole at each other? The quick conclusions you drew about each other based on dress, posture, voice, and so on? Remember the first tentative comments you all made, if you made any at all? Remember how one or more was a forceful presence or even a blusterer? Remember your anxiety?

  Well, what was going on was that you all were trying to find your place in the group. If you stayed together over some period of days or weeks, you all took on roles and settled into a fairly predictable routine of responding to your tasks and to each other. Some people did more talking than others and generally exercised more authority and influence than the rest.

A clear and helpful description of this state of affairs comes from a Sausalito-based organizational consultant, William Daniels, who sketches the typical work group this way:*

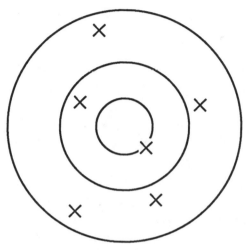

Daniels suggests that we look at this diagram as if it were a topographical map, with the center ring being the top of the hill. The Xs represent people placed at their level of influence in the group, with those on the outer ring having the least influence.

Those at the center maintain some disdain for those on the outer rings and are critical of them, particularly those furthest out, for not having the courage of their convictions. Those at the outer ring complain that they're ignored and that when they try to speak up, their ideas are discarded with little consideration.

Daniels argues that while we may think those at the top of the hill enjoy undiluted power, this is not the case. Rather, they're uneasy that their performance takes place under the

*The following diagrams are from William Daniels' *Group Power II*, University Associates, 1990, pp. 19, 20.

jaundiced eyes of those at the periphery who are all too eager to see them fail. What results, then, is a work group where no one is functioning at full capacity. This generates a compromised performance. Daniels wants to see us achieve a formation like this:

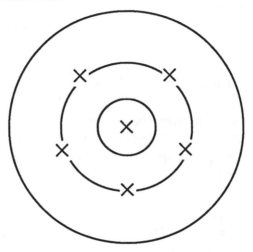

How can this happen? The first step is for the leader, whose position displays higher authority, to begin each meeting with what Daniels calls an inclusion activity. This is what I, copying him, call a belonging exercise. Whatever it's called, everyone starts off on equal footing. Then, if the leader and team commit themselves to the discipline of all the responsibilities I'm explaining here, an equal-influence climate, such as in the second illustration, can come about. Once it is in place, you'll notice that it is likely to be self-perpetuating. Once people learn to work together this way and experience the superior results that come from such a climate, they do not take kindly to its interruption. Please remember that this is an ideal state and won't always prevail. But there's no reason that it can't become the typical state of affairs in place of what most of us are accustomed to.

Daniels's concentric circles set off clearly why belonging is another of this book's seven themes of authenticity. Referring to the ordinary aggregate of people who run our organizations as a "team" has become a cliché—and an inaccurate one at that. "We may call ourselves a team," think many people, "but I don't *belong*." This book is about belonging yourself, helping others belong, and encouraging each other to be at your personal best in the team setting.

A final tip: Daniels cites small-group research to show that work groups accomplish most when they number between five and nine people. Fewer than five is less effective than one working alone. The same is true for larger numbers. My experience bears this out. I say, throw in the leader and you can make it ten. If your department contains a larger number, this won't be a problem for regular staff meetings. But for actual problem-solving—what we can call task-force or project activity—you'll have to divide your group into smaller units.

- *Setting standards*. It's easy for a group to get exhausted from working on a knotty problem and choose a solution of convenience to be rid of it. It's important that a team maintain its integrity by pointing the finger at itself when it feels the temptation to sell out. The team keeps its standards high and is willing to bear extra pain to see a task through to a resolution that it can announce with pride and undertake with conviction.

- *Encouraging*. It's inevitable that a team will get lost and confused. Projects occasionally will seem hopeless and certain responsibilities endless and thankless. Discouragements will set in, and the ship may seem to be taking on too much water. There is no more important time for bonding to show itself than this, when people need to offer each other strength to stay the course and hang on through rough seas. Teams that have the capacity to encourage themselves eventually sort through their confusion. They know the wisdom of Robert Frost's words: "The best way out is always through."

Values and the Maintenance Functions

Learn to rely on three big values to help your team enhance its maintenance functions. These authenticity-inducing values are:

1. Trust comes first.
2. Team primacy prevails.
3. Collaborative style wins.

I'll treat each matter-of-factly.

- *Trust comes first.* Give it. Expect it. Appreciate it. Adhere to the rule that what plays in the room stays in the room. Much confidential and sensitive information is shared when people work together. Treat it with extreme care.

  Discover what's right rather than wrong with your associates. Don't pick away at them. We all have clay feet. Find your common ground.

  Know that broken trust is a sin.
- *Team primacy prevails.* Team achievement, not individual priorities, is what counts.

  Be a nurturer, not an impairer.

  Keep your associates out of trouble by sharing yourself, your time, and your information. Don't let them hang themselves. Grab the rope.

  Realize that total agreement isn't necessary or even desirable. But group spirit is.

  Don't wait for the "team" to "catch on." Sign up or out, now. The train is leaving the station. Get on or get off. "Wait and see" is a formula for failure.
- *Collaborative style wins.* The task-force or ad hoc mentality is *the* perspective. Even your department, though an established function, needs to reach outside itself regularly for people and information to do its work well. Or it may concentrate on the expertise of a particular few within its own house on occasion. In either case, you need to realize you're part of a multidisciplinary network in which you have little or no formal authority.

  Win commitment to the task by showing value in your associates. They matter; they are important to your enterprise. Maintain the "uneasy balance." I've offered guidelines for making a team work, but they can't be legislated, and they don't constitute a magic formula. Carla Paonessa, partner with Andersen Consulting, says this kind of collaborative work is like dancing with a bear. So, give your associates a bear hug!

Seek full voices and superior choices, not consensus! Distinction lies on the narrow road, not the one that travels easy. Sometimes, in fact, you and your teammates will have no option but to hack your way through a dense forest. No road will exist!

Before moving on to the third and concluding question of this introduction, I'd like to make a distinction between *teammate* or *team member* and *associate*, at least from the standpoint of how I use these terms in the book. By team member or teammate, I refer to someone with whom you regularly share time and space in group work, and in a group that has a well-understood identity, whether a department, interregional and multifunctional network, or some other project configuration.

An associate can be anybody you come in contact with in your work. It is a broader term than teammate, though your teammates are all associates. Examples of associates are suppliers, someone in another division or group, your boss's boss, or your subordinates' subordinates.

I'd also like to clarify in a structural sense what I mean by team itself. *Team* for our purposes in this book refers to a well-identified unit of five to nine peers reporting to a boss or team leader. On the other hand, the *idea* of teamwork itself, based on a clear corporate strategy, is necessary on a corporate-wide basis to have across-the-board success. That idea boils down to an attitude and discipline that is fostered in all its teams—like yours, for instance.

Effective teamwork automatically creates interteam linkage. Here's why. Most every peer reporting to a boss in turn heads up her or his department. Teamwork between those peers prompts interteam linkage between the departments they head. Teamwork taught at one level of the hierarchy has the potential to fan out on the next level down. When this is true of a company, it is in this sense that an entire corporation can refer to all their people as a team.

3. *Where does the individual fit in?*

Some people worry that the prevalence of team rhetoric sounds awfully, well, *communal*. They fear a sameness, a group-think emphasis that not only stifles individual initiative and imagination, but manipulates people in such a way that distinctive performance gives way to blandness.

The 20 chapters that follow refute this outlook. I have written them to put such thoughts to rest. As a matter of fact, another of the seven themes of authenticity running through this book is that you the reader are challenged to move out of your comfort zone and express your uniqueness. Each chapter and the essays that comprise it espouse one broad behavioral value designed to tap into your authenticity and thereby enhance your competence and self-esteem.

Here's a pleasant paradox made apparent to me in my years as a management consultant: I can say with confidence that most executives identify the high points in their careers as those times when they were part of something, when their work was bigger than their job. This was when they were stretched to the limit (and sometimes beyond), bonded with peers, bosses, and subordinates alike. Over and over, I have listened to executives from all industries exclaim that in such times they felt most united with others in pursuit of some worthy end and yet were called upon for what was most distinctive about themselves. Another way to capture this thought is to remember the old chestnut spoken between lovers: "I love you for what I am when I am with you." Right there in that little gem is a working definition of empowerment.

A second paradox is this: Each of the book's essays forces you to address a single aspect of your individual thoughts and actions. Yet the purpose of having you examine your own behavior in 100 thin slices is to discover just how much you're linked to a network— one that can make a difference, good or bad.

It's one thing to lay out broad guidelines and prescriptions, as I've done so far, to ensure team effectiveness. It's something else altogether to understand, by way of nitty-gritty instances, if you're supporting or thwarting a team effort, if you're part of it or outside it. Your network can be healthful or destructive, and nothing makes this more clear to those around you than the thoughts you think or the words you speak or the actions you take at, say, 3:31 on a particular Wednesday afternoon.

Keep in mind as well that the team style won't come about if it's merely some executive's pet project and identified as his or her program. After all, for both you and the company, it must become a mind-set, a way of life. Not merely a component of the business, it then emerges quite simply as "the way we do things," "the way we run our business." The team is bigger than finance. It's bigger than marketing, engineering, operations, human resources, research and development, data systems, or sales. It's bigger than hierarchy or its lack, quality, or the bottom line itself. It's bigger than all these because it *carries* them. Finally, it's bigger even than vision, because without the team there can be no truly comprehensive vision.

And yet . . . yet . . . viewed from another perspective, the team is smaller than all these, too. While the team is simultaneously overview and foundation, it is also microscopic and incremental. It's a look, a thought, a decision, an admission. It's a commitment, a question, a bold leap, a word of forgiveness, a dawn meeting, a midnight drink, a hesitant phone call, a frank opinion, an acknowledged fear, and a commanding presence. It's all this and much, much less.

The remainder of this book, then, is given over to 100 such "lesser" examples of how team takes place and how you can be a team catalyst. You'll notice that in many essays I use non-business events to draw lessons applicable to the challenges of management-by-authenticity. This will annoy some people and, regrettably, strike others as irrelevant. Yet I will persist, with the conviction that since business is a human enterprise, we'll do well to take our learnings wherever we find them. We in business already suffer too much from tunnel vision.

OPENING

Enthusiasts soon understand each other.

WASHINGTON IRVING

I

Being Accessible

Investing in Others

I begin this chapter by stressing the importance of theme 6: *A team-catalyst is an individual who takes upon himself or herself the responsibility for modeling actions and attitudes that support shared competence.* I do so because this theme pertains not only to this chapter but to all subsequent chapters as well.

Let us start by recognizing that there's no more convincing way for you to promote shared competence among your associates than by modeling accessibility before them. You be the authentic example! You'll of course continue to learn from those you admire, but remember that executives with whom you spend time and have tasks in common are keeping their eyes on you. Invest yourself in them.

Give thought to the following:

- Praising/thanking them for their daily accomplishments
- Making your smiles genuine
- Going to lunch with them
- Learning to coach them

- Not withholding criticisms of their performance until a formal review

—— 1 ——

POKES AND STROKES

Not long ago I attended a meeting where the featured speaker was Dr. Mark Tager. Tager, a doctor of medicine, consults with corporations on health and fitness programs for their executives.

Though his major focus is fitness, Tager also gets involved in broader executive development concerns and has found himself in a position to do research and make observations on a wide range of executive behavior.

The personable doctor told the story of hearing one boss boast that he regularly gave positive feedback to his subordinates on their job performance. So Tager went to one of those subordinates at random and asked if this was so. The subordinate laughed at Tager's question and said, "Come with me back to my office and I'll tell you exactly the last time he told me I was doing well. It was so unusual I wrote it down on my calendar."

All of us in the audience laughed too, because it struck a familiar note. Most of us have played both characters in his anecdote. We've overlooked and been overlooked.

Tager says his research shows that most bosses are miserly in their praise to subordinates for work well done, but generous in distributing negative criticism. Says Tager: "The ratio of pokes to strokes is about 4 to 1."

Pokes

For many years I've wrestled with the notion of constructive criticism. Some people, including me, deliver it so gleefully. You know what I mean? We put on our sincere faces and speak in soft tones, but we're hard of heart and can't wait to deliver the bad news.

24

Yet people do deceive themselves, get a bit slovenly about their performance without fully facing up to it, and need to know *we* know they're not putting out. Maybe the best model for us here is the coach—the athletic, music, drama, or debate coach who unselfconsciously pushes her subject to the wall until he gets it right. No glee. Just concern for getting the performer to do his dead-level best.

Strokes

Staying with the coaching idea, I notice that when the subject gets it right, that's where the glee comes in. And that's where it belongs. The mentor takes genuine pleasure in seeing talent at work. That, I'm sure you know, is authenticity at work—in both giver and receiver.

I've always liked Ken Blanchard's (coauthor of *The One-Minute Manager*) thought of catching your subordinate in "the act of doing something right." After all, along the road to superior performance are thousands upon thousands of little steps that can be taken boldly or haltingly. That subordinate who is praised for one bold step is far more likely to take another and another.

Then when the missteps come, as they inevitably will, the boss who has built up a backlog of trust through daily support is in a position to offer a no-nonsense prescription for the subordinate to regain the right footing.

TAKE ACTION
---

1. Be a team leader who finds something in a subordinate's performance you like. Then say so.

2. If this is difficult for you, get into the habit of keeping a calendar to remind you to do so. Better you do that than your subordinate!

2

JUDGING A BOOK BY ITS COVER

I've lived in a high-rise apartment building in Chicago for almost 20 years. About ten years ago, I became aware of a woman in our building whom I've come to know only as "Mrs. Simon." She's a winsome person who draws favorable attention to herself in simple, elegant ways. She sparkles, and does it with poise.

Oddly enough, you can learn a lot about people over time as you ride elevators with them, exchange brief greetings in the lobby, share space and washing machines in laundry rooms, wait your turn as you exit and enter the garage, and observe how they respond to building attendants.

One day a couple of years ago, our daughter, Laura (when she was home from college), closed our front door behind her as she crossed the hall to the service porch. She went there to dispose of a couple of boxes that housed bedside lamps delivered to her by a local department store. When she returned moments later, she discovered she had locked herself out. She went down to the lobby to find the building engineer for a master key, but learned from the doorman he would be away for at least a couple of hours.

At the time, Mrs. Simon passed through the lobby on her way to an appointment and heard this tale of woe. Without hesitation, she insisted that this young damsel in distress—known to her as no more than a familiar face—stay in her apartment until the engineer got back. "Unfortunately, I can't stay to keep you company," she said, "but make yourself at home." Laura protested briefly, then gratefully accepted her invitation.

A Smiling Disposition

You can imagine that a disposition like Mrs. Simon's is readily marked by genuine smiles. She laughs easily and doesn't take life too seriously. You may wonder, though, if I'm glamorizing her gesture. Isn't this just a neighborly thing to have done? Perhaps, but this simple act of kindness to a relative stranger—who, for all she knew, could be a kleptomaniac, or a slob who might in a matter of minutes destroy her well-appointed apartment—seems characteristic of her entire life and being. So, out of curiosity, I've paid more attention to her actions since then. The effect I see that she has on most people is overwhelmingly positive. There are times, apparently, when it's possible to judge a book by its cover.

Authenticity

The genuineness of a smile allows us to have confidence in judging the book by its cover. That is, the authentic smile is a window on the warmth, caring, and integrity that exist within.

It's better not to smile at all than to be known for a fake smile. I know a banker who has gone far up the ladder. Today he is an executive vice president for all operations of his large downtown bank. And I know for a fact that he's good at what he does. He's not peaked out, and he is looking for new worlds to conquer. I also know that for some reason I trust him, and so do his associates.

The peculiar thing about him, however, is that he doesn't smile. Even more peculiar, he's proud of it. I sat with him in his office one day and was surprised to hear him tell a new associate that he doesn't smile. Why not let the recent recruit find out for himself, I thought. Yet it was obvious he took pleasure in making this announcement about himself—for my benefit, I suppose, just as much as for that of the new kid on the block.

The literal truth is, he smiles more than he thinks. To be sure, his smile, when it comes, registers as little more than a slight crack in fine china. Yet there it is to see for anyone with a sharp eye and sensitivity to the spirit of the moment. So this fellow's not terribly demonstrative, and I think he ought to do a little work on that score, yet I'm convinced that his minuscule, authentic smile, rare though it is, is one of the reasons I believe I can trust him.

Authenticity in general, and genuine smiles in particular, are characteristic of teams. They feed on each other. The quality of smiles among a team of people is markedly superior to that of a group of strangers or competitors who happen to be collected in a room. Basically, the smiles of the former are windows; those of the latter are shutters.

One night many years ago when I was first married, my wife and I returned home from a cocktail party. We were in a taxi, pulling up to the front of our apartment. As I reached into my pocket for money to pay the driver, I asked my wife if she'd had a good time. She thought a moment before making a crisp three-word reply, one that caused the driver to erupt with a belly laugh and gave me an expression I'd use the rest of my life. "My face hurts," she said.

In his monumental best-seller, *Bonfire of the Vanities*, Tom Wolfe similarly describes the visages of all of us who join the fake set. He calls them "boiling faces."

TAKE ACTION

1.   Check out your smile. You know how it feels. Stand in front of the mirror and smile your smile. Would your face hurt if you kept it up? Make sure that what others see isn't a boiling face.

2.   Check out the smiles of your work group. Are the smiles you see genuine? If so, there's a team there, or you have the makings of one.

3

OUT TO LUNCH?

In Cupertino, California—one of a string of towns in the famed Silicon Valley—is the headquarters of Grace/Horn Ventures. Located in a sleek, dazzling, mid-rise office building along Stevens Creek Boulevard, Grace/Horn Ventures is the nerve center for W. R. Grace & Company's entrepreneurial interests.

Here a small cadre of marketing and financial experts evaluate small businesses for investment on behalf of their associates sitting high atop Grace Tower, 3,000 miles away at 42nd Street and Avenue of the Americas in New York City.

Years ago when I was a recruitment consultant, I did a search for the president of one of these fledgling businesses. In the process I worked closely with Chris Horn, president of Grace/Horn, and Bob Pedigo, executive vice president.

One morning, Bob Pedigo, my candidate who ended up in the job, and I were meeting in the Grace/Horn conference room. When the time for lunch arrived, Pedigo simply had his secretary send out for sandwiches.

Later, our business completed, and while the three of us were disposing of our paper plates, plastic tableware, and pop cans, I complimented Bob on keeping our luncheon simple and not interrupting the flow of our conversation with the mechanics of travel to some restaurant.

"Oh, are you kidding?" he asked. "This was a fancy one for me. My normal lunch is an apple at my desk. Takes about four minutes total."

A Diagnostic Tool

Now I'm not picking on Bob Pedigo. He's a delight to work with and he was supportive of me in my efforts in every way. Moreover, he was a marvel of decorum the first time he laid eyes on me. My attire was totally inappropriate for the occasion, and while others would have burst out laughing, he merely smiled, shook my hand, and said it was nice to get acquainted.

We met that first time for breakfast in a Hilton hotel at the northwest tip of the island of Oahu, where Grace/Horn's start-up company was located. While my work has taken me to all sections of our country and to some foreign lands, I had never been to Hawaii, and it showed. Bob greeted me in a faded navy polo shirt, khakis, and loafers. I stood there awkwardly in a navy pinstripe suit, white shirt, polka-dot tie and shiny black shoes, looking as if I were calling on The Morgan Bank but couldn't find the elevator. There was not a suit or tie to be seen in any corner of this vast and crowded restaurant.

We got on quickly and well, got the job done, and have stayed in touch. I've thought repeatedly of his expression "an apple at my desk" as a description of his typical lunch, however, and have come to use it as a diagnostic tool in my work.

Here's what I mean. When I interview executives for either an executive development or team-effectiveness assignment, I want to get a sense of their management style. I want to know what they like most about what they do, what they like least, what they've accomplished, what they're most proud of, how they got this job, what's ahead for them, how they make decisions. I pay attention to how they dress, what their offices look like, how they talk with people on the telephone, how they relate to the secretaries, their posture, their speech, and on and on.

Sooner or later I ask them, "And what do you do for lunch, usually? Do you go out with your customers, suppliers, and associates, or are you pretty much an apple-at-the-desk person?"

Give Yourself a Break

It would be poor judgment on my part were I to draw sweeping conclusions about a person's management style based purely on whether he or she ate lunch at his or her desk. For example, because they don't believe in sidewalks in large parts of California (a sure sign of lack of civilization!), a fellow like Bob Pedigo has to put up with the hassle of jumping into his car every time he wants to break bread with anybody away from the office. That might cause a lot of people to brown-bag it.

On the other hand, company cafeterias and, in small operations, kitchens offer the opportunity for all people to spend useful time with their associates if they're so inclined. So the person who stringently avoids such contact and works through lunch is making a statement about accessibility and the warmth that goes along with the sharing of self.

The break provided by time out for lunch has purposes all its own. It's bound to help clear the mind and offer benefits in emotional elasticity and cardiovascular functioning. But all kinds of positive business payoffs take place as well at the midday hour when people who work together can share simple good times in each other's company.

TAKE ACTION

1. Be accessible. Be known. Be warm. Be real. Be a sharer of self at lunch.

2. Lighten up. Work, work, work through lunch won't make you more effective. You may do more chores, but you'll probably accomplish less. Your teammates need *you* and your accomplishments more than your scurrying.

4

THE SIGNIFICANCE OF SMALL MOVES

Consider these small moves:

- A high school student proofreads her term paper one more time even though she's sick of it. She finds two spelling errors and one glaring error in punctuation, and straightens out a clumsy sentence. She gets an A— instead of her usual B.
- A busy, pressure-racked executive sits in a house of worship. A passage of scripture, some word from a wise man of antiquity, breaks through, and he has a flash of insight. Something gives between his shoulder blades, and he steps out into the day with a lighter burden.
- A somewhat timid market researcher decides he is going to speak up at the next meeting. He does so, overcoming his fear that he may look stupid, and wins surprised nods from his peers and a compliment from his boss. He leaves the meeting feeling ten feet tall.
- A boss is growing increasingly irritated with a subordinate who is griping about her behind her back. But she's embarrassed about it as well, and is hesitant to confront the problem head-on. She steels up her courage, however, and goes to her subordinate's office. She says, "Bill, I'd like us to talk about something that's come up that I perceive as a problem." Bill is swamped right at the moment, but they agree to meet at 10:15 the next day.

- A homemaker with two children, now both in school, trembles over the thought of embarking on a master's degree in nutrition. She picks up the phone and calls the university admissions office. She has them send her a catalog and application.

The Need for Coaching

Little things. Always, there are the little things. All great accomplishments come about not only because someone had a big idea, but also because small moves were made by one or many people integral to the job at hand.

Sometimes the little moves are clear to all and require only rearticulation and coordination among those trained for the task. This is true when musicians in a symphony orchestra play their notes. Other times the small move is not clearly indicated, or if it is, can be the source of anxiety, doubt, embarrassment, or exhaustion. Such is the case with the previous examples.

To do well in life and work, it seems we all need to make small moves we often don't want to make. Most individuals have ambition—or at least dreams—but it's apparent that those who realize their ambitions back them up with tight little corrective actions. Somewhere in their lives were influential people—parents, siblings, teachers, friends, neighbors, or others—who taught them the significance of small, painful moves.

My point here is: Because most successful people have been beneficiaries of such coaching, of being encouraged to take small steps when they don't want to, it's obvious we can be of enormous help to our subordinates if we're willing to learn how to be their coaches.

The Five Rs

I think of coaching as providing encouragement to subordinates who need to take tight little corrective actions. This is true whether subordinates are embarking on a new opportunity or persisting in some problem behavior that needs attention. This is team development by way of skill building, really, and is accomplished by taking small steps. Such encouragement from you is necessary to affirm your subordinate's faith in self and to overcome evasion, fears, and excuses.

Here are five guidelines:

- Rehearse/visualize. Put yourself into your subordinate's shoes. What does he think? What resistance will she present? How will she feel? Don't be flat-footed and poorly prepared.
- Review/restate the problem or opportunity. Give your subordinate ample time to vent his or her side of the story. Be a listener. Be ready to change your mind if you don't have the whole picture. Own up to your own role in why the problem exists or why new measures must be taken.
- Remove the blinders. Make sure your subordinate understands you're not crying over spilt milk, but raising the bar for high standards. Focus discussion on the future. Ask what are the alternatives to current performance and how we can be better.
- Respond with a plan. Be proactive. Win buy-in by collaborating with your subordinate on goals, accountabilities, deadlines, and payoffs. Ask for a commitment to it. Get your subordinate to take the first small step *now*.
- Recycle/renew/revise. Coaching is a process, not an event. It's never over. Coaching is your job as team leader. Stay on the case.

Learn from your subordinate and the process itself. Delight in his or her growth and show it. Be receptive to new data and modify approaches if indicated.

TAKE ACTION

1. Recall how often you've said to yourself, "It's time to . . .," and know the fear of making small corrective moves.

2. Show you care for your subordinates by taking those small steps toward them. Learn to be their coach.

——— 5 ———

THE TEAM'S PERSONAL BEST

At the beginning of this chapter, I urged you to praise and thank your subordinates for their daily accomplishments. Here, the subject is holding criticisms in abeyance until the date of an annual performance review, and my urging is that you not do that.

The core of all these essays (as if you didn't know) is the team. Even when one of these essays seems to focus solely on how you can improve your individual performance, its purpose in doing so is to enhance your contribution to the subunit and overall organization of which you are a part. It is to make you more the collaborator, facilitator, leader in some instances, follower in others.

Imagine then, for the sake of the subject of this essay, that you are the coach of a team. Hockey, basketball, tennis, swimming, baseball, football, track and field, whatever. The long season has just begun, and you have high hopes for a championship campaign. The competition will be fierce, of course, but you have a first-rate lineup of players. Some are more gifted than others, but all in all, they make up a fine crew.

Now imagine that as the coach in charge of the operation of this team, you set this rule for yourself: You will withhold criticisms of your players' performance until the season is over.

Feedback

Absurd? You bet! Ludicrous? Oh yeah! What team could make progress if the coach remained silent about observations of their performance? If you acted like this, you simply wouldn't be a coach.

It's a good thing that the concept of and the word *coaching* has entered the executive suite in a big way. It has made clear how ridiculous it is to think we should withhold criticisms of our subordinates' performance until the "season" is over. We need people who are performing at their personal best every day if we are to compete effectively. How can they do so if they aren't coached?

34

Naturally, people get messages on how they're doing. There are smiles. There is additional responsibility given out. There are invitations to lunch or dinner by the boss. There are perks and company-financed MBA programs. There are promotions and raises. There is the trip on the company plane with the big boss and . . . there is also the absence of these things.

The point is that most people know basically if they're making it or not, but such mere basic information doesn't supply the support they need to perform at their personal best. An individual's personal best comes from incremental improvement—from intense, detailed, steady feedback from the lips of someone who knows what quality is and enjoys seeing it in the performance of his or her charges.

Between the Lines

I have just spent the past two days interviewing the president of a company and the nine people who report to him. This is a successful company, battling it out with two other able competitors for overall top position in their market. They do not yet face serious foreign competition, but if they are to prevail in their business, their margin of success will be based on team effectiveness—effectiveness in turn based on the members of the team performing at their personal best.

The vice presidents all feel fortunate to be working for this particular boss. They think he is gifted in strategy. They believe he has them on the right course, and they're equally in awe of his pragmatic sense when it comes to marketing.

To a person, however, they're put off by his distance, his aloofness, his a bit-too-frequent sarcasm, and his discomfort with confrontation on a one-to-one basis. One executive says, "He expects us to read between the lines too much. He should just tell us what he thinks. We never really know."

My job as a team-effectiveness consultant in this case is to get this group of vice presidents to tell the boss what they want from him—straight, steady feedback on their performance. The dual advantage of this process is that the president himself will get feedback on his performance that he so badly needs and wants.

35

That's the beauty of how good teams work. Feedback flows in all directions. Such authenticity becomes the norm.

--- *TAKE ACTION* ---

1. Let your subordinate know what you want from her that you're not getting. Be specific: "Norma, you almost always wait until all people speak their minds and then straddle the issues. Next meeting, I want you to be the first with your ideas."

2. Be a good team member by giving the same kind of feedback to your peers that you give to your subordinates. Invite the same kind of feedback from them and from your boss as well.

FAST TAKES

on

Being Accessible

- In general, the ratio of pokes to strokes in business is 4 to 1.

- Prescriptions delivered to others to improve their performance are more credible when supported with a backlog of trust.

- Genuine smiles are windows; fake ones are shutters.

- Habitual lunch at your desk is an exclusionary statement.

- People are more likely to make necessary small moves if you step in and coach them.

- Coaching is not an event. It is a process.

- Coaching doesn't come naturally; it must be practiced to be learned.

- Authentic feedback flows in all directions.

II

LISTENING

More Than Being a Blotter

The title of this chapter makes clear that being a good listener requires far more of you than being an expert receptor. The exchange of ideas between people takes place when the parties to the exchange realize their role in the listening process is to be proactive.

Good listening generates people moving toward each other—even when what they're doing is airing and clarifying disagreements. Therefore, the content of this chapter deals with, among others, theme 4: *The authentic state of humanity is union, and, ironically, this enhances one's uniqueness.*

Master the listening process. Begin by giving thought to the following:

- Looking beyond the literal content of an associate's comments
- Speaking your opinions even though you don't know your associate's thoughts on the matter
- Converting your questions to statements to clarify your position

- Making yourself available for discussion with subordinates and peers
- Admitting when you don't understand something someone is saying

—— 6 ——

NOT WHAT THEY SAY
BUT HOW THEY SAY IT

I live close enough to my downtown Chicago office to walk to work. One day a couple of years ago, shortly after midmorning, I left the office to walk home to pick up my car and drive to the suburbs for a luncheon meeting with a client.

About a block from home and 30 yards distant, a man was walking toward me. From the clothes he wore, I guessed that he was an engineer of one of the local high-rise apartment buildings. His walk was sprightly, but he had his head down, as if thinking about where he was going to get what he didn't have and needed for his work.

As we came right upon each other, he looked up. There was an instant of blank expression on his face. Then he broke stride, gave me a big grin, half-saluted, and spiritedly said, "N-nice to see you, Mr. Rumsfeld."

I gave him a big grin back, and replied, "Hi, how are ya?" and kept walking.

For a moment there, I had the double pleasure of being some sort of personage while making this man's day. I knew that Donald Rumsfeld, President Ford's secretary of defense and later the CEO of G.D. Searle, lived in our neighborhood, so I gathered my greeter had seen him somewhere, although not with great acuity. Mr. Rumsfeld and I do not look much alike—a fact that will come as a relief to Mr. Rumsfeld.

Non-Bankable Words

This case of mistaken identity meant, among other things, that the literal content passing between this man and me isn't what the

Hollywood producer would call bankable. But the exchange was not without its instructive elements. I learned how this man reacts to people he likes or wants to impress, and I surely know how he feels about Mr. Rumsfeld. And of course I gloat at being taken for a big-time operator.

A few weeks later, the man and I ran into each other at about the same spot, this time at the end of the day, and we just smiled at each other and exchanged hellos. I thought I detected a little sheepishness in his face. In any event, he didn't call me Mr. Rumsfeld.

Now we run into each other all the time, have formally introduced ourselves, and frequently stop to pass along pleasantries and small talk. We had a good laugh over his promoting me to former defense chief of the United States.

About a month ago, I was subject to a viral attack of labyrinthitis—an inner ear infection that causes severe nausea and vertigo; to stand up is to throw up and fall down. I was flat on my back for three days. By the fourth day, I was wobbly but able to make my way and regaining strength.

It was a warm day, and I ventured out to nearby Lincoln Park to practice walking. Between drills, I sat on a bench to rest. Along came my new friend Bill and I asked him to sit down and visit. He told me I looked a little pale, and I told him of the damndest bout I'd ever waged with my body.

We chatted at some length. I learned he's not a building engineer, but a retired conductor of the Chicago and Northwestern Railroad. I learned he's a widower of nine years and still misses his wife terribly. He learned I'm the parent of a daughter who's about to graduate from college. He learned I'm a consultant. We also talked about religion, politics, and the Chicago Cubs.

Unspoken Cues

What's going on here? This is a short story of two people moving toward each other. It's a story of a relationship that's authentic, yet began on the basis of thoroughly inaccurate information being passed between both parties. Nonetheless, goodwill was communicated and fostered by way of posture, facial expressions, and tone of voice. In fact, goodwill was the real message. Stories like this are written every day in the corporation.

On the other hand, every day in corporate life, stories are also written where the absolutely proper or accurate words are spoken between parties, yet the exchange is decidedly inauthentic. In such accounts, the people are moving away from or even against each other.

We need to be sensitive to the messages our teammates send us that go below and above their literal words or even their lack of words altogether. They may be angry with us, more than even they realize, and have trouble putting their anger into words. So what we get is high-sounding subterfuge. Or they may respect what we do, but haven't learned to be forward about paying compliments. So what we get is silence.

We'll do our share in enhancing team efforts if we train ourselves to be alert to these unspoken cues that tell us the real story.

TAKE ACTION

1. Ask yourself, "Why is my teammate telling me *this* . . . *now* . . . *here?*"
2. Then, "*How* is she telling me?"

— 7 —

A RISKY OPINION

I'm sitting across the table from my client. He's hosting me for lunch at his downtown club.

This is a client in whom I truly take delight. Time spent with him is a joy because he has a bountiful sense of humor while the workings of his mind are something to behold. When it comes to the art of managing people in a large organization, this is the most imaginative person I've ever met.

Though I'm the guest, this luncheon was my idea. I requested it because I want to share some views of mine with this man who might take what I say as bad news. Though I like him a great deal, we haven't been working together for very long, I don't know him all that well, and he just might be offended enough to terminate our relationship.

Since he's vice president of human resources of his large specialty chemicals company, this could spell a loss to me of many thousands of dollars in fees. Counted up over a period of years, that number could be staggering.

A moment ago, I wrote that my host is extraordinarily imaginative. And nobody revels in the expression of that imagination more than he does. Where he gets hung up, unfortunately, is in his all-too-frequent seeking of "strokes" from his associates. He seeks more attention and praise from his boss for his initiative than is good. He seems to be saying by his actions, "See, whatta ya think of that? Aren't I a good boy? How about a pat on the back?"

I'm here to tell him that I believe if he keeps this up, he'll get into trouble. His career with the company will be cut short. People will lose patience with him no matter how talented he is.

The Telling

I tell him. But I begin the conversation this way: "Sam, if you don't mind, I'd like to spend some time talking about your management style. I think you know I'm a fan. I've learned a lot from you that I've been able to use here, and elsewhere as well. I want to hear from you how you think things are going for you, but again, if you don't mind, I'd like to talk first."

Sam usually smiles a lot and his enthusiasm is boundless. On this occasion, however, he is appropriately subdued. He looks me straight in the eye and says, "It's all yours."

After I tell him, he remains quiet. He nods slowly several times and bites his lower lip, all the while staring at the tablecloth. He picks up his coffee cup and just before putting it to his lips, says, "You're right."

The Response

We then make good on the first part of my introduction to the conversation. That is, he talks about his management style. Only now, he's focusing on what purpose his attention-getting serves; how that purpose is negative and gets in the way of his otherwise standard-setting performance.

Near the end of our time together, he tells me he has a question: "Does Will (his boss and CEO) know we're having this conversation?" I reply truthfully (I might not always): "No, but in hanging around him and some of the others, I've been picking up signals."

On the street in front of his club, we part company. Just before we do, we shake hands and he says, "Thanks for being a friend."

————————— *TAKE ACTION* —————————

1. Don't be apologetic about what you see. You won't always be right in your opinions, and you must be prepared to admit it when you aren't, but be willing to call 'em as you see 'em.

2. Show the courage of your convictions by being willing to speak first. Even though you risk offending a teammate or other associate whose views you don't know, over the long run this practice will win you respect and increase your self-esteem.

——— **8** ———

NOT VINEGAR, NOT SUGAR

Imagine we're sitting face to face in a room and I ask you any of these questions:

"When was the last time you had your hair cut?"

"Do you think it's a good idea to promote Kay into that job?"

"Why do you do it that way?"

"Do you think it *was* a good idea to promote Kay into that job?"

"Have you done all the research necessary on this?"

43

"Why do you persist in this?"

"How do you do your work with all this clutter around you?"

"How do you do your work with that radio playing so loud?"

"The meeting is supposed to start now—with everybody here. Bill, where's Charlie?"

"When are you going to get to the point?"

"Why are you so quiet in meetings?"

"Are you prepared to stick it out?"

"How long has it been since you won one?"

"Oh?"

"Really?"

Be honest now, most of these questions have a sting, don't they? At the least, they put us on guard. Often, they flat out make us bristle.

There's a familiarity to them, too, isn't there? None of them strikes us as strange. That's because we ask and are asked questions just like these every day of our lives.

Now let me ask this question: How much quality communication is taking place between two people when such questions are asked? How much good listening is shared between them?

The Conversion

Imagine again that we are teammates sitting in a room face to face. Instead of asking you any of the earlier group of questions, I convert them to statements. Suppose I look you in the eye and say any of the following to you:

"You're looking a little shaggy, Jim. If you want to make a good impression in your presentation at Roundtree tomorrow, you'd better get a haircut."

"I've got some real doubts about whether Kay can handle that job. I'd appreciate talking it over with you."

"Maybe I've got a better way than you. Maybe I don't. Tell me why you do it the way you do."

"Kay's not gotten up to speed on that job the way we'd hoped. Let's get together to see what we can do to help her out."

"Tell me what research you've done on this."

"I'm having trouble understanding your persistence on this when the signs strike me as arguing against it. You've gotta have a reason. I'm dying to know what it is. Tell me."

"I could be wrong, of course, but it seems you could feel and work sharper if you'd clean up your office."

"I could be wrong, of course, but it seems you'd be more composed if you turned down that radio. That might reduce your complaints that nobody comes to see you, too."

"I hate starting a meeting without everyone present, but if we go ahead, maybe Charlie will be on time next time."

"Harry, you always make great points, but you sometimes lose your listeners by talking around those points. Make them, bang! Then explain them."

"I get the impression you don't speak up at meetings because you're afraid your comments will sound stupid. Am I right? No? Terrific! Then tell me the real reason."

"Right or wrong, Linda, I sense you get bored easily. This project's gonna take slogging it out. I have to be convinced you're willing to do that."

"You seem to have gotten down on yourself, Doug. I can't imagine anyone better than you at what you do. Do you see that job? Go get it! Here's how I think I can help you.

"No!"

"I don't believe that for one moment!"

The Impact

Feel the difference in impact the statements have on you. Consider your visceral reaction to them. Smoother. Softer. Hopeful. Helpful. Authentic. See how the recipient of any such statement feels valued as a human being, is treated with respect, is induced to listen, and is encouraged to respond in a positive way. Real communication takes place. Subterfuge, sarcasm, and judgment are replaced with telling it like it is.

Be a practitioner of such positive impact. Such practice takes a little longer, but the payoff to both parties in the exchange is far superior to that generated by the barbed question.

—————————— *TAKE ACTION* ——————————

1. Make the point with yourself that questions aren't always wrong, but are *often* wrong. They may not accomplish what's best in a situation.

2. When converting questions to statements, don't evade the issue. Don't jettison your discernment and high standards. Just let your teammate know what is really on your mind.

—— **9** ——

A MODEL OF PROACTIVE CONTACT

Bob Kaplan is a friend and associate. He's the director of executive leadership for the Center for Creative Leadership, a not-for-profit organization headquartered in Greensboro, North Carolina. It is committed to research and training in executive development. As you can tell from his title, Kaplan is a key player.

I first came to know Kaplan a few years ago when I was invited to speak to the assembled research staff in Greensboro. He attended and was the first person in the audience to ask me a question. His curiosity and penetrating mind were apparent from the outset. We spent time together in his office later that day and found we had many work interests in common. We agreed to stay in touch.

The Center staff is composed of high-talent, full-time professionals, but I have become increasingly familiar with its operations by virtue of serving as occasional "adjunct staff." This means that in certain projects the Center takes on, I am asked to participate as one of the members of the consulting or research team.

In this way I have become better acquainted with Bob Kaplan. We have worked closely and spent hours together off the job as well. We've laughed together, haggled, and disagreed. We've paid each other heartfelt compliments and leveled with each other when the other's not been at his personal best.

An Admirable Balance

Perhaps what I admire in Bob Kaplan more than anything else is the way he is able to maintain exemplary contact with his associates at the Center without compromising devotion to his own work and growth.

Kaplan is a team worker par excellence. He's bright, energetic, and positive, and of course that all helps. But he's pensive, determined, and disciplined as well. He has high standards for himself as much as for his subordinates, so he'll hide himself away now and then for thinking and planning. This allows him to return to his collaborations with his team as a contributor at the top of his form.

Whenever I've worked with him I've marveled at the way he directs himself masterfully through his routine of contact and withdrawal. After an all-morning meeting where we've been hard at work with a client, the walk with him to the Center cafeteria is invariably a lesson in networking. Along the way, he'll stop two or three people to talk briefly about some project, ask a question, offer an opinion, pay a compliment, schedule a meeting, share an anecdote, make an introduction, whisper a word of caution, agree to some proposal he's read, or turn thumbs down on another.

I notice that this is the case with him whether we're exiting the men's room, heading for the drinking fountain, or standing in the Center's parking lot at the end of the day before we go our separate ways.

The Broken Code

Between these high-energy, high-efficiency bursts of activity, I notice Bob will shift into a lower gear with ease. This person who the casual onlooker might even think is garrulous and the stereotypical extrovert, is a careful, orderly, quiet type who is a very, very good listener. One gets the impression that he truly knows what's on the minds of his people and the clients they serve. In all the hours we've logged together in his office, for example, he has yet to take one phone call. That's a courtesy important to extend to any visitor, and it lets me know he has low tolerance for distractions.

If you were to ask Bob Kaplan's peers and subordinates if he is readily available to them for discussions, they would answer you in one voice with a resounding yes. But I think I've broken the code. I believe I've discovered a secret of his. He makes himself available by making *them* available.

He goes to people. He doesn't wait for them to come to him. His idea of a break is to get on the move. His walk to the cafeteria, as you've seen, is not just a means of conveyance at mealtime, but a chance for an encounter, a good-natured, authentic linkup in some way with someone with whom he shares tasks. I'm always amazed at how much he gets accomplished this way week after week. These frequent "chance" encounters often eliminate the need for meetings that would take up to an hour or more of both parties' time.

And what's nifty is the twist he's given to availability. He's made it proactive rather than reactive.

─────────────── *TAKE ACTION* ───────────────

1. Follow Kaplan's lead. Don't *be* available. *Do* available.
2. Use such proactive accessibility to keep your ear to the ground. This will alert you to the ways your teammates need more "follow-up time" from you.

─── **10** ───

GETTING SMARTER
WITH DUMB QUESTIONS

A friend of mine for almost 15 years just took a job as vice president of human resources for one of the nation's major investment banks. He's a good-natured person with a quick wit and a broad smile, so I wrote him on the Friday before he settled into his new office: "Dear Dick, I've sent you this note because I want you to have at least one piece of mail in your first week in your new digs."

He wrote back that in his first week he was able to find the men's room in short order and that in fact he had received three pieces of mail. Mine meant the most to him, however, because the second was supposed to go to someone else but accidentally was placed in his in-box, and the third was labeled "Occupant."

When I got his reply, I picked up the phone and called him. We exchanged pleasantries, kidded around some more, and then I asked how it was going for him. He said that this looked like a good move for him, the juices were flowing fresh, and the place felt right for him. Then he told me a story that proved the point.

Early in his second week, he was making the rounds with the key officers of the firm to get acquainted with them and learn what their expectations were for him. In one of these meetings, the managing director of corporate finance launched into a discussion that went over the newcomer's head.

My friend knew that the man expected him to understand the subject (it had something to do with investment syndication and I don't understand it either) and, wanting to impress this fellow, considered trying to get by with his smile, an assortment of assuring nods, uh-huhs, and beating a hasty retreat.

He thought better of it, though, and instead did this. He cleared his throat, and when his discussion partner completed a sentence, held up his hand, and gently pushed it toward his partner as if to say, "Whoa!" *Then* he smiled his broad smile and said, "I can tell from your comments you think I should know this subject, but the fact is I don't. On the other hand, I expect to when I leave your office. Can we start over? Tell me: What's a syndicate?"

The Listening Process

Like so much else, listening is not an event but a process. It's not just a clear hearing of what another person says. When it's done right, listening is a psychological contract—unwritten, and perhaps only sensed, but as real as rain. There are emotional elements to listening, such as when I feel condescended to by your speech and tell you, rather than complain to others, that I wish you wouldn't do that.

In a similar vein, suppose I'm talking too much and notice that you're getting bored. I stop, admit it, and ask you to tell me what's running through your head. Overbearing as I've been, this means I've remained engaged in the listening process. I've caught on to the error of my ways. Unless a run-on mouth is habitual with me, proving that I don't learn from my mistakes, this admission on my part is likely to win your appreciation, and you'll continue to contribute to our thinking partnership.

When my friend Dick interposed his admission of ignorance, he was holding up his end of the psychological contract. He risked looking stupid. What he got in return, however, was respect. The officer who was speaking to him was left with no choice but to conclude that here was a listener, a learner, a person who was placing value on the time and contribution of both parties to the discussion.

The Team Process

Nowhere is the psychological contract to listen and admit ignorance more in evidence than on the thinking team. How can any team solve problems or agree on initiatives until its members become comfortable with spotlighting what they *don't* know about a subject?

The partnership of team effort implies the readiness of all its members to shine light into dark corners. They might say, for example, "Lois, I don't follow that at all. Tell me what I'm missing." Or, "Chuck, you've spoken about that three days in a row. I've asked for clarification and you've given it. I'm embarrassed to ask a fourth time, but it still doesn't make sense to me. Does anybody else have this trouble, or am I alone?" A few nods may be forthcoming, and Chuck's fervor will have to be buttressed with clearer thinking.

Chuck and everybody else on the team will benefit from this.

TAKE ACTION

1. We have all been in groups or classes when somebody else asked the "dumb" question we were afraid to ask, and virtually the whole group sighed in relief at having it answered. Therefore: Ask dumb questions!

2. Be glad when people ask you dumb questions. Say, "Thank you for asking." This will keep them from *doing* something dumb.

FAST TAKES

on

Listening

- Every act is a form of communication.
- You won't get the opportunity to listen to the best ideas of others if you won't share your own.
- Quality listening is an exchange process that requires quality talking as well.
- The right words often don't convey the authentic message.
- "A question mark," said Frederick Perls, "is a hook on the end of a statement."
- The balance of contact and withdrawal makes you a fresher listener.
- Taking phone calls while in conference means you're not there to listen.
- The thinking team admits its ignorance.

III

ENCOURAGING

The Art of Empowerment

By now, you've no doubt suspected that virtually all seven themes of this book weave their way into each chapter—one way or another. In some cases an emphasis on one is quite clear, as with vision in chapter XX. But even there, as you'll see, the other themes are present as well. Despite my attempts at organization, they all become inextricably linked.

Such is true with this chapter, to be sure, but let me move on to theme 5 in particular and show its importance to the subject of encouragement. This theme is as follows: *Belief in men and women as social beings is a lofty one and is best authenticated with down-to-earth performance.* The act of encouragement is a social act. It is other-centered rather than self-centered and finds numerous nitty-gritty outlets. Make yourself an encourager by giving thought to the following:

- Showing enthusiasm for a teammate's courage through your voice, facial expression, and gestures

- Not imposing your ideas of how a job should be done
- Encouraging your *boss*
- Lobbying for *top management* team effectiveness
- Encouraging yourself to reclaim some neglected strength

—— **11** ——

BEING THERE FOR SOMEBODY

John Donne, the early seventeenth-century English metaphysical poet, wrote, "No man is an island." No better imagery exists for expressing our need for each other, for our need to have others need us as well.

In thinking about the latter in particular—our providing intervention for someone else—my mind automatically turns to the subject of encouragement and what our role should be in the encouragement process.

An early and brilliant model for us in this regard is the great Viennese psychiatrist Alfred Adler. This pioneer of the "social" school of personality was the first to write extensively about the therapist's responsibility to encourage a client to pursue the life tasks of work, love, and friendship rather than to lean on excuses for avoiding them.

Whenever I read Adler, as I do from time to time, I'm struck anew that encouragement itself is not some bland, mild word of support, but instead means "to make courageous." That changes my understanding of the word. Doesn't it change yours?

Face to Face

Perhaps it's the references to voice, facial expressions, and gestures in the first bullet point on page 52 that make me think of the therapist–client relationship. Such an exchange is an active engagement conducted on a face-to-face basis over the long pull. Therefore, it serves as a good teacher for us, and it's clear that we can apply some lessons from this particular relationship to our team relation-

53

ships. Adler, for example, was an active listener and observer, insightfully piecing together a client's pattern of living. He would concentrate on what a client avoided and would not hesitate to put the client's feet to the fire, have the client move toward those responsibilities that frightened him or her, then applaud every inching move forward as an act of courage and authenticity.

Small Signs, Big Idea

There's no question that in an executive's life, good performance crowds out the mediocre or bad. By that I mean if a person on the job can be induced to act on something he or she believes in but is afraid to try, that person is likely to find some success at it, no matter how halting or small, and be more eager to build on it in the future. This leaves less time and room for inauthentic effort.

The first such step taken by women or men who are teammates of yours is an act of courage that is wholly theirs. They are on the line, out in front, and exposed; the butterflies are in *their* stomachs. It is their knees that are knocking. You, of course, know they won't die, but they're not at all sure!

Your role—first, last, and always—is to be there with the small sign: a grin, a blackened frown, an angry voice expressing authentic concern, a joyful one celebrating your associate's getting the picture, a gesture of exasperation or one of "go for it." These are a blend of the three-steps-forward, two-steps-back philosophy of accomplishment. This is life, and your being there with these small signs is the big idea.

───────────── *TAKE ACTION* ─────────────

1. Be there for somebody.
2. Get your body into it.

12

HONEYCOMBS OF LEARNING

An evolutionary change in the authority structure of American business has taken place over the past generation. I have seen it firsthand in my consulting practice and have verified it in my research.

When I entered management consulting in 1965, all I or my associates had to do to win a choice assignment was to get the ear of a company's CEO and convince *him* we had something to contribute.

Today, that may be just the beginning of the sales effort and is no guarantee of work won. Generating the CEO's consideration is an important step but not the only one, and often, not the most critical. Consider the following examples:

Example 1. The president of the largest manufacturing company in its field is a social friend of mine—has been for many years. We've spoken of my work and he's expressed genuine interest in it. A year ago, he wrote a letter to me about that, stating that he thought his company should discuss with me my helping them in executive development. He sent a copy of that letter to his vice president of human resources, the person with whom I would work closely on such an assignment.

I followed up on the president's suggestion and called that man frequently. He neither took my calls, nor returned them. When we run into each other at professional meetings, as we do occasionally, he's always cordial, and even asked me once to call him so we could arrange to get together. I did, of course, but was met with the same behavior.

You might cite the man for stupidity. I certainly would call him discourteous. But no matter what, he's under no threat of reprimand in not acting on his boss's recommendations. He has a mind of his own that has concluded it has no interest in my services, and he feels secure in the way he expresses it.

Example 2. My book *Inside Corporate America* is a study of 1,086 top and middle-management executives in the 115 headquarters, subsidiaries, and divisions of 13 major corporations. Based on more than 400 questions, one such query directed at those executives is this: "Are you free to exchange operating information with your peers in other functions without approval from your boss?" Ninety-three percent of the top executives and 87 percent of the middle-managers replied "always" or "usually."

Power and Influence

When Harvard Business School professor John Kotter wrote his first-rate book *Power and Influence*, his publisher sent me a copy for review. My response, which ended up as a dust jacket blurb and pertains to team functioning, is relevant to this essay: "There is the meaning of authority, which we understand pretty well, and the meaning of influence, which we don't. But more important than either is the ability to exercise the power of influence. That's what *Power and Influence* is about. Anyone who takes to heart the lessons of this penetrating book will be sure to enrich his or her ability in a most important area."

Eroding Authority

> Oh where, oh where
>   has authority gone?
> Oh where, oh where can it be?
> It's all drained out of the boss's big stick
>   'Tis a network of thee, me, and we.

The point of this doggerel and chapter is not that your boss has no authority over you, nor you over your subordinates. That would be incorrect. Rather, it is that with the wider dispersion of data throughout organizations—largely by virtue of the computer—our corporations are becoming honeycombs of learning more than centers of production.

As I'll point out again in essays 36 and 96, people are being called upon increasingly to collaborate to understand what all this data means. And while to my mind hierarchy is as inevitable as death and taxes, there's no question that the dividing lines between individuals' levels and functions are getting blurred in the service of teamwork disposed not to reporting data but interpreting it. This is as true in the factory as it is in the office. And even though you see words such as "superior" and "subordinate" scattered throughout this book, they increasingly are giving way to "associate" and "team member" throughout business.

If your bent is still barking out orders, you're headed for extinction—fast. Telling your associates how to do their jobs is the fastest way I know to freeze yourself out of the action.

———————————— *TAKE ACTION* ————————————

1. Ponder what it means for your corporation to be a honeycomb of learning rather than a facility that's a center of production. Are you going to be a functioning team member in that network?

2. Want specific help on this? Buy and read Kotter's *Power and Influence* (see "A Closing Word," page 338).

——— **13** ———

AN ETERNAL VERITY

Don't you love people with big world views? I do. One such person whose company and work I enjoy is Bruce Buursma, columnist for the *Chicago Tribune*.

Buursma currently writes on sports, but this is something new. For some years, he was the *Tribune*'s religion editor. He has traveled throughout the world covering the exalted (such as the Pope), and trekked low country and bayou roads in search of stories on the fallen (such as Jim and Tammy Bakker and Jimmy Swaggart).*

He's reported on schisms among Baptists and Lutherans, Oral Roberts's special messages from the Almighty, Pat Robertson's run-

*Shortly after I wrote this essay, Buursma was promoted to West Coast bureau chief for the *Chicago Tribune*. From that region of the country, he was called on to cover *anything* of major importance for the *Tribune* reader. Now he has become a business columnist for the financial pages and lives in a yet-larger world!

ning for the presidency, and the Episcopal Church's unwillingness to ordain women as priests; and he's explicated such heavy theological doctrines as incarnation and transubstantiation, and itemized the differences in religious practice between Orthodox, Conservative, and Reformed Jews.

These days, he concerns himself with split-fingered fastballs, fake bunts, double steals, torn rotator cuffs, pulled hamstrings, three-point shots, Michael Jordan's wardrobe, spinnakers, and bogeys. I ask you: How can you not be in wonder of anyone who is equally at ease with the perceptions, spirit, and vocabulary of a clergy robing room before the administration of a sacrament, and a locker room after a championship game?

Just Like the Rest of Us

Over lunch one day, when Bruce was winding up his assignment as religion editor, we got to talking about some of the people he'd followed and interviewed along the way. I wanted to know who among those concerned with the eternal verities had most won his respect.

He cited several names you would recognize, and I then asked him what they are like. "Well, for the most part, they're just like the rest of us." He then told me he'd just returned from a large ecumenical gathering in New York City. Two clergymen, whose names are household words to anyone the least bit interested in religion, delivered major addresses.

He later met with one of them, who asked Bruce, somewhat surreptitiously, how he thought his address compared to that of the other luminary on the program. Buursma told me that he'd noticed this quality among all great personages he'd observed firsthand: "They want to know how they're doing."

Your Boss

Your boss may not be a great personage, but she's one individual under heaven who's almighty important where you're concerned.

And though she may not be exalted to those outside your organization, she has an abundance of power over you. Of deep significance, however, that you may not have thought of, is the power you have over her.

The power I refer to is the power of encouragement.

It is common for us to look for encouragement from others. There seems to be no end to our appetite for being on the receiving end of cheerleading. We feel alone in facing many of our tasks and often doubt our ability to perform well. We wonder if we'll measure up to what is expected of us.

That friend or associate or boss who urges us on with a smile or kick in the pants is someone to whom we feel indebted after we haltingly approach some undertaking and find we were up to it after all. Were it not for that person's intervention in our lives at that point, we might still be in the wings wishing for what might have been. Instead, we're stronger, more self-confident, and ready to take on a little more risk the next time around.

Just as we've been the beneficiaries of support for our capacities to perform well when we've had our doubts, we've also experienced the joy of being there for a peer or subordinate of ours who benefited from the right word at the right time from us.

But what does not occur to most of us is how much our bosses need encouragement from us. We often lack empathy for the anguish in their lives when they doubt their ability to perform or make the right choice for the businesses or functions for which they're responsible.

Like Bruce's religious leader sitting at the pinnacle of his ecclesiastical hierarchy with literally millions in his flock, your boss wants to know how she's doing. No matter how surreptitiously she might send out the signal, she wants to know that somebody who matters to her believes that she can do it—whatever "it" is— or that she has done it, and done it right. *This is an eternal verity.*

Believe me, you matter. Let her know.

TAKE ACTION
---

1. Take a break from wondering if you're scoring with your boss by considering what she needs in the way of support from you.

2. Don't be a phony, an apple-polisher, or a manipulator. Be authentic. Just be there *today* with a kind word for what your boss has accomplished or is about to undertake.

— 14 —

ENCOURAGING TOP TEAM DEVELOPMENT

About five years ago I visited with the CEO of one of our very largest companies. We were in his office having a cup of coffee together. He was hunched forward in shirt sleeves, the index finger of his right hand curled through the cup handle, his left hand palmed around the cup itself. He sat in a chair at the end of a rectangular coffee table. I sat adjacent to him at the near end of a long sofa in this smaller than expected, well-appointed room.

He was about to sip from his cup when he suddenly put it down and shifted his body directly toward me to make a point more firmly. "The hardest thing for me to get used to in this job is the way these guys who report to me won't grab the ball and run with it. It's as if they come to me one by one and ask, 'What do I do now, boss?' It's exasperating. I want to scream, 'Go look in the mirror, man!' "

Does it surprise you that people—people in their late 40s and up, senior officers of one of America's corporate giants, most with grown children, living in the right towns, driving the right cars, belonging to the gilt-edge clubs, making over a half-million dollars a year—have trouble taking initiative? "Is it possible," you ask, "that these very executives who are walking specimens of corporate success don't know what to do next?"

Self-Starters?

It's not at all the case, actually, that they don't know how to take initiative. Rather, it's more that they've gotten out of the habit, and this CEO's plight is as common as Volkswagen Beetles on college campuses in the 1960s.

It is true that top executives *and* junior executives often don't take initiative, but for different reasons. Big organizational life gets tricky, and the differences in the pushes and pulls of these two executive ranks is one of the ways this occurs.

Remember when you first went to work as a professional? The boss who hired you told you—you were probably in your early 20s— that she wanted you to be a self-starter. She wanted you to have ideas and push them. She wanted you to be decisive and aggressive. But what did you find out? You found out this wasn't the real picture. Every time you tried to go off on your own, you got your wings clipped. You were told in a thousand ways, "This is how we do things around here, and we expect you to follow suit." You quickly learned to check and get approval before you launched virtually anything. You learned *not* to be a self-starter—at least not to be what you meant by that term.

So the corporation by its actions ends up letting its young people know that it doesn't want them to be self-starters because they don't know enough. Later, though, after learning the ropes and chafing somewhat in the process as they advance through their 30s and climb the ladder, the winners reach age 40 and qualify for top management. "Now," the corporation says, "you've got the knowledge and experience. You've got the responsibility and the authority. Now we *really* want you to be self-starters." This time the corporation means it, but these thoroughbreds have forgotten how to leap from the gate!

Development at the Top

Corporations are wising up. This CEO made this evident to me five years ago. He wanted badly to take measures to put red blood back into his blue-blood management. He confirmed the most exciting, promising trend in the boardroom today: executive development for top executives. Years ago, executive development was treated chauvinistically by top executives. "Executive development?" they'd ask, then reply, "Oh, that's for my guys."

All that is changing. The theme of lifelong learning so central to the professionals in the field of continuing education has moved onto the headquarters floor of corporate America.

To my mind, the way this development is best implemented is by focusing effort on top management team effectiveness. The top executive grows—gets the juices flowing again—by full participation on the team. Recently an editor of the *Wall Street Journal* asked me what I mean by team effectiveness. I replied, "Authentic communication between mature adults." This is exactly what the CEO wanted, but didn't have, among all his direct reports.

Full participation on a thriving team generates ideas, creates initiative, and puts members to the test. It reawakens dormant desires and self-confidence. And when this happens at top management, it sets an example for the rest of the organization. *Team* effort becomes the norm throughout the company with the result that those junior executives won't be as confused as they were, either.

―――――――――――――――― *TAKE ACTION* ――――――――――――――――

1. Climb aboard the team train. Lobby among your boss and peers for embarking on team development for your group.

2. Urge your boss to do likewise among *her* boss and peers. If the team message isn't coming down from the top, help send it up!

―― **15** ――

WITH WINGS OF EAGLES

For two days, I conducted a workshop with six high-potential executives of the international technical services group of a major food company. These people serve as advisors and trouble shooters to plant managers around the world.

One of the participants flew in from London. Another one, from Singapore, directs a staff responsible for plant services that are carried out in ten time zones! Whenever a plant is planned or built, major equipment purchases are made, or something big goes wrong with work flow or product quality, these people are on the case.

Another of the attendees, however, was particularly fascinating to me. He was a little more senior than the rest. He had served his time in the field, including Canada, Puerto Rico, and the Philippines, but was now a staff person back at corporate headquarters. His job is coordinating, and he reports to the vice president of technical services.

This fellow—let's call him Lew—gives the impression of being cynical. He also has a quick wit, is a good storyteller (though his stories have a sarcastic edge to them), and draws people to himself naturally. Whether we were at breaks or lunch, he would be at the center of virtually every conversation.

What Scares Us to Death

During the first morning of the workshop, I laid out a conceptual base for what we'd be working toward during the rest of the workshop; namely, how the attendees can create more impact for themselves on plant managers and associates through team problem solving.

The conceptual base I refer to is what I call "the team style profile" and is made up of 20 dimensions that coincide with the 20 chapters of this book. When I got around to item number 10, reclaiming your unique strengths, I noticed that cynical, hard-surfaced Lew truly got intrigued.

In this part I said that what we're really, *really*, REALLY good at—where we could stand head and shoulders above all others— scares us to death. This concept of authenticity is not easy to get, but Lew is bright and curious and was taken by this thought. He began to lean forward in his chair.

Even those things we're good at *now*, for which people rely on us—those cultivated abilities that make someone say, "See if you can get Ken to do that for us," or "Ask Lisa if she'll analyze this for you"—are arenas that frightened us silly earlier in our careers.

What I'm getting at, of course, is the need for exercising the courage—for encouraging ourselves—to stay a little bit frightened by running on the learning track. "This," I said, "is how you have an impact on people and events."

Yet One Level Deeper

A more advanced stage of learning, however, is to go one level deeper into the recesses of our beings to discover what is most unique about ourselves that we have neglected. Lew wanted to know more about this, so I continued.

We all care about something down to our bones, but acting on that care requires a boldness that terrifies us. The boldness required is dramatic precisely because the care runs so deep. And because we're frozen from taking the bold steps, we bury that care, putting it beneath the level of our awareness while we busy ourselves with other concerns.

That care is different for each of us, and it never leaves, even though we try to ignore it. Yet were we somehow to summon up the will to act on the care, it would be inevitable that we have a powerful impact on people and events by virtue of the conviction that pulls us. It isn't a matter of juicing up something artificial. Rather, it's a matter of scraping off layers of aged and accumulated inhibition and getting out of the way of our own passion.

I don't pretend to know Lew's neglected care, but I know it has something to do with the affiliation of people, and therein lies his potential uniqueness on the job. I asked him to take the lead in a team problem-solving project and he did an impressive job.

Near the end of the workshop, I asked all participants to complete a writing assignment that included laying out five goals for themselves. Two were to be immediate, reached within a week. Two were to be intermediate, reached within a year. One was to be long-range, reached in three years. Then I made them share their goals with the rest of the group.

Lew's "softening" in the workshop was apparent. He said that for his two intermediate goals, he was going to take a stand on his values, which he's kept partially under wraps, and that he was going to master the techniques of team problem solving.

At the very end, I insisted that all participants tell one quality they appreciated in each other. At that moment, Lew blushed blood red, but he loved the activity. This confirmed that he was chipping at the barnacles all around his neglected strength. His blush could be our blush.

TAKE ACTION

1. Look under the rock. See what you have kept in hiding.

2. Give that little creature light and air. Feed it. Nurture it. Then give it wings.

FAST TAKES

on

Encouraging

- Good performance crowds out bad performance.
- Encouragement isn't bland, mild support. It's an authentic intervention into someone's life.
- To make courageous is to be courageous.
- Giving and receiving encouragement needs to be done in more equal parts.
- Your boss needs encouragement from you.
- It's a common misfortune to get out of the habit of taking initiative.
- Blue-blooded top management can be induced to greater initiative with a red-blooded team-effectiveness transfusion.
- Encouragement needs to flow in four directions: up, down, across, and inward.

IV

BEING AFFIRMATIVE

The Discovery of Options

Theme 2, *The need to belong is a powerful human force that finds expression in teamwork,* serves as a foundation for this chapter. People want to feel their work is bigger than their jobs, and being affirmative accomplishes this.

Affirmation is a way we bind ourselves to others authentically. It's an expression of hope and high purpose. It's a declaration of trust in associates, the belief that in concert, no matter how daunting our prospects, somehow we can find a way.

Without affirmation there's no team. To be affirmative, give thought to the following:

- Engaging your teammates' strengths
- Acknowledging discouragement to put it behind you
- Avoiding unrealistic goals
- Enjoying *performing* your tasks as well as *completing* them
- Celebrating your accomplishments

67

16

DIVING OVER THE DUMMIES

The high school I attended was a large one. It numbered more than 3,000 students. It was good, too, noted for its college preparatory academics, special education, arts, and athletics.

On the athletic director's staff was a man by the name of Orin K. Noth who coached the sophomore football team. O. K. Noth was a wiry little guy who bellowed like a rogue elephant and struck the fear of God into his players. He was a stickler for discipline, and his job, I later figured out, was to get the school's most promising athletes ready for varsity play the following year.

I wasn't a football player, so I escaped his scornful glances and acid tongue. I did, that is, until I found myself in gym class under his care for a six-week-long section on tumbling. Six torturous weeks those were, with my being raked over daily for being the most physically inept creature on the planet.

The following six weeks were devoted to basketball, where, thank goodness, I had a modicum of ability. The dear raspy-voiced fellow came around and shocked me by saying, "Oh, I see Mr. Cox is a basketball player." He watched, gave me pointers, encouraged me to go out for the junior varsity team the next year, and lo and behold, I did and made it.

However, baseball was my main sport and first love. I was pretty good with both bat and glove and played varsity my junior and senior years. In the spring of my junior year, Coach Noth came around again as a spectator and said, "Oh, I see Mr. Cox is really a *baseball* player!"

Though this man was never my team's coach, he was always there watching and did what was right. Noth was more than O. K.

Limitations

In tumbling class, Noth never allowed me to relax. He kept pushing and pulling and spent just as much time putting us laggards through the paces as he did with those for whom the drill was a cakewalk.

When I finally dived over five dummies and finished up with a graceless somersault, he laughed so hard he dropped his clipboard. Then he applauded, chortled, and said "Cox, I guess you'll be all right."

It was obvious my heart and skills weren't in tumbling, yet the coach was not going to take that state of affairs at face value. He wasn't going to focus his energies on my limitations, but used the process of tumbling to teach me to act on my strengths. The strengths in this case were mental. The truth was, I was *afraid* to dive over five dummies. He made me make my body perform.

Strengths

In the midst of anybody's limitations there are always strengths to be found and engaged. Never lose sight of this in your work with teammates. One of the greatest gifts you can offer is to convey that you have paid attention to your associates and have spotted or sensed some ability or attitude in them that sets them apart from their peers in a positive way.

Then, if you're committed to being a true collaborator, you'll urge them not to neglect those strengths but to make good things happen by grabbing hold of the opportunities they present.

———————————— *TAKE ACTION* ————————————

1. Think not what people can't do, but what they can do.
2. Then tell them.

—— **17** ——

THE VALUE OF DISCOURAGEMENT

A friend of mine called to tell me he'd been fired. He's not what you'd think of as a close friend because we've known each other only through professional involvements over the past three years or so, and live in different regions of the country. Nonetheless, we have a great deal of respect for each other; the chemistry, as they say, is good between us, and I have a lot of feeling for him.

There was a tremble in his voice. He was hurt and stunned at his firing, and was probably embarrassed to be calling me about it. He wondered what my reaction might be, I suppose, and if I might think less of him somehow. He also wanted support and advice, of course, and I'm pleased he didn't let embarrassment keep him from placing the call.

My friend (let's call him Mark), is brainy and sensitive. He's enormously gifted and has an eye and ear for his work. He sees what others of us don't see, and hears what others of us don't hear. On the other hand, he misses some signals in his relations with teammates that he shouldn't. He can be argumentative for no good reason, distant, and resistant—particularly to new things and people. Later on, he can bring more ideas to a project than anyone. But when he encounters something new, he's inclined to put on the brakes.

He had gotten into trouble at his company, where he'd served with distinction for 13 years, because he was at odds with his boss, the CEO recently brought in from the outside. The new boss was revving up the engine while Mark was siphoning his gas tank. Or so it seemed to the CEO. As a result, my friend was history.

Pain and Embarrassment

In our phone conversation, Mark began to describe his ordeal since being given his walking papers a few days earlier. He's divorced and lives alone. His teenage son lives with his mother in a distant city. So other than spending time with empathic associates at work, he struggled through his pain in relative isolation.

He was sick. Sick. He told me how he threw up repeatedly over the weekend. He knew he'd been a bad actor—had been a cantankerous adversary to the CEO at first—but he'd been given a warning and thought he'd made real strides in cleaning up his act. Apparently, he hadn't made enough and was now feeling totally inadequate, immobilized, mired in discouragement.

The issue here is not who was in the wrong and how this rupture could have been avoided. True enough, if Mark had been more willing to move out of his comfort zone, he could have seen value in what the new CEO wanted to accomplish. And had the CEO shown a little more patience and understanding, he could have brought Mark under his wing and had a loyal supporter. But that was history, too, on that Monday not long ago when Mark called me, and he had to get on with his new life.

Shunning Denial

My first response to Mark was merely to listen to him; to let him get his story out. After all, this man cares deeply about his work and loved the company. He's not an opportunist who manages his career with an "up, periscope" mentality—always keeping his eye out for the next jump up the job ladder somewhere else. He was shaken to his roots.

Then I told him that his terrible sense of discouragement was normal, understandable, and would even serve a good purpose. He found the first part of that statement hope-inducing, but the latter part surprising.

He had suffered a loss, I told him, and it was important that he was acknowledging it—facing it fully. He knew he had a hand in that loss, and it was important that he own up to that as well. People who lose a loved one, and who do not mourn that loss fully, who deny the impact of it on them, will find that it continues to gnaw at them like a low-grade infection.

Facing his discouragement, then, was the only way he could put it behind him. The discouragement would pass, I said, and he would begin to reclaim his beliefs in his talents and enjoy a resurgence in his energy even though he was now completely sapped. He would come to know later, if not right then, that there's no value in ignoring discouragement. To do so is de-authenticating.

The story has a happy ending. After some months, Mark landed a job that offers him a real growth opportunity. He's got to sell himself all over again, to be sure, but he should do just fine. Being cautious about new situations, he's not as convinced of this as I am, but it's the right place for this now-wiser person to put what he has learned to work. Moreover, he's taken the plunge and remarried. That's another good start!

———————————— *TAKE ACTION* ————————————

1. When discouragement comes your way, don't deny its existence. Talk it over with your teammates. They know how you feel already anyway. Remember *Mad* magazine's Alfred P. Newman? "What, me worry?" Likewise, no good purpose is served by bravado's rhetorical question: "What, me discouraged?"

2. When discouragement comes—and it will—own it: Live it, accept it, breathe it, taste it. Then you'll be able to spit it out.

—— 18 ——

STAIRS AND LANDINGS

This past week, I attended a national conference sponsored by a Chicago organization called the Center for Ethics and Corporate Policy. I'm board chairman of this group, so I had a welcoming role and was a convener of one of the conference's plenary sessions. Other than those responsibilities, however, I was free to be a fly on the wall and the beneficiary of a program full of rich thoughts and opportunities for learning.

One of our keynote speakers was Andrew Sigler, CEO of Champion International, the forest products company headquartered in Connecticut. Sigler was chairman of a recent ambitious ethics project undertaken by ten member companies of the Business Roundtable (200 of the largest corporations in America). He and representatives of the other nine companies were in attendance to present workshops on how they are attempting to weave an "ethics perspective" throughout their operations.

Sigler's speech was titled "Ethics: A Corporate Asset," and it was a dandy. He told the conferees how ethics as a word itself can get in the way, and he prefers language such as "acceptable standards" or "acceptable behavior" as a means for setting guidelines for suitable, responsible corporate performance.

He said ethics is not ethereal at all, but a down-to-earth, everyday thing—such as a concern for safety in your plants. Then he said something fascinating: "When you're setting high standards for yourselves, and you've got everybody in the company thinking and talking about them, you've got to realize you're never going to get there. You're aiming for perfection, and if you're not careful you'll end up on a downer."

Stretch Goals

We readily might see that fostering an ethical perspective throughout a company as far-flung and complex as Champion is a recipe for frustration without stopping to realize how hard we can be on *ourselves*. We too, as persons, are subject to downers that are of our own making.

It is well known that in any endeavor, if we fail to grow, we die. Growth comes in many forms, however, so it is important to know that I'm not referring only to growth in size. The expression "use it or lose it" comes to mind and captures the thought that utilization of some resource—all by itself—is growth.

When we call upon resources of ours that we previously have allowed to be inert or dormant, we become engaged in growth. This is an authenticating, stretching process, a test of our elasticity, of reach, of courage, of affirmation, of hope. It is to act on a goal, whether we have fully articulated that goal for ourselves or not.

It is essential that we set stretch goals for ourselves at proper intervals. These are intervals and actual goals that you, of course, must choose for your own life. But it is imperative to keep in mind that the balanced life is made up of cycles and rhythms, advances and withdrawals, actions and reflections, stairs and landings. There is a time to reach and a time to savor what you have reached—even when what you reached falls below your expectations.

Unrealistic Goals

Andy Sigler pointed out that plant people can build up thousands of accident-free hours, and then "Some guy gets careless, slips off the bottom rung of a ladder, and breaks his ankle. The people want to kill him!"

73

"See what I mean?" he asks, and then says, "You've gotta find ways to celebrate your victories." Those thousands of hours of plant safety is a victory for factory teams, he's telling us all, and he wants to find ways to help those teams celebrate it rather than be down because their string is broken along with an employee's ankle.

When a goal we set for ourselves is a long-range one, we'll want to savor our milestones along the way, acknowledging there will be failure and disappointment to slow us down and divert us. Such milestones are short-range or intermediate goals in support of the longer-range one. They let us know we're heading in the right direction and are exhilarating in their own right. They are a confirmation of our strength, an expression of our growth, vitality—our authenticity. They keep us looking up, forward.

Some long-range goals may indeed be impossible, a reach for perfection that can never be grasped. If Wade Boggs of the Boston Red Sox wants to be acknowledged as the best hitter ever to play the game of baseball, he's sure to fail. No such concurrence is in the cards. But as a young boy he wanted to make the team somewhere. He did. As a young man, he wanted to make the team in the majors. He did that too. And now he has a string of American League batting titles behind him. Though he wants to be his personal best, it's likely he'd agree expecting to be the best of all time makes failure a surefire certainty.

TAKE ACTION

1. Discouraged with a project right now? Take time out to see how far you've come, how much you've accomplished. In most cases, this will come as an uplifting, pleasant surprise.

2. Don't torture yourself with unreachable short-range goals. Stretch yourself, and do what you can. Your team expects no more from you than this. You mustn't either.

—— **19** ——

WORKING ON TOMORROW'S TIME

It's 8:23 A.M. I've had breakfast, brushed my teeth, read the *Wall Street Journal* and a local paper, run a facial tissue over my shoes lightly (hoping to give them a tad more luster), and I am sitting in a chair.

I'm in a hotel room in San Francisco, making use of some time before I catch the elevator downstairs to attend a meeting at 9:15. From where I sit, I have a sweeping view of East Bay and have my eyes fixed on the San Francisco–Oakland Bay Bridge—the one that was damaged slightly in the 1989 earthquake.

This brings back memories for me. I recall a seventh-grade geography class taught by Florence Murdoch. At one point, we charges studied a picture of this magnificent bridge in our textbooks while she explained that it was the longest suspension bridge ever built. Opened in 1936, stretching more than eight miles connecting the cities of Oakland and San Francisco, this two-tiered structure holds my fascination far more than its showy sister, the Golden Gate.

This bridge's design engineer, Glenn Woodruff, undoubtedly had a goal—a clear end in mind as to its ultimate purpose and sheer beauty. He knew, obviously, when he undertook his task that its completion lay years in advance. I can't imagine, however, that despite his desire to see it built (construction began in 1933), put to use, and viewed as the wondrous structure that it is, that he did not find his day-by-day, nit-by-nit design work on it anything but glorious.

In his own way, he was a Luther Burbank—growing a new breed of rose and stopping to smell it at the same time. He shows us by example that the future need not be today's abductor.

Lost in Time

It's common for us to say or hear, "I can't wait 'til this thing's over." We're referring, of course, to some project or involvement that's onerous to us. Such encumbrances are inevitable now and then, and our sense of dread is understandable. We have no option but to grin and bear it.

On the other hand, people we think of as gifted are those who make what they do look easy and are tireless in their pursuits. Their ease of execution in their craft is borne of practice, familiarity, and focus. A major-league second baseman, for example, is art in motion as he takes a lob from the shortstop, pushes off the bag, pivots, throws to first, leaps high to avoid a sliding base runner, and watches on his way down as the double play is signaled by the first-base umpire. All this activity is accomplished in less than two seconds, but its mastery has been years in the making.

The instant pivot is a marvel of body and eye coordination that becomes second nature only to the player who has done it thousands of times. But who's counting? The hours spent and the repetitions completed in order to "get it down" and "keep it down" are frozen in time to the devotee who finds only exhilaration in such routine.

Killing Time

The exhilaration of practicing for the exemplary double play would be nonexistent were it not for its integration into a larger whole. The significance of the double play derives from its part in the game, a season of games, a career of seasons, and the advancement of the sport of baseball itself.

By focusing our attention solely on the future, our current work is robbed of its significance. Yet a present stripped of its connection to the future is likely an artless, zestless pastime. Our expression "killing time" is a tip-off. There's little to be gained by this point of view. Rather, what we seek is to make time come alive. What we long for is to make our tasks today serve some useful purpose for tomorrow.

The second baseman in the quest of a World Series victory who painstakingly drills himself, and the bridge builder who begins a project by putting lines on paper years before the ribbon-cutting are people who offer lessons to the rest of us. Simple questions we need to ask to spur affirmative attitudes in our daily undertakings are these: What is my company here for? What am I here for?

Though the questions are simple enough, giving authentic answers to them requires considerable reflection on our part and results in goals that demand accomplishments of us. Mere work or labor in isolation from final purpose breeds boredom and resentment. On the other hand, accomplishments toward some worthy end stretch us, confirm our abilities, and add to the joint efforts we share with our teammates.

Any one of you who becomes an exemplary practitioner of your craft knows the full importance of the activities of the present, and you invest yourself in time. Your commitment and joy in participation is apparent to all onlookers. It's paradoxical that sheer pleasure comes to the person who commits this unselfish act. Such devotion inspires dreams in others.

TAKE ACTION

1. Extricate yourself from some harmful either/or attitudes. Good work is not a matter of keeping your eye on either today or tomorrow, one exclusive of the other.

2. Yes, by all means stop and smell the roses. But be sure to grow the roses first and keep the garden tended.

— 20 —

ONE FOR ALL, ALL FOR ONE

In essay 15, I described a workshop I conducted among a half-dozen technical service executives with a large consumer foods company.

You'll remember that I gave the participants a writing assignment. I sent them away from our meeting room for an hour to have them look back over their lives to identify three high points. I wanted them to think about those high points and see what's missing in their lives now that was present then. I asked them to identify and write down what passions or values were attached to those high points that are missing now. "See how you can recapture those passions and values in whole or in part," I urged them.

Then, as you'll recall, I had each executive draft five job-related goals that would be shared with all five associates when the group reassembled. Two of the goals were immediate, to be reached within a week. Two of them were intermediate, to be reached within a year. The last was long-range, to be reached within three years.

When the executives returned in an hour, they were highly charged, partly because the writing assignment forced them to get reacquainted with themselves, and they liked whom they met. Another reason is that the goal setting, based on the convictions of those reasserted selves, filled them with hope and power.

Sharing Goals

When we reassembled, I asked for a volunteer to go to the flip chart and list her five goals, bullet-like, and talk them through with us. "Tell us what these goals mean to you. Tell us why you chose them."

After the volunteer completed her list and commentary, I asked the group what they thought was the value of such sharing. It was clear that the atmosphere in the room had changed. Ned replied, in effect, for everyone there. "Well, it helps me to know these folks' agendas. And I can see that it helps them to know mine. And it helps me to *know* they know mine and them to *know* I know theirs."

The volunteer had just made herself much better known, then, and she was more authentic to everyone even though these people had been working together for at least months, and in some cases years. The rest were eager to follow her lead and lay out their goals.

This process led to a different kind of bonding between these people, and even though one would return to Singapore, another to London, and still another soon would be reassigned somewhere offshore, they will gather with greater ease at their next joint meeting. Moreover, from halfway around the world, they'll be of greater support to each other in the interim.

Celebrating Accomplishments

Sharing goals is one side of the coin. Because we've seen that it can have such a beneficial effect on a group of associates, let's flip the coin over and look at the other side.

Whereas goal sharing helps create bonding, even when some of the goals are mutually exclusive, and working together to reach those goals advances it, the joint celebration of accomplishments hardens such bonding to all assaults. Let us take such pause. Without joint celebration of accomplishments, a team becomes less of a team.

The "I" and the "we" become united in joint celebration. That's because the goal that I share with the team rises above my purely personal concern. When I discuss it, it becomes clear that ultimately my success depends on the team's—the business's—success. I don't invent the goal in a vacuum. Though my goal may be in conflict with someone else's goal, it won't be in conflict with *all* that person's goals, and it certainly won't be in conflict with *everyone's* goals.

In addition, as I share my goals, other members of the team see how my goal can be modified from the way I express it, and I may agree that their suggestion is an improvement. The others may make their suggestion while stating if they modify one of their own, our efforts will dovetail easily. The rest of the team members listen to our exchange on this item and nod or offer their views of how this fits in with them and their goals. Lose-lose and win-lose become win-win.

Teammates working together to achieve such joint goals will inevitably run into roadblocks and outright failures. Goals may need to be modified again or rejected outright for poor timing or faulty judgment. But never mind, some goals will be reached. And at such times of triumph, the team must stop and kick up its heels to celebrate their joint accomplishments.

TAKE ACTION

1. X marks the spot. Don't make the mistake of ignoring a milestone you've reached by looking on to the next one. Make sure your team stops to savor its victories.

2. Remember, your team member's victory is a victory for you; yours is a victory for her or him.

FAST TAKES

on

Being Affirmative

- In the midst of anybody's limitations there are always strengths to be found and engaged.

- *Any* process can be used to teach someone to act on his or her authentic strengths.

- Owning up to our own hand in our losses is a first step to rebounding.

- Facing discouragement squarely is the first step in putting it behind you.

- Savor what you have reached, even when it falls below your expectations.

- Find ways to celebrate your victories.

- Mere work in isolation from final purpose breeds boredom and resentment.

- The goal you share with your team rises above your purely personal concern.

V

SHARING

Your Time, Who You Are, and What You Know

As we all know, sharing is an act of union. As a result, theme 4 again is the obvious one that applies to this chapter: *The authentic state of humanity is union, and, ironically, this enhances one's uniqueness.*

Teamwork depends on your giving what is distinctively *you*. What gives a team richness, texture, and ultimately resourcefulness is the diversity (uniqueness) of its members and an artful linking of their diverse gifts. It's in contrast to your teammates that you become more aware of your uniqueness!

To be a true sharer, give thought to the following:

- Viewing your work as what you owe of *yourself* to a community
- Not resenting team meetings called by your boss
- Not resenting team meetings you call for your subordinates
- Not withholding information useful to your teammates
- Making sure you're heard when you have strong opinions

——— **21** ———

TAKING BY GIVING

In the past four years, John Shad has captured our attention. As chairman of the Securities and Exchange Commission during most of the Reagan administration, he made good on his personal crusade to crack down on insider trading. Then, after serving in this post with distinction, he became our ambassador to the Netherlands. Following that, he became chairman of Drexel Burnham Lambert, the investment firm with a cloud over its head due mainly to the highly questionable machinations of Michael Milken, its notorious junk bond king. Shad's task is to make sure the firm cleans up its act. There's no one better for the job. When asked if he took on the assignment to be window dressing, he convincingly replied, "That's not the kind of man I am."

Be that as it may, as Shad was preparing to leave the SEC for the Netherlands he truly turned our heads by awarding a grant of $20 million from his own estate to the Harvard Business School to establish a teaching program in ethics. Harvard, in contrast to their customary poise in the face of such magnanimity, seemed bewildered by it all. "Ethics? Ethics? My God, how do we blend that into a business curriculum?" they seemed to be asking.

As an indication that the school was looking a gift horse in the mouth, *Business Week* quoted a junior professor who offered, "They (the administration) still have to sell this to 100 tenured faculty who think the whole discipline (ethics) is garbage."

John Shad is a graduate of Harvard Business School's heralded class of 1949. That class has been the subject of much media attention over the years. It includes such accomplished executives as C. Peter McColough, retired CEO of Xerox, John Grant, retired CFO and an architect of American Standard's turnaround in the late 70s; and James Burke, retired CEO of Johnson & Johnson. Burke in particular won our admiration for his ethical handling of his company's Tylenol crisis in 1982. The public came first. I'll have more to say about him in the concluding chapter.

A Giver

Shad made his career and fortune on Wall Street, rising to the rank of vice chairman at E. F. Hutton. Perhaps ironically, his concern for ethics came about because of Hutton's own hanky-panky in its scandalous check-kiting scheme that took place after he left the firm to head up the SEC. But I doubt it. He seems like a giver to any enterprise he's a part of and cringes when people only take, take, take. He spoke well when he made his grant: "Those who go for the edges—like high rollers in Las Vegas—are ultimately wiped out."

Shad, therefore, is an example to us. This forthright, uncharismatic, diligent man has achieved a performance level and financial success few of us aspire to. But his example isn't about that, as such. It's about giving what we've got to the system. That translates to giving our gifts—what is distinctively us—to those with whom we share tasks. Most intensely, this means we share with our teammates. In the broader scheme, we can be expected to offer the same to all associates.

Ethics and Performance

Giving what we owe of ourselves is, of course, ethical. Yet an added twist in giving what we owe is to go out on a limb like John Shad has and give voice and action to cares and beliefs we have about our businesses that may make us unpopular. This may result in others thinking of us as self-serving, self-righteous, or naive. Or we may occasionally have to be willing to be the messenger who brings bad news.

Consider this example: A senior officer of one of our largest forest products companies hosted me in his office recently. "You know," he said, "our competition from around the world now is fierce. Fierce! When I think about the way we shirk our responsibilities in telling all our people—our own staffs, workers, unions, officers, board, and public—of what we need from them to compete successfully, I'm convinced it's not a technological or even financial issue. It's an ethical lapse. It's our own cowardly way of selling out."

The man who spoke those words is no pussycat. No prude. No killjoy. He simply cares about the stewardship of his business. He cares about the ethics of performance. He knows the health of any enterprise is based not on what we take but on what we give. He understands that a company, an industry, the industry of our nation, is a commonwealth built upon shared competence, and that when the commonwealth is abused by persons who "go for the edges," it isn't long before its moorings go wobbly and its entire existence is threatened.

Now why does Harvard's faculty have such a hard time figuring that out? Giving is the ultimate return on assets.

—————— TAKE ACTION ——————

1. Think through the ethics of your own performance. See that keeping your competence from your teammates and associates, whether intentionally or because of reticence, is an immoral act. It is withholding your authenticity.

2. Don't be fearful of making an occasional display of what cynics might label self-righteousness. Follow the lead of our forest products officer. Call 'em as you see 'em!

NOTE: Even John Shad's efforts weren't enough. Drexel Burnham collapsed and declared bankruptcy in early February 1990.

—— 22 ——

TEAM: THE ORGANIZATIONAL ATOM

As I write this, I'm in the midst of preparing a team-effectiveness workshop for a chief executive and the eight vice presidents who report to him. Two weeks ago, I completed the first phase of this project when I met with the CEO and these executives in their boardroom and outlined our objectives for the three-day workshop.

My purposes in that meeting were to get acquainted, make sure we were on track together, and answer any questions they might have. I also confirmed that I'd be spending an hour or so with each of them over the next day and a half.

I then laid nine self-addressed, stamped envelopes on the table in one stack, and nine copies of a brief team-achievement inventory (see appendix D) I've designed in another. I told them that filling out the inventory would take less than five minutes of their time, that their anonymity was assured, that this information would help me plan a workshop that would be useful to them, and that I'd appreciate their sending them back to me as soon as possible.

The two-page inventory asks respondents to rank on a scale of 1 to 5 eight characteristics of the management group they are a part of. Those characteristics are: (1) mission/goals, (2) initiative taking, (3) involvement, (4) feelings/emotional investment, (5) leadership/facilitation, (6) trust/candor, (7) decision making, and (8) resourcefulness and growth.

The group is punctual. All but one of the inventories are back already. The last one that came in, however, had this note written at the bottom: "Frankly, this material does not seem germane to us as a group." Obviously this fellow doesn't know what constitutes team effectiveness. Where a group stands on these eight factors is where it stands on authenticity and success.

If I hadn't faced this kind of problem before, I might be anxious about the workshop. As it is, this person will probably be turned around easily. He'll be turned around by participation. Showin' is better'n tellin'.

The Process Is the Team

In my consulting activities, I'm fond of saying, "The client (by client I mean the client *organization*) has the answer." The late genius Marshall McLuhan said, "The medium is the message." I copy him by saying, "The process is the solution," and as a follow-up, "The process is the team."

The empowered team is a collective state of mind where ideas are food and puzzlements are challenges. It is where conflict is positive because it is out in the open. Responsiveness is paramount. Whether established department or ad hoc task force, the team is a thinking organism where problems are named, assumptions challenged, alternatives generated, consequences assessed, priorities set, admissions made, competitors evaluated, missions validated, goals tested, hopes ventured, fears anticipated, successes expected, vulnerabilities expressed, contributions praised, absurdities tolerated, withdrawals noticed, victories celebrated, and defeats overcome. Finally, it is where decisions are backed when the boss says yea or nay to this option or that.

The team, then, is the organizational atom—the locus of power—and if executives are going to take upon themselves the responsibility for sensitizing their organizations to the source of their own energy—for the sake of not only surviving, but thriving—then they must start there.

Meetings Aren't the Team

What gets called the team most often isn't. The "management team" of most companies is usually a case of mistaken identity. Meetings aren't the team either, though a team can't exist without meetings.

In its June 21, 1988, issue, the *Wall Street Journal* good-naturedly pointed out the banal quality of the lion's share of meetings executives attend. The article was titled "A Survival Guide to the Office Meeting" and stated that executives spend an average of 17 hours a week in meetings and another 6 in preparation for them. This, at best, is a group-groping for a team, but a team it decidedly is not.

Given this colossal waste of time and corporate resources, of bridling high-talent executives in the same room under the guise of accomplishing something distinctive, I can understand your irritation with a boss who runs meetings poorly. On the other hand, we might now finally be induced to see the opportunity for the team, and realize what tremendous resources we're wasting.

You will mark yourself with above-the-crowd qualities, therefore, if you do all you can in your own sphere to convert this waste to an investment in making meetings work.

86

TAKE ACTION
---

1. Master the art of running meetings with you in charge. This isn't difficult, but it requires your full commitment to learning how. If you haven't done so, now might be a good time to read the introduction to this book. It gives specific advice for assuring the essential elements of effective team meetings.

2. Remember this at all times: Anyone who is making a meeting work—really work—is making the team work.

—— 23 ——
WINGING IT WON'T WORK

I serve as chairman of the communication and public affairs committee of a large downtown church in Chicago. (I'll have more to report on this in essay 61.) Being chairman of this committee carries the additional responsibility of serving on the church's Session (analogous to the board of directors), plus occasional duties on a subcommittee of that board.

In short, I attend a lot of meetings for this one entity alone. This, of course, says nothing about meetings connected with my business or any other organization I may be involved with in one way or another.

I find myself resenting some of these meetings more than others at different times and for different reasons. But perhaps I can offer the generalization that I frequently resent the meetings I call more than the ones I'm called to. I'm quick to add, however, that this resentment is not legitimate.

It's not legitimate because the meeting I'm called to allows me to be far more passive and uninvolved if I so choose. That meeting where I'm member, not chairman, gives more leeway for faking it, not participating, or serving only in a perfunctory way. It's easier to get away with being lazy in this setting, avoiding my responsibilities to be a contributor.

It's also true, to be sure, that we sometimes don't like to attend meetings others call because we *have* sought to be contributors, and our efforts have been shut out or rejected by them. We may in fact be overly sensitive in these cases and exaggerate the degree to which our thoughts were shunted aside. Or we may not fully admit to ourselves that we presented our views poorly. Yet there is no denying that hordes of meetings are dominated by petty tyrants or power-grabbing cliques, and we're correct to conclude that our time so spent is a waste.

Nowhere to Hide

The meeting I call can generate resentment because I'm front and center, and I know that if it's going to be productive, it requires careful preparation on my part. Moreover, as leader of the meeting, I have to be fully mobilized, thinking all the time, even though—if I'm doing my job right—I'll be talking less than the others present.

An irony in all this—and you're probably already ahead of me—is that the meeting I chair that I resent is made productive only by not allowing it to be the kind that I prefer to attend as member, namely, one where I can fake it and just run through the motions. What this means, at bottom, is that as chairman I have no place to hide, and must make sure the attendees become *participants*—that they have no place to hide either.

Meetings Are Work

Does all this sound just a mite too convoluted to you? More importantly, if meetings are such a pain, as we all seem to think, why not just dispense with them? After all, everybody complains about them, about their frequency and poor quality.

There's just one problem: It is the primary way that knowledge workers work today, and, despite their complaints, the *only* way they're willing to work. Remember the last time something was done in your organization and you thought the idea should have been run past you before it was acted on? But it wasn't, and it made you madder'n hell, or hurt your feelings.

What that meant, as you well know, was that you were left out of the "loop," or that someone acted in isolation and you weren't the only one madder'n hell. That loop you were left out of, or that didn't exist when you and others thought it should, is nothing more than a committee or work group that meets to generate or evaluate decision-making alternatives.

So the old view that work is something we do between meetings is baloney pure and simple, and we need to stop deceiving ourselves this way. Yes, we do work between meetings, no doubt. Not only that, some of this work is in isolation, by way of individual thought or experimentation or further study. But the typical purpose of that effort is "homework" to contribute to the data base or the analysis of the data base that will be undertaken in future meetings of the work group, committee, or task force the "home-worker" is a part of.

The key point here, then, is that a meeting, whether you are called to it or call it yourself, is work itself and work to prepare for. When you call it, you're more on the spot, sure enough. But if you run your meeting well, it will end up a delight to all.

TAKE ACTION

1.   Stop thinking of meetings as something to get over with so you can get back to work. Meetings are work, not an interruption of work.

2.   Because meetings are work, stop demeaning them. Prepare for them, whether you're called to them or calling them. Winging it won't work.

—— 24 ——

LIFE TRANSFUSIONS AND ANTSY DRIVERS

I'm always amazed at how one's memory works. It's so efficient, calling up what's necessary to make a connection that another part of the mind wants made. Just like the computer that has been properly programmed, it does a rapid sort and generates the appropriate data.

Such was the case a few moments ago when I asked myself what would be a good example to help make the point of this essay. With this mere prompting, I immediately was taken back to a true story I heard on the radio when I was nine or ten years old.

The story was told by host Don McNeil on a program called "The Breakfast Club." The show was broadcast before a live audience from Chicago's Allerton Hotel. My mother usually had it on in the kitchen as I ate breakfast before heading off to school.

The story, which I haven't thought of in years, is this: A young boy was very sick. His parents were told by the doctor attending to his case that he needed a special blood donor but the hospital wasn't able to locate one. He wanted to know if they could get blood from the boy's older brother who had the identical, rare type. When the parents asked the older brother, they were puzzled that he hesitated before answering, then got tears in his eyes, then finally consented.

The younger boy was operated on. The doctor told the family in the waiting room that the surgery was a success and that their youngest son would recover to lead a perfectly normal life. Then he leaned down, putting his hand on the older brother's shoulder, saying, "And it wouldn't have been possible without you."

With profuse joy and relief, the exhausted parents thanked the doctor and headed for the hospital exit and their car parked in the lot outside. They didn't notice that the older brother stayed behind. As the doctor turned to leave, the boy suddenly tugged at the sleeve of the doctor's green gown. When he turned around, the doctor saw that the older brother was now crying. The boy looked up at him and asked: "When do I die?"

Debunking Catastrophe

This is a lesson on giving information to teammates that we might advantageously retain for our own career interests. Yes, I know family is family and business is business, and therefore the analogy doesn't quite hold up. Moreover, the "information" provided by the older brother, while life-giving to his sibling, meant death, he mistakenly thought, to himself. So the analogy doesn't make it in that respect, either. No one in business is asking *that* of us.

However, let me stay in the realm of the extreme for a while. Let us ask ourselves the ultimate consequences if we fail in our careers. What happens to us if the worst-case scenario unfolds? What happens if we don't get the promotion? What happens if we're transferred where we don't want to go? What happens if our company is acquired and we lose our jobs? What happens if we lose, lose, lose?

We go on, that's what happens, and that's no big catastrophe. It's the anticipation of failure that's so fretful. Right now, our country is full of executives who were "delayered" out of their jobs by the current move to flatten our organizations. They were anguished by these developments as they approached, but now many find themselves in new careers or new businesses altogether and feel reborn.

Prepared for Failure

The nature of all great winners is that they are prepared to lose. They have an added dimension, some extra resource to fall back on that allows them the luxury of knowing there's more going on in the game than the game itself. They are more flexible, trustful, helpful, more willing to give someone the benefit of the doubt.

Recently I was a passenger in a car with such a driver. We came to rest at a four-way stop. To our left, on the cross-street at the intersection, a driver approached rapidly, lurched to a halt, then bolted ahead without waiting his turn. My friend turned to me and laughed, "If he wants to be first, let him be first."

The sacrifice we make that benefits someone else and strikes fear in our hearts for working to our detriment seldom turns out that way at all. Rather, if we make a habit of it, we engender a spirit of like-mindedness among our teammates. Even those who may have taken advantage of us are inclined to soften up over time. Time is what matters. Authenticity becomes more a part of the corporate equation.

Somewhere in America there's an older brother who grew up and is now in his late 50s. Whatever he's doing, I'll bet he's a winner.

─────────────── *TAKE ACTION* ───────────────

1. Share information. Share what you have. You won't run dry. There's more where that came from.

2. When people take advantage of you, as some will, just accept it. What did that antsy driver add to his life by being first?

─────── **25** ───────

BE YOU, BE HEARD

In essay 30, I'll emphasize the necessity for your occasionally taking risks with your views, even when you're sure to anger those whose sponsorship you seek. In essay 28, I'll argue for balancing that risk-taking by exercising restraint in confrontations, to avoid being labeled a gadfly. In this essay, however, I'll first deal with your self-image. I'll underscore how important it is, as a matter of principle and practice, that you see yourself as *worthy* of being heard—on any subject on which you have strong opinions. This is authenticity—your declaration of self.

Shyness and self-deprecation aren't options. The thrust here is directing toward yourself what the late psychologist Carl Rogers called unconditional, positive regard. Accordingly, right off the bat, let's determine that you have thoughts and opinions that deserve airing. After all, you're not a dummy!

Ordinary Words

Yesterday, a Sunday, I attended a buffet luncheon as a member of the Chicago contingent to an out-of-town gathering of a professional society. We were hosted by the Houston contingent. The mood was casual and relaxed, and though almost a third of the 50 or so in attendance were from Chicago, many of us hadn't seen each other in a while and this provided an opportunity to renew ties.

Shortly into our hobnobbing, the president of the Houston group, Marv, whom I'd never met, stepped to the front of the room where we were standing and greeted us. He did so with warmth, grace, and power, and had no trouble breaking into our already up-tempo conversation. From his first words, we hushed our chatter and listened to him.

He said, "Welcome to all to the luncheon. We're pleased you're here. Many of you know we wanted to have this luncheon for our friends from Chicago, and that's true. But let it be known that today we also honor [fictitious name] Harry Engel," and with that he pointed to a Houstonian we all recognized at once as an unsung hero of our national organization. We all applauded and shouted "Hear! Hear!" Our host then raised one arm high and said, "Enjoy yourselves." I turned to the woman I'd been speaking with before the official greeting and said, "Boy, that Marv. He knows how to make a point."

I wasn't kidding or being sarcastic. I meant it. In a few short moments and with a minimum of words, what easily could have been interpreted as a routine or frivolous luncheon was given a firm purpose and meaning that only a frivolous person could ignore.

Merely reading Marv's words no doubt causes you to wonder what made them so powerful. After all, as I recounted them here, they're so ordinary. Yet I tell you they had an impact not only on me, but on virtually everyone present.

A Forceful Presence

It's difficult to be heard—to have impact—if we attempt to make a point while looking at our shoes. I use this as a figure of speech, of course, to convey what a lack of confidence or being apologetic does to curtail our effectiveness. Others look at the ceiling, or the wall, or even a shoulder, say, of the person to whom they're talking, and the impact of this simple action is deadly to their cause. Such behavior is annoying, first of all, but also lets the person spoken to know the speaker's wishes will be easy to ignore.

Marv didn't look at his shoes or the ceiling or the back of the room. As a matter of fact, although only one of 50 people, I felt he looked at *me*. While our eyes locked for just an instant, he let me know that he believed what he was telling me was important. Most people in the room, I could sense, had the same experience. As a result of this simple exchange, he accomplished the following: (1) The Chicagoans felt welcome; (2) the Houstonians were given responsibilities as hosts; (3) the unsung hero was uplifted himself and spotlighted for the rest of us; and (4) we all were told to enjoy ourselves while participating in this now-important event. All this was made possible by a person who insisted on enhancing the surroundings of himself and his associates by having his point of view *matter*.

Do proper eye contact, tone of voice, pace of speech, and posture all convey that we believe in what we have to say? Some say no and think these indicators of high self-esteem aren't that at all, but simply aspirations of manipulation and phoniness taught by the "positive thinking" genre to those bent on feathering their own nests.

Others see value to such self-management, but attempt it only for big events such as job interviews, giving speeches, or appearing in court. Personally, I like Marv's attitude and think we need to demonstrate belief in ourselves and our ideas in the everyday events of work life with our teammates.

When I look a teammate in the eye, it's not done to be seen, but to *see*. I want to know what's going on in my teammate's mind. When I do this, I make a *listener* out of that individual.

TAKE ACTION

1. Help convert your team's ordinary experiences to extraordinary. Give texture to what is flat or dull. Do so by being what you think you aren't. See. Stand tall. Sit straight. Don't rush your words. You're worth taking time for!

2. Drill and re-drill with this truth in mind: So much of what you are not is your blockage of what you are.

FAST TAKES

on
Sharing

- Giving what is *distinctively us* adds our own authenticity to the pool of shared competence.
- *Giving* is the ultimate return on assets.
- The team is the organizational atom.
- What gets called the team most often isn't.
- Meetings are work, not an interruption of work.
- Meetings are the only way knowledge workers are willing to work; therefore it's imperative you learn how to make them productive.
- All great winners are prepared to lose.
- Look your teammate in the eye to make a listener out of him or her.

REACHING

Men grind and grind in the mill of a truism,
and nothing comes out but what is put in.
But the moment they desert the tradition
for a spontaneous thought,
then poetry, wit, hope, virtue, learning, anecdote,
all flock to their aid.

RALPH WALDO EMERSON

VI

BEING VULNERABLE

An Underrated Strength

Theme 6 has particular bearing on this chapter on vulnerability. Let me repeat it. *A team catalyst is an individual who takes upon himself or herself the responsibility for modeling actions and attitudes that support shared competence.*

It takes a great deal of courage to model vulnerability. Being vulnerable is being authentic in a way that runs counter to many of the creeds of American culture. Yet the team catalyst is willing to do it. She's willing to do it by way of risking failure, admitting mistakes, asking for help, or acknowledging a lack of knowledge or exposure. In so doing, this individual enlists the support of others.

To experience the strength of vulnerability, give thought to the following:

- Apologizing to a teammate you've wronged
- Being vulnerable *selectively*
- Not being intimidated by fear
- Being curious, playing with ideas

—— **26** ——

RIGHTING A WRONG

Last night I finished a novel that had been lying around the house for a couple of years. It has an outlandish plot and absorbing narrative. It turned out, for me at least, to be a moral tale well told and relevant to the subject of this essay. It's *Private Screening* by Richard North Patterson. Weird, yet totally believable, it's fiction that proves truth is stranger than fiction. The plot contains surprisingly little sex and features a wealthy media mogul, his wife, their son who's gone wrong, a rock star, her enigmatic manager, and a terrorist who calls himself Phoenix.

Colby Parnell is the mogul. He's a second-generation, Ivy-League-educated head of a San Francisco media conglomerate, SNI, that includes newspapers and a national TV network. His wife, Alexis, is a failed Hollywood actress he worships. Their son, Robert, grows up with a violent nature and an "unnatural attraction" to his mother. Colby comes to loathe him and banishes him from their house. He is later kidnapped, but Colby resolutely refuses to pay the kidnapper's ransom. The boy is never heard from and assumed dead.

Seventeen years later, Alexis and the rock star's manager are taken hostage by the hooded terrorist, Phoenix. In a brilliantly executed, bizarre scheme, Phoenix gains control of SNI's broadcast facilities and conducts two-sided negotiations over national television for a full week. First, he orders the rock star, Stacy Tarrant, to stage a live, televised concert and raise $5 million. If she refuses, her manager will be executed with all America looking on.

Colby, for his part, faces a second demand from Phoenix. If Colby doesn't comply, his cherished wife will suffer the same termination on national television. Phoenix asks him to apologize and explain why he was willing to let his son die 17 years earlier. After a week of unbearable stress, he's a devastated shambles of a man who babbles pathetically into the camera at the appointed hour, "Lexie . . . You were so beautiful. God help me, I thought he wasn't mine. . . ."

Doing Wrong

Seventeen years after a shattering event in two people's lives, one of them is forced to admit the error of his ways. Presumably, had not the kidnapping of his wife taken place, Colby Parnell still would not have talked of his decision that widened—so long as he insisted on remaining silent—an unbridgeable rift between him and Alexis.

This is a story of such cold barrenness. Such limiting stoicism. Such stifling pride. Such crippling embarrassment. Such face-saving charades. Such life-immunizing deception. Such passive resignation. Such evasive conversation. Such vapid facial expressions. Such running through the motions on some sort of upper-class set of civilities that choke off authenticity. All this is what passed between Colby and Alexis *for 17 years!* All this because a perceived wrong had never been spoken of and dealt with. All this grief was so unnecessary.

Being Wronged

That is not altogether different from what sometimes happens on the job, is it? Another lesson about work performance can be drawn, then, from an unlikely source. Truth about our relationships with peers can be discovered in unexpected corners. True enough, the pace and demand of business life may not allow us to harbor grudges for so long a time as Alexis did, but this should not obscure the fact that we may cut and run from work relationships before resolving our differences. Our problem is left hanging while we scat one step ahead of the sheriff from one department, region, or company to another.

As you read through the pages of this book, you'll note that one of my convictions is that the *you* on the job and the *you* at home are the same person. Moreover, the wrongs we do others whether at home or at work are often a retaliation of *feeling* wronged, whether the feeling is merely perceived or actual. Perception is reality, goes the cliché. Such certainly was the case with Colby, who was convinced he wasn't Robert's natural father. How different his life with Alexis would have been had he been able to apologize for his awful error and be given her forgiveness.

101

Alexis herself wasn't blameless either. She permitted coldness to develop within her house. She could have insisted on learning what drove Colby and Robert apart and worked to heal deepening wounds. In the process, she could have saved her own love for Colby and had her eyes opened to her own culpability in the troubles of this triangle. She too could have made amends.

You may argue that the story is more dramatic than need be for underscoring that in our dealings with others, including teammates, apologies and forgiveness correct serious imbalances. And naturally, I'd have to agree. After all, our work lives aren't made up of kidnappings, death threats, and ransomed rock concerts.

Still, within corporate corridors, permanent estrangements in the name of personality conflicts aren't all that rare, either. Think of the needless loss.

TAKE ACTION
---

1. Don't let wrongs you've done fester. Get at them.
2. Be prepared to say readily: "I'm sorry, I was getting even. How can we fix this?"

—— 27 ——

LILY'S LAMENT

I'm an upbeat person. An optimist. I like to stress the positive side of human nature.

Integral to such an attitude is my conviction that encouragement is one of our gifts—a gift we're privileged to give others because when people are down, they *need* to get back up, and *want* to, and *can* with a little of our help and a lot of their own.

Lily Tomlin wittily catches the paradox of this latter point when she says, "We're all in this together—by ourselves." It's a paradox worth keeping in mind in other ways as well.

You now know that my views are founded on the premise that all of us long for development. We want to push out our boundaries, reclaim our abandoned strengths, and accomplish distinctive things. In short, we covet authenticity. We seek to embrace life to the fullest. Further, we realize ultimately that to experience such development, what is essential is our linking hands, becoming part of a community, being engaged in some sort of team effort.

Yet having said this, as a consultant I'm daily a part of one or another community made up of people of one corporation or another, and there's no denying that some of what I see isn't pretty. People do—or try to do—each other in for their own gain. Like Lily says, we're all in this together—by ourselves. Discretion remains the better part of valor.

A Firm Grasp

It's not easy to get a firm grasp as to which of your associates can be trusted with your most candid thoughts. The same goes for knowledge of your limitations and plans for your new initiatives. Some of us are better at this than others. But none of us always knows who our enemies are. Undeniably, we all get fooled. We miss the point. We don't read the signs and end up with egg on our faces, or worse.

So the point, then, isn't to ignore your enemies, but to make use of your energies and ideas in such a way as to increase the chances of nullifying their gyrations.

A Little Magic

There is some sleight-of-hand that without exception can be called on to work for you and your career. I made reference to it in essay 19 in chapter IV on affirmation and seeking higher purpose. It's this: Make sure you help get done what your company wants done. This simple, straightforward initiative often will neutralize your enemies and avoid the sideshows that getting embroiled with them always entails. Ensure their irrelevance by teaming up with those who share your commitments and by turning in superior performance in areas where it has the most impact. "A good offense is the best defense," goes the old saying. Real accomplishments cover a multitude of sins. They make people overlook your failures. That's what I mean by sleight of hand.

Know who your enemies are as best you can and be nice to them. But be sure to go on the offensive and place your trust in those who value what you share and share what you value. And guess what? By being nice to these adversaries and paying attention to what counts, it's likely you'll even bring some of them onto your team.

TAKE ACTION

1. Be vulnerable, but on a selective basis. You may be suspicious of some people, and rightly so, but the fact is you've got to trust *somebody*. If you're suspicious of many, you've got problems a lot bigger than your career.

2. With those you trust or can bring into your trust, don't be afraid to spell out what you believe in, what you're afraid of, how you've blown it in the past, what you're good at and not so good at, and how you'd like their help. Then, most importantly, be prepared to return support to them in *their* efforts.

28

SAYING NO TO INTIMIDATION

I had a fascinating, revealing experience this week. I received a report on myself based on a series of psychological tests I'd completed recently. It's been more than 20 years since I've gone through an exercise like this, so I was eager to see the results.

The occasion for the exercise came about through a consulting assignment. I'm engaged as adjunct staff to the Greensboro, North Carolina-based Center for Creative Leadership in working with one of their corporation clients. The assignment requires such testing on the part of the corporation's top management, so it seemed sensible to me that I ask to take the tests, too. I did and am glad I did.

I found that at my age, 52, the tests (or "instruments" as they're more usually called by professionals) confirmed what I already have come to know about myself, good and bad. On the other hand, I was reminded of things about myself I had conveniently forgotten, but that call for my renewed attention if I'm to continue my personal growth in some important areas.

As with all such measures, however, the fallibility of this exercise and its judgments at higher levels of ambiguity was amply demonstrated in a few places. One in particular was shown in the psychologist's description of me as "little if at all inhibited by the disapproval or opposition of others."

An Important Decision

Fairly often, we encounter people who say, "I don't care what people think." In fact, we've all probably made that statement now and again. For some, it seems, it's almost a slogan.

Yet, when we stop to think about the statement, what possibly could be more absurd? Not one of you reading this page has not, does not, and will not know the fear of disapproval and rejection of your actions or thoughts at the hands of associates or some audience you deem important.

It was pioneering University of Chicago social psychologist George Herbert Mead who gave us the concept of the "significant other." (That was back in 1934, by the way, and it's cute to see its popularization today with its someone-other-than-spouse usage.) Muzafer Sherif, another social psychologist, gave us the concept of "the reference group," a group to which we "refer" (or defer) for standards and maintaining a respectable self-image. Sherif and Mead come together in the sense that any reference group is made up of significant others.

I may not care, in the abstract, that a group of Shintoists reject my Christianity. But if I were to take up sole residence among them, their rejection of my faith would begin to have an impact—not all of it pleasant, not all of it subtle—on my behavior.

Just think of all the implications embedded in such an innocent question as "What kind of suit are you going to wear to the party?"

Next week I'll serve as a facilitator for a team-effectiveness workshop for a company president and his officers at Quail Lodge in Carmel, California. The announcement reads "Attire will be casual." My God, what if somebody showed up in a suit?!

We don't care what people think? We don't care what our teammates think?!

Making Yourself Stronger

A major issue in our lives and work isn't whether we care what people think of us. That's settled. We care. Rather, it's whether we're willing to make the following statement to *ourselves* on well-chosen (ah, yes, there's always the matter of judgment) occasions: *"I know some key people won't like what I'm going to do, but I'm going to do it anyway."*

"Well-chosen" means you pick your fights with teammates carefully and bring all your resources to bear on the initiative at hand. I'll have more to say about this in essay 34, but for now keep in mind that this is always exhausting, even if the result of your efforts turns out to be exhilarating. So you do so sparingly. To do so often is to dissipate yourself and become known as a gadfly—a loser's label.

It's not fear but intimidation that matters in the subject at hand. You won't always want to act out in opposition to constraining opinions of others. That's far too taxing and counterproductive for all kinds of reasons. But to be willing to make yourself vulnerable— at what are for you critical crossroads—can only make you stronger.

—————————————— *TAKE ACTION* ——————————————

1. Sometime soon, someone will say to you, "Don't worry about what people think; go ahead and do it." Your first response will probably be, "Easy enough for her to say!" Then ask yourself, "Does she have a point in this case?"

2. If after thinking it through you agree she's right, there's nothing left to do but to do it. Swallow your fear and do it.

—— 29 ——

LIVING ON TENTATIVES

The week before last, I had occasion to attend a breakfast meeting where Bill Granger was the featured speaker. For years, Granger was a columnist on slice-of-life subjects for the *Chicago Tribune*, and he's a first-rate novelist. He's written several books; his current novel, *Henry McGee Is Not Dead*, is a fine one.

It was clear from the moment he stepped to the microphone that public speaking was not his milieu. "Unaccustomed as I am. . ." would have been a thoroughly mundane but fitting opener for him.

Yet he was a smash. He held up a sheet of paper on which he had scrawled about four or five half-sentences and told us in the audience this was his outline. Then he proceeded to regale us with a handful of stories, complete with his own hilarious commentary, that included Chicago politics (laughable without commentary), his Catholic education on the city's notorious South Side, and the "totally useless, exorbitantly priced baubles" that constitute the bulk of the merchandise at Bloomingdale's brand-new store on Chicago's Magnificent Mile.

Whatever it is that makes a group of insiders laugh at their own foibles, Granger had found our hot button, and for 20 minutes he kept his thumb on it. It was a great way to start the day—flushed through by genuine humor, all of us caught in the act of being ourselves.

We'd all clamored to gape at the new Bloomie's wares, and our politicians . . . well, God love 'em, they're totally ours. Adlai Stevenson had it right. We get the politics we deserve.

The Active Mind Is a Joy

The active mind is a joy to behold, as it was in this case, and it is also a joy to express. It was clear, for example, that as much fun as we were having listening to Granger's spontaneous meanderings, he was having at least as good a time, if not a better one.

Nonetheless, giving expression to what we want to learn and what we've come to learn can be risky. To say to our teammates in unvarnished ways what we think, believe, or hope for is authenticity that makes us vulnerable. The explorations of worlds we don't know in order to attempt mastery—or at least manageability—are forays that leave us less than confident. Robert Frost crystallized our ambivalence about such voyages: "Anyone with an active mind lives on tentatives rather than tenets."

You could say to me, "There you go, using a 'creative type' to make a point with those of us in business. What does Bill Granger have to do with us who work day to day with dull care in corporate life? And Robert Frost . . . good grief, he was a poet! Come on."

Now let *me* ask: When a Bill Granger sits before his word processor day after day for hours, experimenting with ideas that may flop in the marketplace, how is that different from what we do? Isn't that work? Isn't that risk?

And we mustn't forget, when he left his writing and got up early one morning to give a talk, it was obvious he was out of his element—out of his comfort zone.

A Playful Mind at Work

I sat in the front row and don't recall seeing Granger consult his notes even once. Rather, he just sort of loped along, keying from one idea to the next, one notion spurring another, keeping firm eye contact with the audience, a broad-beamed smile on his face, and all the while carrying us along with him.

When he finished his talk, he threw the meeting open to questions. He did so with his ever-present smile and laughingly implored us to "please have some questions so I won't feel like a failure." Of course, hands shot up all over the room, and Howard Christeson, an investment banker with Merrill Lynch, got to him first. Howard said he had just read *Henry McGee* and asked, "How do you come up with a character like that?"

Granger replied that the story is set in Alaska. "Why is that?" he chortled, then answered his own question. "Because I wanted to take a trip to Alaska. After I'd been there, I could write about

108

it." Then he said that he gets an idea about a character or two, and then they just take off, and he has no idea where they're going, what they'll do, or how they'll end up. His comments implied there's always a moral to his stories, a place he plans to end up philosophically and spiritually, but how he gets there as a writer is a product of his unfolding imagination.

How very like his talk, I thought.

But he pulled it off, ill at ease as he undoubtedly was at first. The adventurer in him won out and he set full sail with his stories.

TAKE ACTION

1. Say yes to the adventurer in you. Name your Alaska and go there. Create your Henry McGee and make him come alive.

2. Don't say you lack ideas. Don't say you're not creative. Those statements simply aren't accurate. Say, if you need to, that you're fearful of your own natural curiosity, but then, to repeat, say yes to that adventurer in you.

FAST TAKES

on
Being Vulnerable

- Shyness and self-deprecation aren't worthwhile options.

- Silence over wrongs done creates unbridgeable rifts.

- Personality conflicts are usually unattended estrangements.

- Avoid sideshows with your enemies. Do what your company wants done.

- By being nice to your adversaries, you may bring some of them onto your team.

- Pick your battles carefully to avoid the loser's label of gadfly.

- "Anyone with an active mind lives on tentatives rather than tenets."

- To say to our teammates in unvarnished ways what we think, believe, or hope for makes us vulnerable. This is authenticity every team needs.

VII

BEING DISCREET

Speaking Your Mind Without Loose Talk

To the extent you speak your mind—what you really believe—you seize a measure of your potential and authenticity. Some people call this finding your voice.

When you find your voice, you inevitably become a contributor to those who surround you. You becomes a sharer of who you are, and since you are of value, you give value—even if your ideas occasionally offend.

Theme 2 is highlighted here: *The need to belong is a powerful human force that finds expression in teamwork.* When people speak their minds about what they really believe, they make their work bigger than their jobs. When they make their work bigger than their jobs, they belong.

To find your voice, give thought to the following:

- Creating a little tension on your team
- Speaking your mind to your bosses
- Not speaking your opinions prematurely

- Not glamorizing your role's impact
- Picking your battles carefully

—— **30** ——

LIGHTING SHORT FUSES

It may seem like a small thing. The head of engineering keeps recommending that the general manager promote Larry into the position of director of marketing. The general manager has rejected the recommendation on two previous occasions.

Why doesn't Ed, the director of engineering, just drop it? What does it matter to him who the boss puts into that job? It's none of his concern anyway. Let him just mind his own store in new product development and let Marty, the boss, hire whom he wants.

The top marketing job in this key division is vacant because Barbara, the woman who held it, was tapped by the parent company to take over all corporate communications. Though she wasn't trained or experienced in that field, the chairman had seen her make presentations to his board and liked the way her mind worked. He thought she was just the person to handle corporate relations. She would master the job in due time.

The impressive array of skills this woman possesses, that caught the eye of the hard-nosed chairman, make her a tough act to follow. As a result, Marty is at the point of exasperation in finding suitable candidates, despite the efforts of one of the nation's premier executive search firms.

Stepping Into the Pit

Meanwhile, Ed steps into the pit and lights Marty's short fuse by bringing up once more his thought that Larry is the man for the job. This time Marty explodes, shouting at Ed that Larry's not big enough for the job, that he'd thought about him immediately when Barbara was snapped up to headquarters. "Do you think," he asks acidly, "that I would be laying out $50,000 in fees and take four months to look under every rock if I thought sweet little Larry could do it?"

Ed holds his ground. "Look, I know you doubt Larry's ability. As Barbara's number-two, he was lost in her shadow. But I'm telling you, I've worked with him for seven years now, and as good a manager as Barbara is, Larry's been the guy with the ideas. I spend time with him and our customers together. They love him. As far as they're concerned, he's the vital link to our business. Have you noticed over the past four months how marketing hasn't missed a beat even with Larry's wimpy 'acting' marketing director title? Come on, Marty! Give him the job. Even Barbara told you he could do it."

Marty sighs, slouches in his seat, and throws his ballpoint pen across the office in mock despair. It careens off the wall freakishly and lands in an ashtray at a corner table. Ed laughs out loud and yells, "Three points!" Marty, despite himself, laughs too, and mutters, "Get outta my office. Lemme think about it."

Two days later, "acting" is removed from Larry's title.

The Grit of the Oyster

This hypothetical story illustrates the correctness of being willing to create a little tension on your team. This is so whether Larry succeeds on the job or not. By raising Marty's ire, and even risking permanent damage to the relationship—and ultimately his career, Ed shows that he cares more about the business and his boss's performance than those who merely go along to get along.

One of the strong views behind the concept of team effectiveness is that all members, including the boss, must be prepared to hear unwelcome thoughts from their teammates on occasion. You know from this example that Marty and Ed have a basic respect for each other. Yet, ironically, such respect, trust, and credibility are kept alive only by risking them. It's like the grit in the oyster that produces the pearl.

Here's a real live example of what I mean. I'm currently a team-effectiveness consultant to the CEO and staff of one of our major frozen-food companies. As is typical of my undertaking this kind of assignment, I interview all participants individually after a brief group orientation. During the interviews, one of the questions I ask each is, "What would be the best possible outcome of this project for you?"

It turns out in this case that here is a good team working to become a better one. All have expressed a desire to share competence with each other. So too do they all seek a better sense of each others' priorities. But one member with a gift of clear language has expressed this team's spirit in an arresting way. "Let's help each other be right," he said. "And let's not be afraid to throw open the door to healthy, controlled conflict."

TAKE ACTION

1. When you get that rumbling in your gut that the idea your associates or boss is espousing with great enthusiasm is somehow flawed, don't hold back. If you do repeatedly, you'll deny your authenticity and lose not only your self-respect, but ultimately their respect too.

2. Occasionally, you'll believe in something that your associates resist. If you remain unpersuaded by their arguments, forge ahead even if it risks offense. You may not be right, and even if you are, you still may not succeed. Yet how else will you know?

—— 31 ——

OVERCOMING TIMIDITY

My comments about hypothetical Larry in the preceding essay lead me to attempt to throw added light to its point in this chapter with real-life Phil. Phil Thomas has his own Chicago-based consulting firm these days, specializing in investor relations. But before launching this very successful business five years ago, he ran the investor-relations program for Esmark, Inc., where he was a vice president.

Thomas reported directly to the late Roger Briggs, senior vice president and chief financial officer, and because of the nature of his tasks also spent hours upon hours working with CEO Don Kelly. If you've followed the business press at all over the past decade, you know that Roger Briggs was regarded as a financial genius while Don Kelly knows no peer in mega-deal-making. He has bought and sold companies the way you and I buy toothpaste.

You can imagine, then, that Thomas's job working with these two titans would be slightly intimidating. Well . . . yes, how could it not be? Yet Thomas was up to it, and a good part of the favorable stock price enjoyed by Esmark over the years was due to his efforts.

Thomas knows how to sell an idea and shoot down a bad one. It was not at all uncommon for him to look Kelly and Briggs in the eye after one or both had made a suggestion and say, "We'd be out of our minds to do that!" Then, he often would counter with, "But here's what we could do that might get us the same thing." Then he'd go out and get it done on Wall Street. Outstanding guy.

A Stakeholder Be

Certainly you can't care about everything around you. Jack Miles, editor of the *Los Angeles Times Book Review*, puts it this way: "A writer who finds everything interesting makes almost everything boring." He seems to be sending us a message: Acknowledge periodic boredom and you'll be in a position to recognize and embrace its opposite. He's not suggesting that we bathe in it, but on the contrary direct our attention to what matters to us.

The important consideration for you is to be authentic. Know what you care about and have a stake in it. Phil Thomas's bold-relief and frequent use of "we" makes clear he felt involved—on the team. His openness and actions mattered—not only to him, but also to his close associates who saw him as part of a joint effort. They depended on him. On the other hand, he was smart enough not to have a strong opinion on every subject.

Without Timidity

You realize, I'm sure, that I wrote first about *identifying* what you care about and have a stake in because this process may give you the power to overcome any timidity you might have about expressing your opinions. You can fight for and carry out to completion—bypassing criticisms, dire predictions, and mishaps—only that which you believe in.

As I've implied, every encounter with your bosses shouldn't entail your playing a role in a high-noon decision. Nonetheless, a steady respect for you is based on your growing confidence in yourself derived in large measure from your having come through with unapologetic, convincing views when your knowledge was critical.

―――――――――― *TAKE ACTION* ――――――――――

1.   Pause for a few minutes and recount those times in the past year when you remained silent but had thoughts to offer your bosses that hindsight tells you would have been useful.

2.   You just have to find some way to get out of this bind. Are you afraid your voice will crack, or you'll look stupid? Is that preferable to being thought a nebbish? Most everyone is fearful when making a presentation. But many forge ahead anyway and win respect. So can you.

―――― **32** ――――

THE COOL ENTHUSIAST

The family council is meeting. In this case, Mom is chairing the session. Dinner is over, the dishes are done, the three kids have put their television, telephoning, and homework aside, and Dad, so as not to be distracted from the importance of the meeting, agreed not to bring any work home from the office.

It's 8:30 on a Tuesday evening in late April. This Denver family of five has reconvened around the dining-room table to begin considering what they will do for their annual vacation trip the last two weeks of August.

As you might have guessed, this is one of those model families, sort of a "Father Knows Best" bunch brought up to date. The kids

116

feel free to speak their minds to their parents while even being fairly decent to each other.

At any rate, because the family vacation is a tradition, ideas about what to do on it get floated up spontaneously throughout the year by any and all members of the tribe. So there's usually no lack of options, and this is made clear by a list Mom has compiled and has sitting atop a pile of brochures she sent away for based on suggestions made by her and the others.

No final decision will be made tonight, but certain ground rules will be laid, including finances and possibly form of transportation. Certain druthers, or priorities, will emerge, while on the other hand, particular options will be discarded for high cost, impracticality, or sufficient lack of interest when carefully considered.

All Eyes on Lisa

As eavesdroppers to this meeting, we find ourselves paying particular attention to Lisa. She's the quiet middle child, the lone sister squeezed in between two brothers who are as different as pudding and peanut brittle. Jim, the high-school junior, is an orderly type who mirrors his easy-going, pipe-smoking dad. Keith, the seventh-grader, is given to flights of fancy, is noisy, interrupts others, and just as easily tunes out, ignoring large parts of the discussion.

Lisa has drawn us to herself with her poise. She's been a good listener. Various points of view have been raised, some of them in direct competition with each other, and she has at times asked her companions to explain their preferences. She wants to test each idea, it seems, to see if the activity could be fun for her and the rest of the family, not just the person who suggests it.

Once, she scolds Keith, saying, "Pay attention, will you, so we don't end up doing something that bores you out of your skull!" Then just as quickly a few minutes later: "See, Keith, that's what I mean. What a terrific idea! Mom, Dad—wherever we go, before heading home, let's spend the last day at Disneyland." Everybody around the table sort of nods and it becomes a given.

Catching the Drift

Lisa, as it turns out, thinks she may want to be an actress. Although the family lives in Denver, they've never been west of that point. They're from Columbus, Ohio, actually, and came to Colorado because Dad was transferred here by his company two years ago.

Throughout the year, Lisa has caught a sentiment developing in the family that they might like to see the West Coast, and concluded that this is the "drift" to their unformed vacation thoughts. So tonight, as the discussion unfolds, she listens carefully to everyone's preferences while mindful of her own. More than anything, she's dying (absolutely dying!) to visit the movie studios. When it's her turn to give voice to her choice, this 13-year-old astounds us with her restraint: "Whatever we do, I'd appreciate it if Mom and I at least have a little time to visit a couple of the Hollywood studios."

Would you like to guess what takes place at the next family vacation planning council? The most important thing is that the decision will be made, and it will go Lisa's way. Here's why.

In the interim, she will ask her mother to call Amtrak and the airlines. She'll volunteer to do it herself, but her mother will insist that she concentrate on her schoolwork. Her mother will call a travel agent to collect information on family rates for the train and super-saver fares for the airlines. She'll also learn about car rental and hotel specials on fly-drive-and-stay programs.

At the next family council, Lisa will propose the following after everyone has expressed their thoughts since the last meeting: (1) a train trip to San Francisco; (2) a two-day drive down the coast to Los Angeles; (3) a Dodgers or Angels game for Dad and brothers, and the studios for Mom and sister; (4) the last day at Disneyland; and (5) flying home to Denver.

TAKE ACTION

1. Don't wear everybody out by wearing your passion on your sleeve. Authenticity does not translate to "undisciplined." Be an enthusiast who keeps cool.

2. When in a team decision-reaching mode, be a good listener. Hear what people think and say that can improve on your ideas. Catch the drift. There's momentum in decision reaching. Don't attempt persuasion until people are ready. Then be prepared and speak with conviction. More often than not, things will go your way.

—— 33 ——

A NAIL IS A NAIL IS A NAIL

A former client of mine is exceedingly able. He's senior vice president of a major corporation. He's had a long, distinguished career, and though he's only a few years from retirement, he gets calls from executive recruiters "all the time," as he puts it. They want him to take a similar post with another company.

Here's the odd thing about this fellow: If he happens to read this, he won't know it's about him until he gets to a specific point or two that finally makes his identity undeniable.

He glamorizes his role. It's a key one, to be sure, and he was even a dark-horse candidate for the post of CEO with the changing of the guard a few years ago. But while no one can dispute he's carried out his duties with distinction, he's made them larger than they are.

"Ignorance is bliss" is too harsh to describe his state of mind. Yet, there is a degree of obliviousness in what he does, both on and off the job. He glamorizes what he does at work, and casts his own glow on his role as family member and citizen as well. A legend in his own mind.

A Grand View of Self

His obliviousness is most pronounced in the way he views his association with objects, people, and organizations. If he's a part of things, they're simply grand, and that's that. His company is grand, or he wouldn't have joined it. But now that he's there and added

119

his stamp, well—it's especially grand. When he looks at his corporation's competitors, he sees little but mediocrity, inferiority.

If he were to buy a can of corn off the supermarket shelf, it would be the finest corn imaginable, not because of the brand or its reputation for quality, but because *he* picked it.

Ironically, some of this man's success stems from his belief that he's somehow special. Many would fear to tread where he walks willfully. Once I was with him in New York. We flew there from Atlanta, his home base. He got André Soltner on the line. Soltner is the chef-owner of Lutèce, New York's Taj Mahal of restaurants. He sought a table for us that night at 7:30.

Mr. Soltner told him condescendingly that the city was full of conventioneers and the night had been sold out for weeks. "Next time," he admonished my client, "call ahead and we will be pleased to accommodate you." My man listened patiently and then said in his most ingratiating southern drawl, "But Mr. Soltner, those folks came to eat. I and my guest are here to *dine*. Do you want to disappoint Atlanta's most discriminating palate?" The room went silent as my client listened to the response. I saw him break into a smile, and then he said, "Thank you, we'll be there."

He didn't get his way entirely. Our reservation was for eight o'clock. When we arrived at Lutèce, we were herded by some lackey past a crowd cooling their heels and brought to Mr. Soltner himself. He wagged his finger at my host, shook his head, and said loudly so the would-be diners wouldn't think he was getting special treatment, "Shame on you, Mr. So-and-So, for being late! We almost had to give up your table." When we sat down amidst the restaurant's rosy hues and fine napery, my client grinned at me from ear to ear. Never had a man felt so special.

The Best, Always the Best

Anyone whose secretary is best because he hired and trained her, whose tailor is best because he chose him, whose neighborhood is best because he lives in it, whose children are best because he sired them, whose opinions are best because he offers them, whose procedures are best because he approved them, whose stories are best because he tells them, whose investments are best because he makes them, whose office is best because he occupies it, and whose decisions are best because he makes them is a person who speaks tiresomely in the first person singular and is sole inhabitant of a glamorized world he has made up. People who know him laugh at him. Many strangers are impressed, but the perceptive ones go away asking, "Is he for real?" They already have formed their answers.

My subject isn't as bad as all this, but he skirts this territory every so often and draws a snicker or two. Were it not for the fact that his work is actually marked with achievement, he wouldn't be tolerated. As it is, however, he is reminder enough that it is all too easy to glamorize our impact.

―――――――――――― *TAKE ACTION* ――――――――――――

1.   The person who glamorizes his or her role is often feeling without a voice and influence among peers and superiors. So this person gilds the lily and shows off to underlings. Is this true of you? If so, find your voice. Use it. Your teammates want to hear that, not some falsetto.

2.   *The Executive Coloring Book* was a best-selling novelty in the 60s that poked fun at executive hyperbole. The salesman in it, for example, didn't call his product a nail. He called it a friction-fastener. Be truthful with yourself and others about your role. Speak it. Don't glamorize. Keep a sense of scale.

―――― **34** ――――

PICKING YOUR BATTLES CAREFULLY

In 1974, I published a little book entitled *Work, Love and Friendship: Reflections on Executive Lifestyle*. In that book, I described 18 negative styles. Here are four of them:

The Adversary: thrives on conflict . . . turns every business conversation and decision-making situation into a power struggle . . . more negative than the devil's advocate, gets abusive . . . holds grudges . . . always wears a frown.

The Diplomat: the exact opposite of the adversary ... gets sweaty palms and hemorrhoids from conflict ... soft-spoken and smooth ... nice-guy image ... will tell lies if necessary to avoid unpleasant confrontations ... beware the annual review of your performance if this type is your boss.

The Abrasive: different from the adversary ... usually smarter and more talented ... lacks finesse to move up to top management because lacks people skills and often has parochial interests ... if can be lived with is often valuable to the company ... but does cause trouble.

The Salesman: the master of double-talk and diversion ... charm and persuasion often distract listeners from an empty head and lack of administrative prowess ... not to be confused with sales executives ... an absolute menace.

These mini-profiles are of four distinct types of non-team players. For all four, words come too easily. Two of them, the adversary and abrasive, are all too eager to pick a fight. On the other hand, the diplomat hasn't the courage to tell you where she stands. And the salesman? Well, he hasn't even thought about the subject.

Too Ready to Pick a Fight

We've been through a long history in American business when the tough guy—the intimidator—was a common character near the top of almost any corporate pyramid. The intimidator might not be the CEO but was probably running one of the key business units or held a critical staff job such as CFO or general counsel.

Typically, the intimidator was a guy who got results and because of this even the CEO didn't mess with him. Oh, the CEO knew all right that he could be blustery and pompous and was in fact a little embarrassed by his style when his name came up in discussions with board members and others, but that conversation usually came to a close with a little chuckle and such words as, "So long as Charlie keeps turning in those numbers, he can growl and scowl all he likes."

Something's changed, though, over the past ten years. The Charlies, despite their numbers, have become something of a liability. It's not "fun" to work for, work with, or even "boss" Charlie anymore. Charlie's just too ready to pick a fight, for the silliest reasons and over the most insignificant issues, just to show everybody, mostly himself, that he's king of the hill.

So the talented people drift away to other divisions or even to competitors where they can truly ply their crafts. Those who remain snicker behind the old guy's back and grow more cynical day by day. Ideas dry up and the business goes flat. Charlie's numbers begin to look sick.

Winning Through Intimidation was a best-selling piece of garbage about a decade ago. Can you imagine such a book being a hot item today?

Not Ready Enough

What has changed over the past decade is that we have started to care about our businesses again. I mean really care, about the quality of our products and services and our customers and clients who use them. Henry Ford said, "A business that makes only money is a poor business." We've begun to take such conviction to heart and realize that focusing on the bottom line doesn't get us the bottom line we want.

So there's no room for the intimidators anymore because we've got work to do and need the best bodies, minds, and spirits to do it. But there's no room for the fakes and flakes either. Those who don't care enough to defend an idea or even have one are going once, going twice, gone.

So don't be a hair-trigger chooser. And for every issue that presents itself, don't be a motor-mouth loser. This message, then, is pick your battles carefully, based on your deeply held beliefs. But pick them! Be somebody who cares and adds value to the business.

We've been forced to care about our businesses because of foreign competition. What a favor the Asian Tigers and Europeans have done for us. They've reawakened us to providing substance over form, performance and quality over running through the motions. Mergermania, payroll cutbacks, divestitures, LBOs, ESOPs, entrepreneurialism, and shareholder value—all going on at once—

begin to look healthy. There's positive energy afoot. One gets the impression that the Carl Icahns may have been doing the right things for the wrong reasons. So what? Let them be pawns. The train's leaving the station: Get on or get off.

───────── *TAKE ACTION* ─────────

1.   Care. Ask yourself: "Is my team really better off with me here?"

2.   Know this: If you're not adding value, you're subtracting it. Is this any way to live?

FAST TAKES

on
Being Discreet

- Teammates help each other be right.

- Mutual respect, trust, and credibility are kept alive only by risking them.

- *Caring* about your business keeps you from going along to get along.

- You can fight for and carry out to completion—bypassing criticism, dire predictions, and mishaps—only that which you believe in.

- At any given time, a drift of initiative is under consideration by your team. It's this drift that's important. It should be fed or starved.

- You're not the only teammate with convictions and feelings. Passions should not be worn on your sleeve.

- When speaking to win others over to your point of view, you must have your ducks in a row.

- Hair-trigger choosers and motor-mouth losers end up being company pariahs.

VIII

NURTURING YOURSELF
AND OTHERS

Mother's Milk for Your Company

A prevalent theme for this chapter on nurturing is 5: *Belief in men and women as social beings is a lofty one and is best authenticated with down-to-earth performance.*

Any time we serve as nurturers of others, it's clear there is an altruistic element in what we do. This isn't to say we don't receive payback from such nurturing. Of course we do, and we all know what many of these paybacks are.

Moreover, taking on the nurturing of ourselves is best done when we keep in mind "the good of the order." What this means is that our self-development ultimately has a goal of increasing our contribution to our teammates and company.

This chapter confirms our social nature in the world of work and asks that it be demonstrated in nitty-gritty ways. To do so, give thought to the following:

- Expressing the child in yourself
- Fostering the feeling of belonging among your subordinates

126

- Being a "people" person rather than a "things" person
- Urging your subordinates to broaden themselves
- Demanding growth and contribution from them

—— **35** ——

THE CHILDLIKENESS IN YOU

Last night, true to my custom, I went for a walk before going to bed. Two blocks from home I approached an intersection where I saw two young couples in their late teens or early 20s out on a double date, having a good time.

Two by two, they were skipping and singing a song I haven't heard since learning it in a grade-school music class taught by the imperious and buxom Miss Phimister.

> Fly's in the buttermilk,
> Shoo, shoo, shoo.
> Fly's in the buttermilk,
> Shoo, shoo, shoo.
> Fly's in the buttermilk,
> Shoo, shoo, shoo.
> Skip to my Lou my darlin'.

Obviously, their inhibitions were in retreat. Perhaps they'd had a couple of beers or had been smoking something, but if they had, bless their hearts, at least they weren't driving. Then again, maybe they hadn't. Maybe they were just being the young people they are. In any event, their verve could be nothing but positive.

The Boyish President

When I saw the young couples and vicariously derived pleasure from their having such a good time, my thoughts fell back to a couple of years ago when I still did searches, and an assignment I'd completed at the time. The search was for someone to be president of a small, start-up food company headquartered in Hawaii. This was a high-risk business; the product was fresh shrimp farmed in captivity rather than caught and frozen at sea. When harvested, they were Cryovac-packed at 37 degrees and flown off to the customer from Honolulu.

The product's taste was extraordinary. (Only a minuscule number of Americans have tasted shrimp that have never been frozen!) But its product costs were high and reflected in the markup charged to the wholesaler and the retail or restaurant customer.

What was required in someone to run this first-of-its-kind business was imagination—a resourceful general manager keeping watch over all aspects of the business, but especially a generator of marketing ideas. The critical need was to present this product to consumers in a way that enticed them to sample it, discover its superior value, and ante up for its premium price.

As is typical of my procedures in a search, I gave reports on three candidates to my client in a face-to-face meeting before he was to spend time with each of them. As a 50% owner of this business, he had questions he wanted answered about all of them. My job was to fill him in on details about their experience and makeup. When we got to the one who later ended up with the job, he asked, "What's this guy like?"

"He's boyish," I said. "Comes off looking ten years younger than his 36 years. He has a little bit of an image problem this way, and isn't as poised as the others. But I like his enthusiasm."

"So what does all that mean?" asked my client.

"Probably that he's more creative," said I.

My client, a wealthy, enthusiastic man in his own right, bent his head forward, arched his eyebrows, and from hooded eyes peered at me sternly. "Please explain that to me," he demanded.

Jack Gray

"Think of Jack Gray," I said, referring to a man we both knew. "Jack is now in his 80s, but just think how energetic and youthful he is. He's as active now as he was before he retired. He's got more irons in the fire than a blacksmith, and his social life is a never-ending whirlwind. No one is faster with the quip than he is and the man still giggles! He's an octogenarian teenager who's never given up his mischievousness and taking delight in life and work wherever he can find it. He brims with ideas. Never have I met a more creative businessperson."

What I didn't have to itemize for my client, but do for you is Jack Gray's accomplishments. Hart Schaffner & Marx (now Hartmarx) is the house that Jack built. Oh, this was an admired corporation before he took the helm, but it was small and nowhere near living up to its potential. Coming out of Hart's Wallach's retail division in New York, Jack shot up through the ranks of this company. He was a gifted promoter who personally recruited Jack Nicklaus and Johnny Carson to be spokesmen for various clothing lines.

He had an eye for operations as well and was an exceedingly able negotiator with the Amalgamated Clothing Workers, Hart's main union. He had a flair for merchandising and was a splendid personal salesman. He had a quick mind for figures and was as shrewd as a fox. He could fire a poorly performing vice president with alacrity yet inspire loyalty from a shy seamstress. When Jack retired as CEO, a tenure that lasted from 1960 to 1976, Hartmarx was by far the world's largest clothing manufacturer. This he accomplished with a bounce in his step, a twinkle in his eye, and the ever-present giggle.

To be sure, my client got the point immediately. I made no claim that the candidate was another Jack Gray, but merely that he had that same boyish creativity, that verve and imagination, that would help him handle this job with aplomb. This he did, by the way, and this venture business took off.*

The lesson for all of us is that we can make our creativity available to our teammates if we'll only own up to that child in ourselves.

─────────────── *TAKE ACTION* ───────────────

1. Don't allow yourself to become old before your time. Reclaim your childlikeness by rejecting cynicism. Enthusiasm feeds the soul.

─────────────────────────────────

*The business, alas, didn't succeed ultimately, though not for lack of expansion, customer demand, or pricing. The Hawaiian waters proved too cold for the species of shrimp farmed and they all died—three straight brood stocks. The venture had to be shut down, and the general manager now heads a major division for a large food company in the East.

2. To get a taste of the power and joy you may have disowned over the years, do something childlike. Write a limerick about a friend, play a game of touch football, ride a bicycle in the rain, or paint your basement yellow. Then bring that spirit to work and share it with your teammates. It's not too late.

—— 36 ——

THE FEELING OF BELONGING

Perry Pascarella is the chief editor of Penton Publications. He launched a recent issue of *Industry Week*, one of Penton's 36 magazines, with an editorial that included these words:

"The corporate message to *tomorrow's* managers might as well be cast in bronze and hung in the corporate headquarters foyer:

We can't promise you how long we'll be in business.

We can't promise you that we won't be bought by another company.

We can't promise that there'll be room for promotion.

We can't promise that your job will exist until you reach retirement age.

We can't promise that the money will be available for your pension when you retire.

We can't expect your undying loyalty, and we aren't sure we want it.

"All the company can promise a manager is: We will support your efforts to make a contribution to our mission so long as you are employed here.

"All it can ask in return is: We expect you to be supportive of our organization while you work here."

The Smart Machine

Let me recommend a book to you that was published in 1988. Its title is *In the Age of the Smart Machine* and it's now out in paper.

Written by Shoshana Zuboff, professor at Harvard's business school, it's a tremendous work, and if you haven't heard of it, don't let that stop you. Get hold of a copy and read it. It's hard sledding but worth every ounce of energy you give it.

The book argues that our absorption with the computer's automating power has kept us from paying proper attention to its second effect: *informating*. The first effect, automating, has a profound impact on blue- and white-collar workers. The computer's informating power affects the realm of management as well.

Zuboff skillfully points out that in the process of programmed instruction directed to all kinds of mechanical functions in plant and office, the computer is also collecting and monitoring endless varieties of information. This information, now available to anyone with access to a company computer terminal, previously passed between people in face-to-face conversations or was stored away in file drawers.

This informating situation leaves managers as confused and fearful about their jobs as plant workers. After all, what's to become of their power, based as it was on their being the keepers of this information that is now available to nearly everyone?

A Hopeless Cause

"Well," you say, after absorbing Pascarella's comments followed by Zuboff's observations on the automating and informating power of the computer, "you're dreaming, Cox, to think that the feeling of belonging can be nurtured anywhere in the contemporary corporation."

You'd have your point in such an exchange, but I don't agree and would like to explain why.

The choice we face in American industry is captured best in a question from a plant manager that Zuboff cites: "Are we all going to be working for a smart machine, or will we have smart people around the machine?" The lesson in this penetrating question is simple yet profound: *Make your subordinates smart and they'll know they belong.*

131

Imagine a policy statement held high in a corporation that goes something like this: "Your first job as a manager is to nurture the competence and self-esteem of your subordinates." Such a policy statement is about making people be smart at what they do, feel good about themselves because they have something authentic to contribute, and feel they belong because such smartness can't be developed in isolation. It comes only from working in tandem with others—in a word, teamwork.

The real message here is that even though the computer makes a vast array of information available with blinding speed to ever-larger numbers, we still don't know what use to make of most of it. What it does mean and can mean is the issue. The more people we include in its resolution, the more we'll know we're on the right track.

Pascarella's litany is persuasive that loyalty as we've known it is gone. Free agency in professional sports is another example of this. But as long as we foster competence and self-esteem in our subordinates, the feeling of belonging is what they'll experience as long as they're with us. And we'll all be better off for it. And maybe, just maybe, with the right kind of teamwork, an even better kind of loyalty can be born.

----------------------------- *TAKE ACTION* -----------------------------

1. Renounce cynicism. Though the external factors may have you wondering if our corporations are in a fatal tailspin, recommit yourself to competence on the job. There is much to suggest your efforts will be rewarded.

2. Make sure you and your subordinates are a team. Remember, they can help you make sense out of the continually increasing amount of information available to you. Count on them. Let them know you do.

—— **37** ——

MAKING THINGS HAPPEN

I have a friend by the name of Joe Conley. He's an executive search consultant. He's an independent spirit—a solo practitioner—with offices in Chicago and New York.

Joe started his own business in 1969, but we got acquainted in 1966 when we were colleagues with the large search firm of Spencer Stuart & Associates. Then, as now, we used to spend time together swapping "war stories" in our work and giving each other the "benefit" of our "wisdom."

I'm being a little facetious here, because whenever I think of Joe, such thoughts usually bring a smile to my lips. He's such a good time! He's an Irishman with a gift of gab, a good storyteller; and our get-togethers are spent with me doing most of the listening and a lot of laughing.

None of this is to say, however, that in the midst of mirth, we don't pass good ideas between us. As you might guess from what I've told you, Joe has a way with words in conversation and has an ear for the well-turned phrase—the kind that locks itself into your memory.

Here's what I mean: In 1967, we were sitting in his office in New York and got to talking about a fellow who recently had left Spencer Stuart. He was someone we all liked and had high hopes for, but ultimately he failed in this people-intensive business. He reached the point where he even hated to pick up the telephone to call someone.

Joe talked with him right after he resigned and told me the man had said, "I didn't make it because basically I'm a things person, not a people person."

Introspection

To be a people person is to care about what impact you have on people and what impact they have on you, and to learn from these exchanges.

Many executives claim to be people-oriented. Some think this because they're extroverted and like to go to parties, or can't stand the thought of being alone for any length of time.

I've interviewed hundreds of executives who proudly exclaim something like, "I'm a people person," but when I examine their résumés I notice they've had too many jobs with too many companies in too short a time. They are always moving on, and few associates are disappointed to see them leave. I keep in mind in these interviews that if they truly had been successful, they wouldn't always leave where they are. People dislike change as it is. Would they want to change *success?*

Surprisingly, people persons may be found in things places whereas things persons might turn up in people places. For example, I've encountered warm, caring, reflective types in accounting, manufacturing, and engineering, and cold, shallow, obnoxious types in sales, human resources, and even public affairs.

To be a people person is to mind (to be introspective about) relationships with people, not just be among them. Some (not all) of our best people persons are introverts!

Nature vs. Nurture

The fact that people persons can be found in both the extrovert and introvert camps triggers thoughts of the ages-long nature vs. nurture controversy. I'm reminded of how some people might blame their lack of people-sensitivity—or their lack of interest in it—on their nature. "That's just the way I am," they'll say, as if their genes have programmed them not to be reflective about their relationships with people.

Executives can get so busy with activities, so mired in projects, so busy in the *doing*, that they're inclined to ask, "What good is introspection for helping me build a plant, sell a product, or design a new compensation scheme? I haven't got time for that. I've got work to do. That stuff you've got in mind is too soft. Besides, I'm doing what I like to do. It comes naturally to me."

Such executives will have a lot more than a distaste for introspection to blame on their genes. Outright failure, for instance, particularly if reaching top management is their goal. Try building a plant, selling a product, or designing a compensation scheme—and doing these in a quality way—without winning the trust of the people who surround you.

Being a people person is learned just as much as being an engineer, accountant, market researcher, or health and safety expert is. You may not be able to get a degree there, but the place you work in is a classroom in people-sensitivity just the same, and plenty of homework is required. Nobody ever said being authentic is easy!

TAKE ACTION

1. Stop blaming your lack of people-sensitivity on your genes.
2. Realize that things don't make things happen. People do.

38

THE TEAM-PLAYING SPENDTHRIFT

Earlier this week, I got a call from Gary Carlson of Bandag Inc. in Muscatine, Iowa. Bandag is a rubber products company with annual sales of around $500 million. The company has just come off two back-to-back record-breaking years. Profits are at an all-time high.

When Gary mentioned that he was with Bandag, all I could recall about the company was that it has something to do with rubber, enjoys a good reputation, and is somewhere near the Quad Cities and the Mississippi River.

He said he had a couple of ideas and questions he wanted to run by me if I had a few minutes. I assured him that I did, and we discussed what was on his mind.

I assumed Gary was in charge of human resources for Bandag. It didn't even occur to me to confirm my suspicion—especially given the content of our conversation, which had to do with executive development—until our discussion ended. Then I asked simply, "Are you head of human resources?" He replied, "No, but I used to be.

I'm VP of planning and development. I did my stint in human resources, but before that I did a lot of other things. That's the way we do it around here."

Small Isn't Beautiful

A few years ago I conducted a study among 1,086 executives in the 115 headquarters, subsidiaries, and divisions of 13 large, well-known companies. Five hundred fifteen of these executives belonged to top management. One of the questions I asked this august group was, "What are the career benefits for the person who has been with a small company before joining your company?" Two percent of these top executives said this experience would be viewed in their company as "very positive." Eight percent thought "somewhat positive," 79 percent "neutral," three percent "somewhat negative," one percent "very negative," the rest "don't know."

I keep these figures in mind whenever I hear big corporations bragging about the "intrepreneural" attitude they foster in their people, the "proprietary interest" they have, the way they spend the company's money as if it were their own. BAH-LOW-NEE!

My experience is that candidates for large company executive positions who come from small companies are given the cold shoulder. They are thought to be from the sticks, too unsophisticated. Yet such people, being from smaller enterprises, have been raised in the cradle of commerce and are likely to have a much broader and deeper grasp of what makes an entire business go. They have a much better hands-on understanding of how its parts hang together and how things get done.

Preparation for General Management

Let me go a step further. Not only do large companies shun large mindscape liberal arts/humanities graduates and ignore candidates from small companies for key executive openings, they don't even do a decent job of training their own executives for broader perspectives.

Returning to the study I cited earlier, I also asked these top executives how effective their corporations are in preparing their young comers for general management. Their answers: 7 percent said, "virtually always;" 31 percent, "generally;" 31 percent, "frequently;" 26 percent, "sometimes;" 5 percent, "rarely/never." Can we call these good numbers for a country that has let Japan eat its lunch? Not on your life.

Imagine, fewer than 40 percent of our companies virtually always or generally prepare their promising young executives to run a business. Most of our time has been spent teaching people to be specialists—to know more and more about less and less. Oh, I know there's a place for that, but over 60 percent worth? No way.

Don't think you have to be Bandag to move people around, to get them thinking about more than what's heating up in their own stovepipe. In fact, at $500 million, Bandag can't claim the simplicity of a small business anymore. This is now a complex organization, and the temptation to squelch authenticity by putting people into their little boxes and keeping them there has to be an enormous temptation for them. Yet they overcome it, as seen in the case of Carlson and many of his associates.

See those people in your department you're so proud of? Be a spendthrift. Give them away to your associates.

------------------------------ *TAKE ACTION* ------------------------------

1. Don't *let* your high-potential subordinates go to other departments. Be positive. Urge them to go.

2. On the other hand, some of *them* may be timid. Gently nudge them into a new arena. In so doing, you'll prove yourself a team contributor.

—— **39** ——

THE ACKMAN LEGACY

From reading these essays, you know that I regularly conduct workshops, seminars, and various programs for management groups. My task in these cases is to do the best job I can as speaker or facilitator. I'm there to help people learn and grow, to catch a glimpse of management life and their larger place in it that they haven't seen before.

One person I can sadly neglect while directing my energies to the growth of others is none other than yours truly. That would be ironic, wouldn't it? So busy teaching that I don't learn, with the result that eventually I go flat and have little left to teach.

So I make a point of attending workshops a few times each year where my role is learner rather than being at the front of the room. In such a workshop six weeks ago I had a learning experience that prompts this essay.

A fellow participant, Mary, was asked to conduct her part in a practice session. Our job as attendees was to involve ourselves fully in each others' sessions and later critique them for design and execution. Mary's session was a wonderful one for me. I won't labor over its details, but it forced us to think back carefully to the best boss we ever had. Mary guided us to think not just of the person, but what he or she did in specific circumstances that brought us to this profound sense of appreciation.

Going Way Back

For me, this experience meant going all the way back to age 18 and a boss named Keith Ackman. Last I knew, he was living in Los Angeles. I haven't seen or talked with him since 1957!

Keith was the membership director of a new and bustling YMCA in Oak Park, Illinois. I was a recent high school graduate. I'd worked for a couple of years as a part-time attendant in the locker room. I'd attracted some attention to myself by memorizing all the members' basket numbers. This sped things along. Members didn't have to wait in line to be checked in. I'd spot them, grab three or four baskets at a time, and get them distributed to the members in a hurry. The members' baskets contained their workout togs, so they could be on their way without delay.

Keith noted this little trick of mine and liked it. He promoted me to attendant in the Y's Businessman's Club, a "health facility" where better-heeled members were willing to pay whopping (at the time) annual dues of $225. There, I met a Yalie by the name of Walter Rose, who was the VP-sales of the Doughnut Corporation of America. Walter was a demanding but exceptionally likable person. He encouraged me to go into business. He also spoke well of me to Keith, and in three months, Keith told me to put on a tie and come upstairs to work directly with him.

Keith taught me to meet the public with poise. He showed me how to be courteous but in charge of a phone call. He had me give tours of the facility to prospective members. When the Y's new chapel was dedicated, he had me give a little speech on what the chapel would mean to young people. He had me officiate at swim meets. He made me host of a golf outing, though I had never played a game of golf in my life (not one since, either!). He had me serve as a timer of panelist presentations at a major conference on community affairs. During one summer (1956) of that year and a half I worked with him, he was cochairman of the national Jaycees tennis championship tourney held on the clay courts at the nearby River Forest Tennis Club. He had me up to my ears in administrative details connected with this event. This was pretty heady stuff for a kid who had just started college.

Growth Demanded

Keith did much more for me than I can treat in this space, including teaching me how to make an adversary into a fellow team member. He forced a confrontation between his secretary and me—sitting in the room with us until we resolved our differences. In that act alone, I learned the enormous value of facilitation. He faced what many bosses run from—and he fixed a problem.

He complimented me often, but he also lectured me sternly. He made me do what I was afraid to do, demonstrating that he believed in me more than I believed in myself. He demanded that I live up to my abilities, and he made clear without words that what was expected from me was contribution.

TAKE ACTION

1. See those people who report to you as birds in the nest waiting to be fed. This is not patronizing. This is caring. This is authenticity.

2. Continue the analogy. Let them be what they are meant to be. Teach them to fly.

FAST TAKES

on

Nurturing Yourself and Others

- Those who seem young and naive often build a better mousetrap.

- Your first job as a manager is to nurture the competence and self-esteem of your subordinates. This is the authentic *you* nurturing the authentic *them*.

- Today's premier experiment with people is teamwork.

- To be a people person is to care about what impact you have on people and what impact they have on you, and to learn from these exchanges.

- People persons may be found in things places, things people in people places.

- Some (not all) people persons are introverts.

- The place you work in is a classroom in people-sensitivity.

- It's critical to think about more than what's heating up in our own stovepipe.

IX

MAKING DECISIONS

Sitting at the Head of the Table

Two themes come into play in this chapter on decision making. The first is theme 1, *Today's management style of necessity is one of quickened response.* The second is theme 3, *Consensus seeking is a time-wasting, leveling influence that impedes distinctive performance.*

You can see how the two go together. We not only need to make quality decisions by engaging the first-rate minds of our teammates, we need to do so quickly and not get ourselves mired down in a de-authenticating process that strips authority to act from the person sitting at the head of the table.

To become a better decision-maker, give thought to the following:

- Using your decision making as a training opportunity for your subordinates
- Not avoiding decisions for fear of being wrong
- Your annoyance with subordinates who want fast decisions on their recommendations

- Rebounding quickly from your bad decisions
- Not inflating the importance of your decisions
- Making your "big decisions" add to your self-esteem

—— 40 ——
VALUING YOUR TEAM MEMBERS

I was in New York City recently, having breakfast with a client in the protective comfort of a club I belong to. He's vice president of human resources of his large company, and there in the wood-paneled, high-ceilinged room, over our third or fourth cup of coffee, he pushed back from the table, crossed his legs, resettled his napkin, and began to talk about what was most on his mind.

He spoke of his boss, the CEO of his company. The boss, also my client by virtue of work I'd done with him, was a subject on which I was more than passingly familiar. Nonetheless, it was understood without words that the conversation taking place on this occasion was to be held in confidence.

My breakfast companion said, "He doesn't use information well. I mean the information that comes out of our discussions. Whether it's generated one-to-one, or stuff that gets thrashed out of a lengthy staff meeting, or proposals or research we give him that he's asked for, he soaks it up like a blotter and that's it. We hear nothing more about it formally, and he never brings it up again in chance meetings in the hallways or elevators. It's as if all our work or discussion has vanished into thin air; and then smack, he announces some decision in an open forum or to the press, and it's often from left field—not at all what we had in mind."

Team Management

At bottom, this man is complaining that his boss doesn't practice team management. He and his associates feel left out of the decision-making process, and this after they've given a good part of themselves to some project or business issue.

Some readers may think I'm heading toward the point that this CEO needs to foster consensus decision making among his top management group. "Do that," they might say, "and the CEO will solve the problem troubling this vice president and his associates."

On the contrary. *I believe consensus is one of the great bogus concepts of our day.* It is incredibly time-consuming to achieve, so much so that it is thoroughly impractical; and when it is achieved, it seems far more likely that what has been accomplished is a stroking of pampered egos rather than selecting a distinctive course of action.

Sometimes a decision-making group will have consensus or virtual unanimity on an issue. This occurs when decisions almost make themselves and hardly any discussion is needed. Most times, however, when knotty issues are presented, each person sitting around the table has a point of view and a stake in events. No matter how sincere you are about the "good of the order," in fact *because* of your sincerity, you will often have strong beliefs in opposition to one or more of your associates. To achieve consensus in a group like this is to have found a common denominator so low that nobody cares about what gets decided. The original issue that divided people has in effect been swept under the rug, and will probably resurface again later in a new form.

Developing Team Members

What a team needs to be taught is the joy and camaraderie of sharing in the decision-*reaching* process. And to enter into that sharing at all times. As a team leader, teach this and you'll really have something authentic! This is buy-in that counts.

The CEO in this case has been getting good information from his people. I know because I've sat in on a few of his staff meetings. He does so because he lets them know he wants their ideas. But he's new in his job, and what I'm hearing at breakfast tells me the honeymoon is over. Information he truly needs has slowed down and is going to stop. He's about to start hearing only what his people think he wants to hear.

His mistake is *not* that he makes the final decision among the competing points of view of his staff, choosing the one option that in his opinion is most likely to lead to an outstanding solution. After all, that's his prerogative and his job.

No, his mistake is this: On those few occasions when he defers his final decision with the comment to his staff that he wants to think on it further, and then decides, *they are among the last to know.*

The bad news is that this procedure has dreadful consequences. The good news is that it is so easily corrected.

Team members don't always expect to be right or have their recommendations adopted by the boss. But for them to remain on the team, their thought and attitude contributions must be valued, and that value must be demonstrated plainly by the boss.

If you're a boss who has counted on your team members for ideas in reaching a decision, then wanted time to mull it over further, then made the decision, then announced it before sharing your thought processes with the team that helped you, you not only have missed out on a development opportunity for each of them, but you have also devalued their work. This is an error you don't want to make and can avoid easily.

----------------------------- *TAKE ACTION* -----------------------------

1. When you make a decision apart from your team that your team helped you make, explain that decision to them before announcing it.

2. If this requires calling a special meeting, by all means call it. It need last only a few minutes. Attendees may not even need to be seated.

—— **41** ——

DECISIONS, DECISIONS

- "Let's do a little more market research on that project. I'm not sure about it."
- "I think I'll give Bill one more chance. I know he has screwed up repeatedly, but he may still have what it takes. He has all the tickets. That's why I hired him!"
- "Think we ought to run this by everybody one more time? We just don't have the full answer."
- "What if she's right and I'm wrong?"
- "What if we're both wrong?"
- "What if we're all wrong?"
- "I'm not put in this position to be wrong. I'm put here to be right."
- "Yes, I know I said this is important, but let's postpone that decision until next month's meeting."
- "I know operations says this is a go situation, but I just don't know. . ."
- "What do you think we should do?"
- "What do they think we should do?"
- "What does Myra think we should do?"
- "Somebody tell me what to do!"
- "I don't think we should move ahead until we have consensus."

A Soft Elitist

To be honest, I'm an elitist when it comes to viewing people and decisions. By that I mean some people come to the decision-making process with more seeming ability and considerably more ease.

Some people come to a decision, no matter how important, and say, "This is a big deal, and my head may go on the block, but let's go for it!" Others, exemplified by the opening litany, come to a decision, no matter how insignificant, with sweaty palms and palpitations. They exclaim, "Woe is me; what should I do?"

146

I need to add, however, that I'm a *soft* elitist when it comes to decision makers, and that the two groups I refer to here are extremes. By this I mean that most of us fall somewhere between these two extremes and can build our skill and emotional strength in decision making.

The first group, in fact, is probably overpopulated with people who are impulsive, impatient, and unreflective and who cannot tolerate ambiguity for any length of time. On the other hand, the second group is likely to have an excess of those known for oversensitivity, hesitancy, overreliance on precedent, and susceptibility to analysis paralysis.

The rest of us come in somewhere in the middle. Some of us are more comfortable making decisions, whereas others would rather make recommendations. Yet the fact is that all executives are called upon to do both. And in the collaborative corporation in the contemporary age, where the distinction between the two is more blurred than it has ever been, make no mistake that the final decision to be made in most cases is still to be made *by one person*. Sometimes that will be you!

Practicing Decisions

In decisions, as with almost everything else, practice makes perfect. Well, not perfect, as you well know, but as close to it as we can get. There are no shortcuts, formulas, or magic manuals that teach us how to make decisions or, more importantly, to overcome our fear of making wrong ones.

But there is a tonic, and that tonic can become constructively intoxicating. It is the tonic of actually making decisions and finding out how good it feels to have done so. It is declaring ourselves on a decision—where we stand—and showing ourselves to all bystanders and listeners that we're willing to let the chips fall where they may.

A good team leader is somebody who gets the shy members of a department or task force to get used to the sound of their own voices and contribute their quality ideas that would otherwise remain locked behind their timid exteriors.

In the same way, we can train ourselves to feel the power of our own resources and express our authenticity by saying, "There is a decision to be made here, and I'm the one to do it. I'll make it." Start with smaller decisions in your personal life and build up to larger ones on the job. For example: "This dress looks nice in red or blue. Which one should I choose? Do I really need to stew? Hell no! Blue is tamer, but I'd be a knockout in red. Red it is!"

Believe it or not, CEOs are often in the position of choosing between option red and option blue. If they are not practiced in decision making (and many aren't), if they have not learned how to live with the sound of their own voices declaring, "Red it will be!", then they are likely to be presiding over a company marked by analysis paralysis.

TAKE ACTION

1. See decisions coming. Welcome them.
2. Decisions are all around you. Do this often: Acknowledge their presence. Declare, "This is a decision point. A decision needs to be made. I will make it. There, I made it. Doesn't it feel good! Don't I feel stronger for the next one! Oh, I made a bad one. Whatta ya know? The world didn't come to an end."

— 42 —

INAPPROPRIATE INTENSITY

I have never been known for my patience. It's a serious flaw. On Christmas Day when I was 12 years old, I went to my brother-in-law, whom I admire, with $15 I had collected in gifts. He was 27 years old and worked for the Speedway Company in Chicago.

Speedway made and sold, among other things, a power drill for do-it-yourselfers. As I recall, the drill, complete with all its miraculous attachments, sold for (can you believe this?) $19.95. I just had to have one, and my brother-in-law told me a few days before Christmas that he could get me one at cost for about $15.

He told me to hold onto my money and pay him when he brought the drill over. Since he and my sister came to dinner at our house once each week, I assumed he would bring the drill the next week. When the time came for them to visit, I had posted myself at the windows at the front of our house on the lookout for them.

When the couple pulled up and got out of their car to come in, I could see that my brother-in-law was arriving empty-handed. My heart dropped, and my first desperate words to him, before he and my sister could shake the snow from their shoes and get through the door, were, "Lloyd, did you leave the drill in the car?"

He looked at me quickly, and curtly (out of character for him) said, "No, I haven't got it yet." Then he broke into his normal grin and greeted the rest of our family.

The following week, I just *knew* he'd show up with this coveted drill, but it was the same story and I was crushed. He knew it, of course, and took me aside after dinner and told me, "As long as you keep asking me about the drill, I'm not going to bring it to you."

The next week when Lloyd showed up without the drill I was somehow able to call upon powers I didn't know I possessed and refrained from any mention of it. Sure enough, right as rain, next week he brought it. He handed it to me happily, and I noticed that it came in a finer-than-advertised blue baked-enamel steel case. And amazingly, it had even more attachments than I expected. It didn't occur to me until much later that Lloyd had added these niceties at his own expense. Such are the greed and self-centeredness of a young boy.

The Teacher

Lloyd himself was extraordinarily patient and was the eternal optimist. His favorite refrain was, "There's no such word as can't." When I got a puppy, it was he who trained her to sit up, roll over, speak for her dinner, shake hands, and so on. He was a good athlete and spent hundreds of hours with me teaching me the rudiments of football and baseball. He bought me my first baseball glove and my first football, took me to my first major-league baseball game

(Chicago Cubs vs. New York Giants) and first pro football game (Chicago—now Phoenix—Cardinals vs. Philadelphia Eagles). He taught me all the things one could accomplish in life, yet he snapped me up short when I got out of hand.

As I think back on my overzealous attraction to that almighty drill and the way I badgered Lloyd about it with my incessant chatter before even offering my $15, I'm reminded of Winston Churchill's description of a fanatic. "A fanatic," he said, "is someone who can't change his mind and won't change the subject." Lloyd saw these strains in me and wanted me at my tender age to learn something about life in this simple exchange.

Caring

It's clear he found my intensity over the drill inappropriate and annoying. This didn't mean he disliked me, but that he disapproved of my actions. The training role for any boss is carried out best when it is combined with caring.

It's common for a subordinate to deliver a recommendation to us with unbridled hopes for our responding in the affirmative almost immediately. If they persist in badgering us while we deliberate for a reasonable time, we'll be justified in our annoyance.

Yet some tolerance on our part is also called for. After all, we usually attach some urgency to an assignment when we make it. When Lloyd wanted me to learn some patience, he wasn't trying to kill my enthusiasm. He just wanted me to know the wisdom imparted by William McFee decades ago: "The world belongs to the enthusiast who keeps cool." Remember Cool-Hand Lisa in essay 32? She had this lesson down pat.

--- *TAKE ACTION* ---

1. Old-time religion taught us to hate the sin but love the sinner. Keep this admonition in mind when dealing with your overzealous subordinate. He or she needs your tempering. Give it with care.

150

2. Be grateful when your subordinates are enthusiastic rather than phlegmatic.

—— 43 ——

THE WELLSPRING OF RECOVERY

- The retired CEO ruminated audibly with his luncheon partner. He had stepped down two years earlier and regretted his decision on his successor. The company was faltering. To his way of thinking, he'd picked the wrong man. He'd even considered lobbying key board members to fire his successor and reinstate himself, then thought better of it.
- The group executive with the specialty chemicals company invested $10 million in a new plant. It was a disaster from the start. The product to be made in it hadn't been researched adequately. It cost too much to make and was rejected by the market at its high price.
- The boss hired an executive presented by the search consultant. The sense among the boss's subordinates, who would be peers of this new hire, was that there was "something funny" about the guy and that he shouldn't be brought on board. They told this to the boss, all in their own ways, but the boss hired him anyway. The new hire, it turned out, was a drug abuser and had falsified his employment record. He was fired within 60 days at a high cost to the company.
- The funds manager violated his hedging formula and invested heavily in a company whose management struck him as superb. The company had just acquired a smaller firm whose product line complemented its own beautifully. Then the company was hit with a $5 billion patent infringement suit from a major competitor, and the president of the acquired company resigned. He was quoted negatively in a *Wall Street Journal* page-one feature on the company's sagging morale. The company's stock plummeted and the funds manager's year-end statement looked positively putrid.

Survivors

It turns out that all four decision makers in the previous examples survived their instances of bad decision making. The CEO is an exceptionally vigorous, effective community leader in one of our nation's major Southeastern cities. He's a model for retirees who seek to remain productive and give something back. His company not only righted itself, perhaps because his successor has since retired, but is now soaring—far and away the leader in its building materials industry.

The chemicals group executive was promoted to the position of president of his company's international division. The international business is growing much faster than the domestic side. The promotion makes him heir-apparent to the CEO slot.

The boss who hired the drug abuser against everyone's advice has been named senior vice president of his corporation. Like the corporation in the first example, this one is the leader in its market.

The funds manager survived as well, though he was the butt of jokes and gossip within his gilt-edged firm, and received rebukes and damning with faint praise from his clients. The latter was a sure sign that he was skating on thin ice. Nonetheless, he is today regarded as a mover among investment analysts and is regularly sought for his views by the business press.

Strong Already

Perhaps the rebound of these survivors can be explained by a statement made by Winston Churchill. (It seems I'm in the mood for him lately.) He said, "Success is going from failure to failure without loss of enthusiasm." After all, most of us have encountered people who have somewhere mastered failure on a grand scale and kept climbing. It defies the imagination, but there it is—undeniable. More likely, though, the exception proves the rule, and we can turn to Jane Austen for at least a partial explanation for the successes of our four examples. "Everything nourishes what is strong already" is the way she put it.

There is strength in numbers, we all know, but there is even greater strength in unity. A tight little band can rout a disorganized army and regroup faster after retreat or even defeat. The four decision makers, all with clay feet, were marked by a management style that kept them in bond with their associates. This saved them from abject self-doubt and embarrassment that is more characteristic of macho types who insist on standing alone when they blow it.

The support we receive from our teammates, even when we disregard their advice and make sincere-but-dumb calls, is a major factor in our being admired later by onlookers for our resilience—our power to rally. Even the retired CEO, embarrassed over his management succession decision, bore his doubts with the aid of a few close links in the community. And today, ten years after stepping down, he is heralded as the architect of the company's number-one ranking. He as much as anyone knows what it takes to be able to rebound from a bad decision.

TAKE ACTION

1. Be prepared for decisions you make that turn out to be dumb. Do so, first of all, by acknowledging your humanity. You simply won't always be right!

2. Second, admit your little foibles and mistakes to your teammates along the way. Don't try to hide them. They know what they are anyway. Have a good laugh together about them every so often. Then when the big boo-boos come, you'll be readily forgiven.

—— 44 ——

THE GOOD NEWS OF PARTIAL CONTROL

I'm the father of an only child, a daughter. Her name, you may remember from essay 2, is Laura, and she's a senior in college. She's wending her way through a psychology major, and I believe she shows exceptional promise in any people-sensitive job. She's perceptive, pretty, and a just-right blend of extroversion and introversion. She's a little shy, but when she gets rolling, she can be the life of the party.

It's Saturday morning as I write this, and I'm aboard United flight 137 bound for San Francisco. I'm mulling over last night and wondering what Laura will think when she sees this in print.

Last night was a wonderful one for me. Laura and her boyfriend elected to declare a brief hiatus from each other, so she was free to join me in a "daughter-daddy" thing for dinner at one of our favorite restaurants.

Dinner itself was nice, but afterwards, inspired by an ideally temperate summer night, the two of us decided to walk ten or twelve blocks across town and go to Dick's Last Resort. Dick's is a fun, new watering hole that has opened in the old North Pier Terminal Building on the bank of a channel that runs off the Chicago River at the edge of Lake Michigan. It features Dixieland music, and it can become a rowdy, foot-stomping place.

The two of us quickly got into the spirit of our fellow revelers, but about an hour into the gaiety, and piercing through the haze of a couple of beers, I had this magnificent little epiphany. I looked across our table to Laura, who was enjoying the music and an animated conversation with our waiter, and realized—perhaps for the first time—that's she's going to be just fine.

Anticlimax?

Were you expecting a greater climax to this little story, more of a barn-burner ending to my momentary vision? Perhaps you're justified in feeling this way, but bear with me while I explain why this is such a big deal for me.

As a parent of an only child, I'm sure I've made all the classic mistakes. I've made Laura too special, doted over her, and have been overly ambitious for her. I've been too unforgiving of her mistakes and have expected her to be an adult much too soon. I've been blind to many of her thoroughly unique characteristics, opting instead to focus my attention on what I want her to be. She's been aware of this, of course, and gave me a Father's Day card by Boynton this last time around that captured the state of affairs between us. The cover read, "I'm so glad you're my dad, and I think you're happy I'm your kid." Inside it read, *"mostly."*

154

What became so clear for me in a moment last night was not only how inappropriate many of my desires are for Laura—how much they are an extension of what I want *my* life to be—but how I've utterly inflated the importance of the decisions I make or have made that pertain to my being her father.

Believe it or not, that fragmentary insight brought an enormous relief. Laura will be what she will be, not what I want her to be, and whatever that is, as I've already noted, she's going to be just fine.

None of this means I haven't had and won't continue to have an impact on her life. After all, part of what she is and is becoming is due to our exposure to each other. But ultimately, where she's concerned, I have little control. The decisions that matter most are *hers*.

A Sense of Scale

It occurs to me, as it does to you, I'm sure, how much we also inflate the importance of our decisions at work. We're inclined to think we have more control over people's actions and thoughts and lives than we do. Moreover, we often delude ourselves by thinking our decisions shape the well-being and future of our enterprises far more than they do.

Cay Rohter is a woman for whom I have high regard. I serve with her on a civic board and have enjoyed seeing her mind at work. For a time, she served as chairman of the board of education of the city of Chicago. I can't imagine a public job more thankless and fraught with political shoals and mind-boggling complexity. Yet she provided a steady hand at the wheel at a time when our city's school system, already a troubled one, could have plunged into total disarray.

Over breakfast with her not long ago, we got to talking about the kinds of executives who are most effective. We catalogued some of the normal traits you'd expect to hear in such a conversation. Then she said something that wasn't all that surprising, yet it got my attention precisely because we're all so prone to forget its wisdom.

"The executives who impress me a great deal," she said, "are those who have a sense of scale of themselves in relation to their organizations. They realize that without them, their organizations would hardly miss a beat."

--------------------- *TAKE ACTION* ---------------------

1. Take a little dose of humility, if needed. See yourself in scale to your total organization. Your team needs what is uniquely you while you're around, but if you're absent or not a giver, the team will find a way to work without you.

2. Don't demean your decisions. Heaven knows, I'm not asking you to do that. But as responsible as you seek to be, realize your control over events is partial, not total. Be prepared to find that this comes as a relief.

—— 45 ——

DOING THE RIGHT THING RIGHT

When we think back on big decisions in our lives and work, the following items might run through our minds:

- Whether or not to play hooky from school
- To try out for a play, or a team; to run for class office
- To break up with a boyfriend or girlfriend
- To make or not make a religious commitment
- To tell a big lie or admit to one
- To do anything solo before an audience
- Whether or not to go to college; what to major in and how to finance it if one goes
- To disappoint one's parents with major actions taken
- To marry someone or not
- To have an affair; to break it off, or divorce; to break off the affair and recommit to the marriage

- To choose an employer, a first job; to hang up a shingle; to launch a career
- To buy a house or apartment
- To accept a job transfer or turn it down
- To look for another job when an expected promotion goes to someone else, or elect to stay to "prove them wrong"
- To build a plant, inaugurate a costly ad campaign, fire someone popular, acquire a company, take a strong stand on a controversial issue, or change careers

Declaration of Independence

One way or another, whether pertaining to the items listed here or a thousand different ones, a big decision is a declaration of independence. Whether we make it well or poorly, it is we and we alone who make it.

Even if we're accused by others or if we ourselves suspect that we have made a decision under the undue influence of someone else, we cannot escape the fact that we have chosen to acquiesce to that external force. Ergo, the decision has still been ours alone. Paradoxically, we have independently chosen to be overly dependent.

I've noticed in my life that "big decisions" in one very real sense aren't nearly as big as I've assumed. That's why I've used quotations marks around the words. Big decisions turn out to be the confirming point for a lot of little decisions I've made along the way. I've taken many little steps, as a diver does approaching the end of the board, but then the moment comes when I have to spring from that board to do the spins and flips that complete the action.

On the other hand, I may reach the end of the board and halt, turn, retrace my steps, and head for the showers. That too could be called a big decision, but it's likely if I look deep enough, I'll be able to confirm other little decisions I've made that led up to it. I may, for example, have skipped practice quite a bit lately. Or I might have gotten into an argument with the diving coach on two occasions recently. Then again, I may even have debated with myself before the season began over whether I wanted to be on the team again this year.

The Process

Just as I've written earlier about other matters, the big decision is not an event so much as it is part of a process. To be sure, it may be the conspicuous part. It may be played out in the presence of many spectators, as when the diver elects not to dive at a midseason swim meet, or some terrified groom leaves a mortified bride at the altar.

These two dramatic examples show the fear that is inextricably linked to any big decision we make. This is so whether we are making a significant investment of our own funds in something, or staking our reputation on some task we've agreed to where we have grave doubts about our ability to perform well.

The diver who walks back off the board and the absent groom are not likely to increase their self-esteem by their decisions. Indeed, their actions may even induce considerable self-loathing. On the other hand, if the diver had gone to the coach before the season and admitted not having the spirit for the competition anymore, the coach might get angry, but the diver would have declared independence in a more honorable way.

Likewise, the groom may have hurt his fiancée by saying he wanted to end the engagement, but both can only be better off ultimately as a result of such action.

TAKE ACTION

1. Today's emphasis on team play in virtually any corporate setting has shown that collaboration is an idea whose time has come. Whatever decision you make, increase your self-esteem by showing consideration for those with whom you share tasks.

2. Showing consideration does not mean conformity. You may well rankle your associates in some decisions you make, but be sure to act with poise and dignity. You may in fact be the only one with the courage or insight at a particular juncture in your corporation's history to point out its lethargy or wrongheadedness. Though your actions may bring initial offense, the authenticity that flows from conviction combined with tact will garner later support and respect.

FAST TAKES

on
Making Decisions

- Consensus typically lacks authenticity. It is a fraudulent concept that wastes time, misdirects a team's energies, evades the real issue, and leads to mediocrity.

- What is significant to learn and teach is the joy and camaraderie of sharing in the decision-*reaching* process.

- In decisions, as with almost everything else, practice makes perfect.

- We can increase our confidence in making decisions by starting with smaller decisions in our personal lives, then building up to larger ones on the job.

- "The world belongs to the enthusiast who keeps cool."

- "Everything nourishes what is strong already."

- Team-style executives realize they'll be called upon to make decisions by themselves, but they'll go out of their way to give credit for their good ones to those who helped them *reach* the decision.

- Executives who inflate the importance of their decisions forget they have only partial control.

X

RECLAIMING UNIQUE STRENGTHS

There for the Taking

Theme 4 returns again with this chapter on reclaiming unique strengths: *The authentic state of humanity is union, and, ironically, this enhances one's uniqueness.*

The key idea of this chapter is that what we have to contribute to our teammates that's most unique about ourselves are strengths that we've disowned! We've discarded them. In the press of our climbing the corporate ladder and the demands we've taken on, we've gradually lost touch with what we care about most deeply. We've gone a little flat as a result of denying who we are.

The union of the team encourages us to reclaim what we've discarded and come alive in a new way. What's reclaimed, of course, are values—deeply held beliefs that define our uniqueness.

To begin such reclamation, give thought to the following:

- Relying less on your "me-too" strengths
- Facing your job with a task-force mentality
- Planning less, doing more

- Listening to your inner voice
- Taking on "do-it-now" tasks from your teammates.

—— 46 ——

ACTING ON YOUR UNIQUE STRENGTHS

Management guru Peter Drucker stated in the simplest, clearest way what it takes for us to be good—really good—at our jobs. He said that the effective executive is someone who has learned how to make his or her strengths productive.

Commitment to Learning

I'm often asked if achievers are born or made. Sincere as the inquiries may be, to be blunt about it, I consider this question wide of the mark.

First of all, *every* person is born with strengths, whether or not they're ever put to proper use. Second, I've never met, heard of, or read about any accomplished person who hasn't had to struggle and overcome failure, disappointment, and sometimes tragedy to achieve the success that wins our admiration.

For people in the first category, only time will tell if they will tap their strengths. For those in the second, a penetrating look at their person's lives will show that they are committed to growing and developing—to learning. Learning facts and skills. Learning from exposure. Learning to build on earlier successes. Learning from mistakes. And learning to rebound from adversity.

Commitment to a life of learning leaves a trail that prompts the casual onlooker to think that such a life was born to win. The most dramatic proof that nobody wins consistently without this commitment is seen in the person born handicapped in some way, yet who goes on to lead a life of distinction.

Commodity Strengths

We all have basic strengths. They are made up of such items as our general aptitudes and interests, formal education and training, exposure and experience. Not only are we aware of these strengths, we're pretty good at using them. For the most part, they got us where we are.

Nonetheless, these strengths aren't unique. For example, you have every right to be proud of your mechanical engineering degree from, say, the Colorado School of Mines, but this alone hardly sets you apart from the legion of other well-schooled engineers. You may justifiably call attention to the professionalism implied in your having become a group brand manager at, for example, Procter & Gamble Corporation, but this alone offers no assurance of success at higher levels in this or any other organization.

Such "commodity" or "me-too" strengths are absolutely essential and signify we know what we're doing. They point to our professionalism. Without them we can't qualify for greater responsibilities. But to do distinctive things in our organizations, to add true value to our joint efforts with teammates, we have to uncover the authentic qualities in ourselves, the ones that set us apart from the journeyman in us, and then act on them.

This demands boldness and can be scary, but it is what generates superior performance in our work.

A client of mine, president of his company, went on television recently to be interviewed about his company and business. "No big deal," you might say. "After all, isn't he the big boss, used to being in charge of things?" The truth is, this man was terrified to go before the camera for a 30-minute show, fearful that this was too much exposure. He worried that he might come off as inept or slip up in the hands of a crafty interviewer and do his company and industry harm.

On the other hand, he had made a lot of noise within the company and at industry meetings that top business executives need to be more accessible to the public and spell out business issues and points of view they believe the public doesn't understand very well.

So he swallowed his fear and went on the air. After a first few nervous moments during which those of us who know him well saw that he had the jitters, he settled down and did a good job. He made many new friends for his company that day and has gone on to become a poised, effective spokesman on foreign-trade issues throughout his industry. Moreover, not only is he good at it, he's learned that he *thrives* on it, and this has made him a more infectious leader within his own firm. He has moved beyond his commodity strengths.

------------------------------ *TAKE ACTION* ------------------------------

1.   Have you caught yourself thinking that achievers are born rather than made and doubting that you came of such noble birth? Strike that thought and declare yourself up to the task of learning how to make your strengths productive.

2.   Begin by asking three close friends or teammates what strengths you have that you are neglecting on your job. Think long and hard about what they tell you. They may not peg you exactly, but chances are they'll trigger an insight that will lead to constructive risk on your part.

------ **47** ------

REDUCING THE UGH! FACTOR

On June 1, 1965, I entered the world of business. For three years prior to that, I'd been a college teacher of sociology. You would be right to think that there was a vast difference between the world I left and the one I joined. Yet those differences were mitigated by my having studied large-scale organizations in my teaching and then joining a medium-sized consulting firm as a personnel and organizational consultant.

My new boss was a management psychologist. He headed the personnel consulting department and set me to the task of my formidable orientation by having me read all sorts of manuals published by the American Management Association, the Conference Board, and others. These manuals contained such data as salary surveys for standard management positions in corporations, general personnel policy statements, varieties of organization charts, and sample job descriptions.

My thoughts leapt back to those manuals when I considered the topic for this essay: job descriptions. I can picture them clearly and remember the texture of their black pebble-grain covers as if I were holding them today.

It's not that their subject matter was all that thrilling that they remain locked in my memory. On the contrary, they were a hovering presence in my professional life for the better part of three months, and no amount of caffeine-laced coffee and spirited commuting to the men's room could ward off their coma-inducing effect on me.

Ugh!

To this day, job descriptions still have the same trancelike influence on me. When I'm forced to see one because of my work, my eyes glaze over and I'm soon reading several sentences twice before noticing it. You know, the mind wanders. The brain exercises its will to be anywhere but here.

I know, of course, that I'm not the only person in corporate life who has this problem. I imagine you do too. Yet it gives us no comfort to say there seems to be no solution to the problem. "After all," we might ask, "what's to stop this dull, lifeless, decades-long march from some personnel functionary's composition desk to the file cabinet?" There, or even in a computer's data bank, the typical job description is laid to rest, never to be consulted again in any meaningful way. "Done," says its author, and moves on to something of more importance.

Task-Force Mentality

There's a way, to be sure, that you can make your own job description come alive. Here's how: Rewrite it. Rewrite it with your behavior. Don't think about how you can live up to some out-of-date, perfunctory rendition of what your work means. Rather, think about what leads to achievement on your job, do it, and then capture what you do in writing. I guarantee you will have a job description that's authentic and will actually be useful to you and your boss.

The way to write this new job description is approach your job with a task-force mentality. Realize that everything you do is information-based. Realize that information you use is power, and the better the quality of information you give and receive, the more power you have. Here I'm referring not to absolute power (nobody has that, anyway) but to the power of influence, to persuade.

Information in turn is generated best in a task-force setting. By that I mean it is interdisciplinary and temporary. No one discipline or department is inclusive or knowledgeable enough to have all the information it needs. In addition, no set of information is likely to have permanent application, given the pace of improvements that need to be made in our products or services.

What this means for you is that even if you're not part of a formal task force or project team, your daily routines are likely to resemble this form of working relationship. This is so regardless of your having a boss, associates, and subordinates who are under umbrellas called accounting, marketing, manufacturing, or whatever.

Don't fight this configuration. Feed it. Go with it. First of all, it's the wave of the future. Second, it's a wonderful way to work. It gives expression to the gifts we all have. It taps the knowledge we've all developed, each in our own ways, and it contributes to real teamwork and joint respect. It opens the possibility of greater trust between people and groups and demonstrates the strengths to be found in mutual interdependence.

TAKE ACTION

1. A moment ago I offered that your job description based on a task-force mentality would be lively and useful to you and your boss. See if I'm not right. See if it isn't fun to write and read. See if you and your boss can't use it to set and measure your performance goals.

2. What we measure we do. What we don't measure, we don't do. Write and use your job description to measure what you believe in. This will ensure your contributing your unique strengths to your organization.

48

PLANNERS AND DOERS

I have a friend who lives in Boston. We've been close for over 20 years. We first met in the late 1960s. He came to work for a company in Michigan that was then part of Martin-Marietta's cement and lime division. I was a consultant to that company; he was a newly minted MBA from the University of Chicago and the president's fair-haired boy.

I resented him a little at first. The president, who'd known him earlier and sponsored him through his graduate work, kept telling me that he'd hung the moon, and I got jealous. But as soon as we got acquainted, my concerns evaporated. He was every bit as talented as the president told me, yet we got on well immediately. Our friendship quickly scaled the bounds of business.

Later, when Martin-Marietta pulled back from the cement business, he joined a large real estate developer in Chicago as a vice president. Then he joined a fast-growing, but small janitorial services company as executive vice president. There, as the number-two person in this firm, he got a taste for what an entrepreneurial, high-risk, high-reward business is like. Though he was not an equity participant in this business and was frankly fearful at that prospect, the notion of founding his own company also had some appeal to him. He stood on the edge of the pool, not bold enough to dive in.

Fresh Perspective

About that time, I invited him to join an experimental workshop I began. This group was composed of eight accomplished executives who met every Saturday morning for eight weeks in early 1977. I

166

wanted to try out an idea that would get executives with distinguished careers to stretch themselves further. My thought was, and still is, that as executives climb the corporate ladder and approach the top, with the time pressures they face, the obligations they carry, and the overall demands on their spirit, they lose touch with much of what they care about and believe in most deeply. I wanted them to reestablish contact with their authenticity.

This workshop was designed to give executives time to step back from work and examine unique strengths they'd neglected amid their perceived job responsibilities. To be a success, the workshop had to have these people approach work with a fresh perspective. It exceeded our expectations and created a bond between us all that exists to this day even though we're scattered throughout the country.

The Reluctant Entrepreneur

The format for the workshop required each participant to provide me a half-dozen early recollections. These are one-time events that a person recalls occurring sometime in his or her first eight years of life. (This is a projective technique developed by Alfred Adler soon after he broke with Freud in 1911. Adler believed that what we remember out of our past, and *how* we remember it, gives an indication of how we view life today.)

Based on those recollections I then composed for each participant a one-page profile that contained four headings: (1) basic strengths, (2) growth-blocking attitudes, (3) style of life, and (4) disowned strengths. I used these recollections as a basis for designing role-playing activities for the executive. All participate in these activities, but the executive whose recollections we use at the moment is center stage. After the role play is completed, I distribute the profile of the executive to all present to see if in the executive's mind, and everyone else's too, his or her behavior in the roles played confirm the profile.

They always do. This is a powerful activity that proves "showin' is better than tellin'." In my friend's drill, it became clear to all that he had made himself a professional second-in-command. One of his growth-blocking attitudes was "I'll hitch my wagon to a star." It was equally evident that despite all his strengths, he was too much the planner, forever preparing but not getting on with what he wanted to give his heart to. "Tim," I said, "you're a seven-eighths man. What are you going to *do* to make you eight-eighths?"

He clearly knew the answer to that then, but still wasn't quite ready. Soon thereafter, he moved to Boston where he became vice president of all facilities of one of that city's largest banks. He developed a reputation as an imaginative leader and built an organization known for its team efforts.

But in 1987, almost ten years after the workshop, he declared himself the entrepreneur he's been all along and started his own business. Like most new ventures, it has had its shaky moments and cash shortages, but its lift-off was successful and he's flying. He will tell you with power in his voice that no matter how long it took for him to realize it, planning is often a substitute for doing. He's corrected that fault in himself, and his team is benefiting from what is uniquely, distinctively him.

TAKE ACTION

1. Plan, yes, but don't plan to death.
2. Follow this rule: Plan your work; work your plan.

—— 49 ——

HARD RESULTS AND THE MEANS WHEREBY

In preparation for this essay, I did some research on what various thinkers from the past have written on the value of listening to our inner selves. Here's a thought-provoking smattering of what I found:

"Many a time I have wanted to stop talking and find out what I really believed."

Walter Lippman

"An inability to stay quiet is one of the most conspicuous failings of mankind."

Walter Bagehot

"In the midst of winter, I finally learned that there was in me an invincible summer."

Albert Camus

"If I were a doctor and were asked for my advice, I should reply: Create silence."

Soren Kierkegaard

"Not all those who know their minds know their hearts as well."

François de la Rochefoucauld

"As long as you are trying to be something other than what you actually are, your mind merely wears itself out. But if you say, 'This is what I am, it is a fact that I am going to investigate, understand,' then you can go beyond."

Krishnamurti

Finally, two observations from Dag Hammarskjöld:

1. "The more you listen to the voice within you, the better you will hear what is sounding outside."

2. "I don't know Who—or What—put the question, I don't know when it was put. I don't even remember answering. But at some moment I did answer *Yes* to Someone—or Something—and from that hour I was certain that existence is meaningful and that, therefore, my life, in self-surrender, had a goal."

Hard Criteria

Numbers saturate our lives. Whether we concern ourselves in our careers with making a sale and toting up our commission, or by serving as a custodian in a leper colony under the direction of Mother Teresa, we are subject to measurement. How many brooms must be ordered in a year? How many beds have to be changed and sheets laundered in a day?

Budgets are not benign. Quotas can be compelling. Return on total assets is a scorecard. Steady annual profit increases are a sign

169

of corporate health. A high stock price wards off unwanted suitors and is a vote of confidence in management.

What we truly measure, we pay attention to.

Soft Criteria

> But just because we say we measure
>   doesn't mean we do.
> And claiming faith in sanctioned numbers,
>   doesn't mean that's true.
> Rather, our need's to stop and hear ourselves,
>   on the theme that's running through.

What I'm saying in this bit of doggerel, of course, is that hard criteria that are often given sanction on high by an organization's top management may very well be ignored despite all rhetoric to the contrary while the soft criteria become what the sociologists call *normative*. The corporate culture rears its head this way and measures the "means whereby" or the "how" rather than the "what." Your boss may like your results, but not the way you win them, and this shows in your lower-than-expected bonus.

Our common error, however, is in thinking that the soft and hard are automatically in opposition. Remember the leper colony. If we don't make the numbers, the enterprise will cease to function. There must be room for both the hard bottom line and the soft means whereby.

For you to be integral to your team, to help quicken it, you are called upon to make your contribution. Make that contribution the best it can be by making it authentically and distinctively *you*. To do this, you'll need some quiet time. (How about that? You could say this book is about the "double QT"—the Quickened Team is dependent on Quiet Time!) You'll have to shut down the whirlwind of your routine and listen for the theme that's running through. Discover this and you'll have your means for coming up with numbers that will blow their socks off.

170

TAKE ACTION
---

1. Follow Krishnamurti's lead, and Hammarskjöld's: Say yes to life and recognize you have a goal. It's there, perhaps buried. Exhume it.

2. Set aside a brief time every day to do *nothing!* That's right, absolutely nothing. Call it meditation if you like, or secular prayer. But whatever label you attach to it, give your inner voice a chance to express itself. Recall the double QT.

50

WHEN ALL EYES ARE ON YOU

Remember? There was that recent time when you looked around the room. Whereas over the past hour the discussion between you and your teammates had been spirited, now silence descended like the dark of night, and all eyes were on you.

Do you remember the statement that brought on the silence? Of course you do. It was made by one of your teammates and was much like the following ones made in similar circumstances. In fact, you've made and heard such statements any number of times.

- "Well, folks, it seems to me we've got a handle on this. Now we've got to sell it to the board. Their quarterly meeting is next week. Not much time to prepare, for sure, but if anybody can pull this off, it's you, Wayne."

- "Someone needs to call Apex and tell them we've screwed up. They're gonna fry us when they learn the shipment will be 30 days late. Better 'fess up, though, and make it clear that even though it's our error, we're delaying for quality reasons. Ron, I think you're the guy to do that best."

- "OK, we're all agreed. If we let the boss push ahead on the alpha project, it'll be a disaster. We just can't let him do it or we'll be guilty of the worst negligence possible. He'll be in here in a minute, and we've got to shoot this thing and put it out of its misery. Janice, we'll be here to back you up, but he's more likely to listen to you on this than any of us. What do you say?"

- "There we are, Herb. We're going to go with your design for the new tractor. The future of this division depends on its being top of the line. We don't have the time we thought we did, so the blitz starts tomorrow. You're in charge."

The "Now" Commitment

Chills run up and down our spines when we face a task and doubt our ability to perform. Ironically, the task may well be one we have sought with vigor, as in Herb's case. Yet when it's placed on our shoulders, we're brought face to face with our unique resources and may wonder what possessed us that we would campaign for it.

Frederick Perls, the founder of Gestalt therapy, defined anxiety as the gap between the now and the then. His definition lays emphasis on the idea that we doubt our ability to perform, but also implies that the sooner we can convert the "then" to the "now," the less anxiety we'll have to endure. His message is to step into the now and put anxiety behind you. Put it behind you by finding out right away that your resources aren't wanting at all, but will serve you and your teammates well. After all, would real fellow travelers ask you to take on the task because they expect you to fail?

All of us have had the experience of being thrown into some task without forethought or planning of any kind. Bang! It was just our job to do, we had to do it, and we did—even surprising ourselves with our finesse, ease, and poise in the process. I'm not arguing here against planning any more than I did in essay 48, but I merely suggest learning from those events and emergencies by remembering we often overplan when we're ready to go right now.

Overcoming "Now" Chills

Yet even do-it-now assignments have some gap in time between the decision to march and when the march begins. This is so when the now gap is a matter of only minutes. I know of no way to overcome now chills except through exposure. By that I mean the more you're willing to accept do-it-now assignments, the more you'll find they are without fangs. The veteran orchestra conductor counseled the young actor one hour before the curtain went up on the opening night of the Broadway musical: "The difference between you and me is that you positively know you're going to die tonight. Though I have my doubts, I somehow sense I'll be alive in the morning."

Let us assume the musical is a success. Six months later, even the young actor, bathing in sweet reviews and enjoying a fatter wallet, approaches the now of each curtain rising with eager anticipation and self-confidence. Let us assume it's a flop and closes in a week. That actor will be anxious that his next opening be a success, to be sure, but when it comes there will be just a tad less look of terror in his eyes.

The now assignment is a blessing because our involvement is more immediate and the anxiety of "then" is reduced. This is true even when making the now commitment, as Herb did, means saying yes to an exacting, complex project that won't be completed—and its success known—for at least three years. Though there will be potholes, confusing signals, and slick surfaces along the road, there will be no question as to who's driving the car.

――――――――――――――― *TAKE ACTION* ―――――――――――――――

1. Be willing to risk failure by saying yes to do-it-now assignments. While many play it safe and remain on hold, you'll become superior by learning from your mistakes.

2. Be pleased for those times when all eyes are on you. Take them as proof that you're viewed as a contributor to the team.

FAST TAKES
---

on

Reclaiming Unique Strengths

- We have to uncover the authentic qualities in ourselves that set us apart from the journeyman in us, and then act on them.

- It's a mistake to fight the "task-force configuration" of your daily work. It's better to feed it, go with it. It's an opportunity to be uniquely you.

- As we climb the corporate ladder, most of us lose touch with what we care about and believe in most deeply. As we do this we lose touch with our unique strengths.

- You'll never learn "the theme that's running through" if you don't take time to listen to yourself.

- Unique strengths, at bottom, are values that provide natural firepower. They don't lack for motivation.

- When you act on a unique strength, people will think you've changed. You won't have changed. You will have become more fully you.

- Acting on unique strengths is contagious. People see your verve and are themselves induced to invest in you.

- The only way to overcome "now" chills is exposure. Repetition is the key to learning.

MATURING

If we really understand the problem,
the answer will come out of it,
because the answer is not separate
from the problem.

KRISHNAMURTI

XI

EXPLORING VALUES

Organizational Savvy and Reaping the Human Harvest

The theme that makes its first formal appearance with this chapter on exploring values is number 7: *Exercising vision is developing an understanding of where you are and where you're headed— both as an individual and as an organization.*

Vision shouldn't be defined as distant clairvoyance. Rather, it's vigilance in the here and now that tells you how what-you-are-now is a *sign* of what you're going to be—good or bad. Such inquiry leads to authenticity, individual and corporate.

To get started on visioning, explore your corporation's values, as a way to both plumb the depths of your organization and tap the strengths of its people. Give thought to the following:

- Looking for signs that give clues to your future
- Being a student of organizations
- Discerning the "little agenda" of your company
- Reviewing your biases on bureaucracy
- Practicing altruism

- Placing high value on our nation's shift to teamwork
- Seeing teamwork as natural
- Being part of a corporate culture that supports team values

---

51

CLUES TO A HIDDEN AGENDA

The man in my office could have been sent from central casting. If anyone looked the part of the top executive, he did. Over six feet tall, trim, gray at the temples, dressed in a crisp navy pinstripe suit, wearing soft, well-shined leather shoes. Age 52.

This man, whose annual compensation was over $200,000, gave only two indications that things weren't well with him—he was tentative and his voice lacked force. You might wonder why, given the fact that he had been running a large group for a Fortune 100 automotive manufacturer.

The reason is that he had just been fired, and he was visiting with me at the recommendation of a mutual friend. Although no longer in shock, he was discouraged and still confused as to why he got the ax.

This was how he put it to me: "It got hard for me to know what the bosses wanted. It seems the company style was management by innuendo. The words didn't match the music." Then he contradicted himself by admitting that he hadn't been totally without signals, saying, "I realize there were times I heard bullets whizzing by my ears, but I didn't heed them." He also admitted he maintained a strange silence through all this. He never once challenged his bosses on either the appropriateness of their directives or on their lack of clarity. He lacked confidence in his judgment, confidence in himself.

They're All Around Us

There are all kinds of signs around us that, if we're alert to them, let us know where our corporations are headed, and on what matters

178

they place great value. They are guideposts to how we can use our gifts to greatest advantage for the sake of our teammates specifically and the business in general.

For example, let's assume you're a financial executive who joined your company because finance and accounting played a dominant role there. Let's also assume you took comfort in the fact that the CEO previously was CFO. But now, to your consternation, that CEO has retired early and the board of directors has surprised everybody, including you, by naming a successor with a sales background!

Moreover, you've heard new lingo cropping up in the corridors and washrooms that says, in effect, "We're not as devoted to the number-crunching as we used to be," or, "We were getting to be too slide-rule in a company that needs to be creative." There's no denying it, these are signs to be heeded.

As the financial executive in this case, you needn't do anything so drastic as leave your company, but you surely must broaden yourself for advancement by having your contribution understood by your teammates and all associates as multidimensional.

They're Reliable

Signs can be messages conveyed with raw blatancy or intriguing subtlety. And as I've tried to make clear, they're ignored at one's peril. It's critical to remember as well that if the signs you see contradict your company's official rhetoric, go with the signs. They're more reliable.

In reference to his one magical year as coach of the Chicago Bears, Mike Ditka said that his 1986 Super Bowl victors were a team of Grabowskis, not Smiths. In so saying, he was getting the sign and the rhetoric together, which is ideal. This meant there was a minimum of dissonance on this most awesome football team of the decade, and it showed in their 15-1 won-lost record and in the way they dominated all contenders.

—————————— TAKE ACTION ——————————

1. Take 15 minutes to conjure up five signs that have appeared in your company or team in the past year that you've ignored. String them together into some theme that is eye-opening for you. Lay

your plans for making a contribution that is based on that theme. Frame your statements of intended achievements around it as well.

2. On a less significant but not unimportant note, suppose your boss drives a Ford. Ask yourself what that sign means about company values. Perhaps it means nothing. But then again, it may mean a lot. For example, on Tuesday, November 28, 1989, the *Wall Street Journal* ran a column-one, front-page story on the firing of Kellogg president Horst Schroeder by William LaMothe, Kellogg's CEO:

"Fast Fall," read the eye-grabber. "Personal 'Chemistry' Abruptly Ended Rise of Kellogg President," ran the headline. "As Cereal Firm Lost Ground, Horst Schroeder Overrode Tradition of Collegiality," read the subhead. "Wrong Home and Wrong Car," read a second subhead. *All this before the story even begins.* You get the idea.

──── **52** ────

MAKING THE FAMILIAR UNFAMILIAR

Let's look at some broad changes in organizational life in American business.

During the past few years, *Business Week*, *Forbes*, *Fortune*, and *Industry Week* all have devoted cover stories to the subject that mergers don't work. Actually, the conclusion the editors of all of these publications reached was not that mergers *never* work, but that most of them don't because the human element is overlooked in making the arrangements for these megamarriages.

Noted anthropologist Lionel Tiger has written, "It is remarkable that knowledge of the essentials of human behavior is so poorly disseminated and translated into action. . . . In most rigorous and technically elegant structures, the weakest bit is still the softest and most familiar—people."

Then, in my own book, *Inside Corporate America* (a survey of 1,086 executives in 13 major corporations), only three percent of the respondents report that "being a student of organizations" has a "very positive" impact on their careers. Twenty-five percent own up to this state of alertness having a "somewhat positive" impact on their careers. Six out of ten responded "neutral" when asked about the importance of this factor to their careers. In appendix B, I show how CEO apathy on this subject is particularly devastating to a company's prospects.

The dismal record of merger failures would seem to bear out the conclusions of our leading business magazines, Tiger's contention, and my findings that executives place an exceedingly low value on understanding organizational life. Moreover, isn't it astounding that otherwise sophisticated senior managers, who intone with grave sanctity their fiduciary responsibilities and commitment to increasing shareholder value, are so eagerly bent on buying what will turn out to be a pig in a poke?

In 1982, I naively told *USA Today*'s New York bureau chief Susan Antilla that I thought we soon would be witnessing the "deconglomerization of America," and she faithfully reported it. I believed that because we refused to get to know who we were climbing into bed with—with predictably bad consequences—we would quit doing it. Since then, each successive year has brought us the largest mergers in history, and the mania moves apace. We are left with no choice but to wonder why.

Spinoffs and Start-Ups

As it turns out, I wasn't totally naive. In some very real ways we are witnessing deconglomerization. As corporations merge, they also spin off what hasn't worked for them. Whether financed through public offerings, LBOs, or their purchase by smaller companies, these "rejects" often thrive when set free from their elephantine masters.

Further, we have had an entrepreneurial boom that's unprecedented. Small businesses have been sprouting like weeds over the past decade. This in turn helps explain the drop in our unemployment in the face of cutbacks, operations shutdowns, and spinoffs. These armies of hourly workers, middle managers, and top executives who were jettisoned in mergers for reason of "redundancies," "discontinued operations," and "going to a flatter organization" through "de-layering" have landed safely. Otherwise, our ranks of the unemployed would have swelled. Many have joined entrepreneurial start-ups. This has been a profound shift, and all things considered, we should be amazed at how little upheaval and strife took place in the process.

As we study business organizations in particular and organizational life in general, we are faced with one inescapable conclusion: Things aren't what they seem. For example, earlier in essay 34 and later in essay 82, I sally forth with the notion that merger mania just might be good for us, and that we shouldn't be put off too much that we're doing the right thing for the wrong reasons.

Explicitness Preferred

Things would go far better for us, though, if we would do the right things for the right reasons. If we were more explicit about the true purposes of our "technically elegant structures" as Tiger calls them, we could manage their positive effects proactively rather than experience their bounty merely as inadvertent fallout from bad plans and bloated rhetoric. We need to be students of organizations.

For example, if mergers do in fact help correct organizational flab and laziness that have hindered American competitiveness, and if they do foster and support entrepreneurialism in their own way, and if they can be managed well by organizing them into small decentralized profit centers, then let's stop apologizing about them and get good at it! Let's not lie anymore by saying, "We anticipate no major layoffs." Rather, let's become expert grown-ups who manage the spinoffs and layoffs with pride and enthusiasm. Let's do this with an eye to how this can be a growth experience for people.

To improve our judgment in managing technically elegant structures, whether in the merger game specifically or any aspect of organizational communications, we have to get explicit about our purposes. None of us is smart enough to be such a student of organizations in isolation. We need the collaboration of our teammates. We need to test each other's thinking as well as be inspired by the offbeat view of that colleague who comes at the task from a different angle.

TAKE ACTION
---

1.   Contemplate Tiger's observation that the weakest and least understood bit in our structures is the most familiar: people.

2.   Starting from that point, join with your teammates in making the familiar unfamiliar. Study anew. What we think we know, we often don't. There's no better lesson for anyone engaged in increasing team-effectiveness.

— 53 —

THE LITTLE BIGNESS
OF CORPORATE ESSENCE

One of the most-read columns in the *Wall Street Journal*, I'm sure, is the one that bears the heading "Who's News." For years, when my practice was predominantly executive search, it was to this column I turned first each business day.

If you're not a regular reader of the *Journal*, let me remind you that this is the column that daily lists the names of executives who have been promoted or recruited to top management positions in our largest, best-known corporations. It holds fascination for anyone engaged in climbing the corporate ladder and is a quick way to gauge who's doing what where.

Sometimes the column might just as accurately be headed "Who's Firing Whom" because those named to fill key posts are just part of the story. Often, the people they're replacing are named as well, and just as often they're described as leaving the company "to pursue personal interests." As we all know, these are code words for forced resignation.

Today, with my practice predominantly top-management team-effectiveness consulting, I no longer turn first to "Who's News"

183

when I pick up the *Journal* each morning. Though I still read it faithfully, I do so for different reasons.

The main one is that the editors added a nice twist to the column a couple of years ago. They often begin it with a brief profile of a CEO, recently appointed, and the challenge the CEO faces in running the company. These frequent digests, strung together by any thoughtful reader, provide a comprehensive overview of the major contemporary management issues of our global economy.

The Local Option

A slogan we've heard a lot of lately is "Think globally, act locally." Business executives speak it when calling attention to the need for thriving in worldwide markets by producing quality products and service in each location where their company has a facility. It is a way for any organization to rally itself for taking care of details while it paints the big picture.

What I find as an inescapable lesson from reading the real-life short stories and adventures at the beginning of each "Who's News" is how much the CEOs have to devote themselves to the local option. That is, their chief challenge is always organizational—in other words, people—even though the task may be called "quality," "distribution," "share price," "capital needs," "new products," "government relations," "volume," "margins," "Asian threat," or "return on assets." These are all measurements, subject to quantitative analysis, whereas their first concern, truly, is the means whereby. That's the local option. That means people. That means thinking small. That means teamwork.

Who Saved Whom

When I give speeches to audiences of business executives, one of my favorite questions is this: Did Lee Iacocca save Chrysler or did Chrysler save Lee Iacocca? I choose him only because he and the Chrysler story are so well known, and I couldn't care less what any person's particular answer is.

The real answer is some of both. Most others would have failed where Iacocca succeeded. He was the right person for the time. But Chrysler was right for Iacocca, too. He had failed at Ford and he might well have failed elsewhere.

I believe all CEOs like Iacocca succeed not because they are miracle workers, but because they tap into a corporation's little agenda. That little agenda is controlled by the people. It has been in existence for years (usually decades), long before the new boss takes the helm; and a CEO who doesn't learn what it is and build on it hasn't got a chance.

Case in point: If you were to read *Out of the Cracker Barrel*, a history of the National Biscuit Company published by Simon and Schuster in 1969, you'd be amazed at how much of the little agenda of Nabisco survives today. Despite the wrenching—the RJR/Nabisco jumbo (largest ever) leveraged buyout, the political maneuvering, the wrecked careers, the corporate relocations, the coming and going of Ross Johnson as CEO, the appointment of Louis Gerstner as his successor, and the possibility that Nabisco may yet again become a free-standing entity—much of what this company was, it still is!

There's a negative and positive side to any little agenda. It can be proactive and growth-producing, or it can manifest itself as a circle-the-wagons mentality with Custerian consequences. After all, and this will come as a surprise to many, strong cultures can kill a company.

Iacocca's distinction is that he affirmed the people of Chrysler doing what they believed in, and had always believed, that called out the best in themselves. Tapping into such deep-seated belief will always produce a winner.

─────────────── *TAKE ACTION* ───────────────

1. You don't have to be CEO to benefit from paying attention to the little agenda. With the help of your teammates, figure out what it is and articulate it. It's the essence of your company. Hint: It's not necessarily what your current values statement says it is. That *may* reflect more what well-intentioned top management wishes you were.

2. Support what's best about it. Tap into its proactive, authenticating elements. Then there will be consonance in your team's actions and thoughts, and together you're likely to inspire the same in other teams you're linked with.

—— 54 ——

THE BUREAUCRACY COP-OUT

I have the pleasure and good fortune to serve as chairman of the board of a not-for-profit, three-year-old community organization in Chicago. The organization is going places and I'm enjoying the ride. It's my second year in the job.

As is typical with most such entities, in our push to offer expanding programming and services to those from whom we hope to win favorable attention and funding, we sometimes have trouble making ends meet.

The time lag that exists between the development costs of new programs and the income we receive from the subscription of those services means that we have to be entrepreneurial and nimble. We have to live by our wits in meeting the needs of our market. Such management by opportunity may not speak volumes for a systematic operation, but it works wonders for interim financing.

Funny, isn't it, how it's not only the big, for-profit corporations that have to balance the long- and short-term skillfully? Small, not-for-profit, altruistic organizations have to do that too!

Our executive director understands this long- and short-term trade-off superbly. He combines the ability to generate income-producing programming on short notice with the conviction that we need a more formal discipline of the organization's vision, mission, strategy, goals, and tactics. In short, we need a plan for ensuring our superior performance over time.

We set about this by asking one of the brightest, most sensitive, and savvy of our board members to be responsible for developing this comprehensive process. He runs the marketing operation of his successful corporation to boot, so we knew we were in good hands.

186

Milestone or Millstone?

Yesterday, the executive committee of the board met to conduct its ordinary business and also to hear the proposal for this planning process. It had been prepared by our fellow board member with assistance from the executive director and associate director. If we on the executive committee liked what we heard, we could recommend its adoption to the full board.

As expected, our associate came through. His document displayed hard work and quality thought. The central feature of his plan was to put our standing committees to work, subject to various timetables, by engaging them in the revalidation of our vision, mission, and goals, and the implementation of our strategy and tactics. It's neither important nor possible to spell out the details of the plan here except to say that it asks a lot from the people who serve on our standing committees such as executive, development, program, finance, human resources, and public affairs.

Killer Bureaucracy

All seven of us on the executive committee save one thought the plan was a knockout. We saw it as a discipline to build structure and capture the spirit of the organization in such a way as to ensure a long, distinctive future.

The lone dissenter, bless his heart, had the courage to stand up to this formidable group pressure. He voiced his opinion that he saw all this as killer bureaucracy in an organization that was small, imaginative, and strapped and needed to remain entrepreneurial.

"Why create all this machinery?" he asked. "Why not let Dave (executive director) and Karen (associate director) do their thing? Let them take the initiative. Let's not tie their hands with this superstructure. If I wanted to really get something done, the last thing I would do is give it to a committee!"

Sounds convincing, doesn't it? Strike a responsive chord with you? Does it jibe with your feeling bogged down by the bureaucracy in your company? Want to shout "right on"?

Well, as much as our committee needs dissent so as to avoid group-think, our sincere dissenter is dead wrong in this case. He's wrong because whenever there's growth, bureaucracy is inevitable. If you don't want bureaucracy, don't grow.

Bureaucracy gets a bad rap. The straightforward definition of bureaucracy, when stripped of its negative hype, is "the organization of people and tasks on a large scale." Try running an expanding organization without that.

Any small company has three choices: Grow, be merged or acquired, or go out of business. The first two require bureaucracy.

A fascinating point about bureaucracy is that its trajectory has changed. It used to be a rigidly vertical, overly layered, top-down, order-giving phenomenon based on authoritarian attitudes. Today it's a collaborative, more horizontal entity based on influence, persuasion, and networking. If our little community organization is going to continue to grow, it's going to have to make use of the collective brainpower of our committees. If we do this, we won't be bogged down. Instead, we'll soar.

The lesson for you, moreover, keeping in mind the thoughts from the previous chapter, is that you aren't called upon to give expression to your authenticity in a vacuum. Rather, this expression takes place where people and tasks are organized on a large scale. Your department, just like one of the committees of our not-for-profit organization, exists within the ever-present, undeniable hierarchy and offers the opportunity for the team and the obligation for you to reap the human harvest.

TAKE ACTION

1. Don't use "bureaucracy" as a cop-out for not getting things done. A bureaucracy is people. Where there are people there are potential teams.

2. Don't fight bureaucracy. Manage it.

----- **55** -----

CODE WORDS FOR TEAMWORK

It was yet another one of those routinely clever cartoons in the *New Yorker*, making its point so well. A man in his late 50s is on a weekend stroll through the woods with his young grandson. The path they're following is densely lined with beautiful, tall trees in full foliage.

The man is portly, nattily dressed in soft plaid blazer, suede vest, tie, and a short-billed cap that announces to the world that this well-heeled grandfather is being sporty and lighthearted today. So much so that he's giving his grandson, absorbed with the surroundings, the benefit of his advice.

Which is: "It's good to know about trees. Just remember nobody ever made any big money knowing about trees."

There, in a good-natured instant, we're brought face to face with the corporate image. Come Monday in the executive suite, this sanguine grandfather will convert to a tyrant in hot-blooded pursuit of self-interest.

Yet though this image is accurate for some, it needn't be for you, and there's clear evidence that companies whose values run along this worn-out line are headed for the ash heap. If we define altruism as the sharing of self, time, and information, what corporation can be without it and hope to survive? And when we stop to think about it, we realize that the sharing of self, time, and information are also code words for teamwork.

Evolving Altruism

Considering grandfathers, I was fortunate to be indirectly exposed to a particularly brilliant, figurative one. In college and graduate school, my main professor and advisor, Clyde Vedder, was a sociologist who was a protégé of the late Emory Bogardus. Bogardus was a professor at the University of Southern California who for decades had an aura about him. Students revered him. He was a scholar of international renown. His personal library contained some 17,000 volumes, and his monumental work, *The Development of Social Thought,* went through four editions before he died in 1973.

First published in 1940, this book traces social thinking from preliterate peoples to modern times. Any reader exposed to the breadth of knowledge presented in this survey would be hard pressed to come away from it without sensing that the march of human history is an inexorable one toward greater cooperativeness.

It's no accident that Bogardus was one of the best-known American sociologists in Japan during the 1930s and 1940s. His ideas had great currency there among scholars. I believe we have over-glamorized Japan's management and already are seeing signs that all is not well there. Still, there's no denying that the "Japanese miracle" wrought since World War II has been based on a style of operation much in line with the kind of sharing and cooperation that Emory Bogardus considered inevitable in all advanced societies. Tired as we may be of hearing about that style, and knowing that it too has shortcomings, we nonetheless have much to learn from it.

Corporate Ties that Bind

Even more important than learning from the Japanese style is our becoming convinced that we can improve on it. There's no question in my mind that we can and will. True enough, we still have throngs of self-serving, shortsighted American business executives who prefer to conduct their affairs in bankrupt, old, cynical ways. They manage their businesses for short-term results that enhance their compensation and pad their personal net worth. Then they get out while the gettin' is good. Or before they're found out and given the heave-ho by increasingly feisty boards or new owners. The new owners may themselves be rapists and pillagers, as we know all too well, yet as I mention in essay 52, some are undoubtedly doing their acquirees a good turn.

Nonetheless, our drift is clearly in the direction of linking hands and pulling together. Ironically, this has been forced on us by the Japanese, who have shown by whipping us repeatedly that cooperative efforts bring forth permanent results superior to those produced by intimidating tyrants and rugged individualists absorbed with today.

For example, it is true that Japanese quality is far in advance of ours. It is shocking, moreover, to learn that our implements of defense (weapons, vehicles, systems) would come to a virtual standstill were it not for the microchips the Japanese produce and we import for use in the manufacture of those implements. The quality of our chips is too haphazard and substandard to be counted on.

On the other hand, the technological lead we maintain over Japan in chips and most other products is impressive. I agree with Milton Friedman, who said in an interview in the December 12, 1988, *Forbes* that the technology development in Japan is still largely derivative.

The Japan style relies far too heavily throughout their organizations on the mediocritizing commitment to consensus. It isn't consensus I advocate in this book, as you now know, but teamwork. There's a difference. Consensus is a leveler whereas teamwork is a rich, authentic collaboration that stimulates full voices and superior choices. It insists that good ideas come about and survive through the test of high-spirited debate and reason. Teamwork learned and done right prompts, then accommodates, individual brilliance and resourcefulness. Then it closes ranks around execution.

Teamwork is altruism. It's insisting on and rewarding the giving of one's personal best to the enterprise. America has a stake in mastering teamwork and is making progress. We have a bent for it once we understand it. It's here that our Japanese neighbors will eventually learn from us. Ultimately, such shared learning will allow us to link up with them more productively. This, rather than competing with the Japanese, is one of the true global challenges of the future.

TAKE ACTION

1. Get behind the cause. Teamwork is our global proprietary product. Learn how to "do" team—it's an acquired skill. Evangelize your company.

2.   Recognize once more that consensus is a leveler. It's more appropriate for routine matters. To excel in a fast-moving, demanding environment, superior options need to be developed. Then one option from among the competing several needs to be chosen as most likely to achieve outstanding results. This requires that teamwork be carried out on a sophisticated level, and not be used merely as a cliché.

——— 56 ———

IS TEAMWORK A FAD?

I'd like to follow up on the message of altruism and teamwork of the previous essay. In this essay and the next two, permit me if you will to wax a wee bit philosophical on the relationship between values and teamwork.

It is November, 1989, and I'm reminded it has been 11 years since the tragic, charismatic event of Jonestown. When Jim Jones persuaded several thousand people to hand over their possessions in favor of a more humble life in Guyana, probably no more than a few had any inkling that he was undermining, in fact changing, their values. What gets lost in our memory of this ghoulish episode is how subject we are to a shift in values, even though we give strong voice in support of the ones we leave behind.

Given how desperately sick Jonestown was, what might induce terror and wonder in us is our subjectability, willingness, and even eagerness to shift values under other, more ordinary life circumstances. Yet to court and make such changes is not all bad. On the contrary, in many instances it's desirable and necessary. Such is the case with us in American business as we evolve from pride in "rugged individualism" to increased commitment to team values. This after all is the promise of "corporateness," isn't it?

Values are many things to many people. Among our various ways of thinking about values, two come to mind quickly. They sometimes are described as having either—take your choice—a lot or a little to do with morals or ethics. At other times they are spoken of as priority-rating systems. Whether viewed as benchmarks for tolerance of the thoughts and behaviors of others or our own willingness to cope with inconveniences to reach goals or cultivate laudable character traits, it's ironic that these coded systems often seem to be developed impulsively and observed without consistency. Aren't we business executives guilty of falling for fads? And despite my sermonettes on the team in this book in general and in the previous paragraph in particular, isn't there some possibility that teamwork is just another one? Perhaps.

Unquestionably, our proudly itemized, strongly defended commitments are always vulnerable to circumstances. At numerous points in our lives, they tend to change with the wind and be discarded with hardly an afterthought. What good can come from such will-o'-the-wisp? Almost perversely, however, history reveals that such malleability deserves to be looked upon as an evolutionary or survival benefit. The Adolf Hitlers, Jim Joneses, and Charles Mansons who have managed to nullify mass or individual values with bizarre inspirational rhetoric and fanatic philosophies are far outweighed and outnumbered by occasions of positive value revision that favorably affected civilizations.

For example, Moses, a stutterer, eventually led his beloved but cantankerous people to new life in the promised land. Their 40-year search ended only after replacing random, self-serving tribal values with more beneficial goal-oriented standards of performance. Though not solely values in themselves, the Ten Commandments Moses brought from God to his people certainly reflected principles supporting group cooperation and cohesion. They introduced both new, valued objectives for orderly communal behavior and worthy expectations among these wanderers. In so doing, they also established overall community standards and a system of measurement of performance. The Israelites thus were provided with their first formal behavioral code. By coming together, they ended their aimlessness.

Corporateness as Evolutionary Force

Advertising, public relations, and publicity campaigns by corporations and nonbusiness organizations alike regularly apply sophisticated and effective methods for the purpose of revising material, aesthetic, and sometimes moral values. Though often viewed with consumer skepticism, such communications serve an educational as well as the more readily criticized persuasive function.

Media coverage of controversial issues influences how focal points of controversy are perceived and evaluated. Criticism of television's treatment of significant topics is common among viewers. Still, such programs prevail, television enjoys steadily increasing popularity, and values are formed, altered, and re-altered via television on a daily basis despite all carping.

As individuals in Western society, we're influenced by our major institutions. Time after time in our lives our values undergo change for better or worse as our institutions undergo change. The fact that we accept such change, whether consciously or not (more often not), indicates that some new priority or desired commodity is given sanction by some institution in which we have invested authority and trust. We are willing to trade some of our old values for the new institutionally approved ones, and so are enabled to participate in the institution's objectives and benefits.

But it's not a one-way street. Individuals have an impact on institutions as well. For example, the American corporation provides the best, strongest, and most consistently successful example of inculcating personal value systems. This may seem surprising to some. After all, corporations are chastised for depersonalization and indifference to personal goals, values, and objectives and are accused frequently of bungling careers and destroying lives. Yet upon closer examination, it's undeniable that the corporate enterprise is successful overall by virtue of institutionalizing the values of its employees and interweaving its own values with theirs to produce a richly textured fabric. In so doing, the corporation achieves its own set of goals as well as those of its people. To one degree or another, it becomes whole cloth.

Early Orientation to Team

Looking back, our first value-*changing* experiences occurred in our early school days, scouting activities, sports, dating, college sorority or fraternity initiations, and other adolescent experiences. But for most of us, the corporation provided the first startling value alteration experience of our adult lives. Most likely it was in this environment that we were first seriously encouraged to shed our self-serving, indulgent values and involvements in exchange for values and objectives that were more team-oriented. Today, that emphasis moves ahead with even greater force. Increasingly, we are asked to work within teams rather than primarily as individuals. To be sure, as I underscored in the Introduction, individuality is tolerated and indeed sought in corporations, but it's also true that newcomers' common experience on entering corporate life is that their primary attention moves from individualized values to those of the larger group.

People who adapt to these new team values are at ease and excel in this environment. They and the corporation hold the same objectives in common because they are developed in common. Those. who won't find ways to express their authenticity for the corporate good instead find life in their corporation difficult to grow in and are ultimately rejected by that community. This is so, in other words, because they do not contribute their unique strengths to its daily tasks or to those that will enhance its future.

Wandering lifestyles that lack long-term goals and direction, such as experienced by Moses' followers in the Egyptian desert, make evident the need for well-defined and -applied values. Without such alignment that directs expectations, individuals and corporations alike will roam aimlessly, greatly limited in meeting and satisfying their longed-for levels of achievement.

Teamwork, then, is not a fad. This evolutionary force that fosters our moving ever closer to the promised land of corporateness is indeed a survival value for our businesses and world.

TAKE ACTION

1. See teamwork not only as a value itself, but as an evaluator of values and an implementor of adopted values as well.

2. Help create alignment for your company by mastering the skills of teamwork. Heed the prescriptions of this book's introduction.

—— 57 ——

A NATURAL ACT OF MAN

No matter for whom the bell tolls or who responds to it, we know that everyone is affected by its chime. In essence, socially there really are no individuals. Even Mendel, the monk who was diligent enough to discover genes amidst the peas in his solitude, ultimately established his worth through various sorts of relationships with others. He had to *commune*-icate his discoveries to others. Together, we cooperate to achieve common goals and interests. Intense sociality is especially true in all primates, among whom we human beings pride ourselves as the summum bonum.

As such thoroughly social animals, we exchange values and adapt to new ones with some considerable amount of flexibility only by encountering one another in our lives. As I showed in the preceding essay, not a great deal of thought goes into which of these values we will acquire. We often unwittingly adapt to get along. Some will be common-sense values that can be rationally justified. Others will be conventional values, not necessarily rationally justified but adopted for pure reasons of conformity. Conventional values, routinely and easily adopted, are usually more emotionally motivated than common-sense values, but they don't necessarily make a fellow a bad guy.

Locusts, Ants, and People

Like all social animals, we change qualitatively when we are in groups. Degrees of qualitative change vary among individuals, but none of us escapes the syndrome. Some, like the locust, are quiet, pensive creatures who become excited in groups. Locusts even change their color en masse through accelerated endocrine levels. It isn't such endocrine acceleration, however, that causes flushed color alterations in human social settings.

Ants too are an excellent example of group interaction. To some extent, all viable groups' behavior runs parallel to that of the anthill. The anthill itself is the major organism. Individual ants are biologically simple, mobile cells, seemingly more *parts* of an animal than sovereign entities. It's as if they are circulating through connective tissue in an intricately woven matrix, informing the entire community about its surrounding environment. Food is found, enemies are observed, and the hill's maintenance requirements are met. The direction of the sun's movement is monitored so effectively by anthill citizens that Alps mountaineers use their long, amoeboid nests as pointers to the south. So efficient are these insects that if they are fortunate enough to avoid human interference, their nests can last as long as 40 years. In contrast, over 90% of human commercial enterprise fails within the first year of inception.

Ants, of course, are not possessed of human brilliance. They don't have the task of choosing and applying values to their lives. They are simply in charge of surviving. We on the other hand have options, opportunities, or burdens of selecting ways to survive. Choosing from numerous alternatives that include education, friends, mates, lifestyles, careers, and life purposes, we direct ourselves toward our goals. Even with human brilliance intact, we often launch ourselves toward these goals with only limited knowledge of likely obstacles or consequences that might result from our choices. Based on what we value, we often embark on lengthy programs and incur long-lead-time obligations while blind to short-term consequences.

Wanderers, for example, even if they have developed the finest, most admirable values, will experience devastation if unprepared to commit to sociality with the various individuals and groups they will encounter during their excursions. As in the case of the anthill, individuals lose preeminence, and the self is curtailed in its grandiosity at the group level. Is it really so meaningless or inauthentic to see ourselves as simple yet elegant satellites, interpreters to and from the outside world, for the long-term benefit of a worthwhile, collective enterprise? I say no.

Early in our existence we develop certain values. These usually are in support of loyalties that may or may not be challenged later in life. Loyalties to family, nation, religion, political parties, and sometimes even sports teams tend to be passed within families from one generation to the next. Such loyalties reflect the values of our families, but families themselves interact with the larger society so that a core hybrid set of values gain exposure to young offspring. In youth we are usually eager to go along with these values, being the social creatures we are. We seek acceptance and approval from peers and relevant authorities, so we value the things we are taught to value.

New Values, New Goals

In adult life we begin to assess our values more critically, discarding some bequeathed values of youth and acquiring new values that reflect our own goals more directly. We select groups to join that share our values and value what we share. Those groups are, in one fashion or another, crucial to the individual pursuits of our most treasured goals.

Our group affiliation gives a fairly accurate indication of what our individual values are. For example, labor unions are not at all likely to have any corporate managers for members. National Rifle Association members are not likely to seek membership in the Audubon Society. Corporate managers seek out professional groups that give aid in the development of their careers and job skills. Those professional associations provide continuing education and opportunities to meet peers, exchange ideas, and benefit from contact with others who share similar values and management beliefs. Today we call it networking.

Let us get even more specific and think about your corporation and your work group. That group reciprocates by assisting you and all its members who support it. It supports and shares your values and helps all of you to win your fellow members' financial, emotional, and voluntary backing. Without such backing, the group cannot exist or effectively live up to its charter. The mutual benefit to group and member alike, then, is dependent on mutual exchange and gratification of its individuals and the group as a whole. When this occurs, a team is in place. So the adoption of new values and new goals isn't limited to young people just breaking out from the upbringing of childhood and adolescence. It's heartening to see positive value shifts and individual growth take place throughout one's adult life.

Such is the case with executives who have rediscovered exhilaration in their work by relearning the lesson taught by Aristotle: Man is a social animal. Teamwork is natural.

--------------------------------- TAKE ACTION ---------------------------------

1. See your authentic place in the whole. Take your place proudly.
2. Be natural. Live up to your nature. Be a team contributor. Ultimately, it is the way of all the world.

—— 58 ——

LISTENING FOR THE RIGHT NOTES

Corporations come by their values no differently from any other complex organization, such as a not-for-profit multi-hospital system, a metropolitan school district, or the U.S. Navy. The corporation's goals will be different from theirs, which in turn will make some of its values different, but its goals will emerge from its culture in exactly the same way. If we define the culture of any organization as the "man-made aspects of its environment" (I think that will hold up), then it's obvious that the values of the corporation also are an integral part of its culture. Those values are adopted to serve the corporation's goals, both those that are clearly articulated to its people as well as those that aren't but are somehow sensed, which may in fact be the more significant. (The latter is what I meant by the "little agenda" in essay 53.)

It's common today for consultants and executives proudly to espouse "management by values" or "value-based management." This is a bit silly because all corporations manage themselves based on values. The issue is, are the values by which they're dominated "good" ones? That is, do they serve a central purpose that in turn serves the wider good of all society? It's undeniable most do. This is not to say we can't do better. I wrote in essay 56 that teamwork is a value that expresses our commitment to evaluate values. Team is the gyroscope. The medium is the message. The process is the solution.

Management by What Values?

In a corporation, the ability to spread common values to those inducted into its ranks, the ability to make favorable decisions in the face of changing values, and the ability to resolve conflicting values between and among its members are essential to its success and growth. Considering that it takes many years for an executive to rise through the ranks to enjoy advanced success within the corporation, you'd think, wouldn't you, that the individual could be counted on to give a fairly clear description of the distillation of all these value gyrations if asked? To be sure, by the time a person reaches top- and middle-management levels, he or she is intuitively familiar with the values and needs of the corporate organization. Yet articulating them is not so easy. The fascinating juxtaposition of numerous values of the organization as a whole with those of its greatly varied management staff comprising a pluralistic whirl results in various interpretations of a corporation's image. What is it? What does it stand for? How does it behave? By what core values is it managed?

One way to project such images is to ask weird questions! As recorded in my book *Inside Corporate America*, when managers were asked to name an animal that in their mind best symbolized their companies, they produced a wide variety of responses. Given that people see things differently, it was understandable that 77 different animal classifications were named as corporate analogies. More captivating, however, is that when asked what characteristics of the animal chosen made it a good analogy of their corporation, executives gave many different responses for the same animals. One executive might see a parrot analogous to her corporation, which she sees as a collection of copycats and yes-sayers. Another would see a parrot as colorful. Still another might see it as abrasive or grating. It's worth noting that far and away most animals and characteristics were positive and given positive meaning. For example, many antelopes were named, but no one selected a tarantula.

People often see part of themselves interwoven with entities regarded as positive, but not so in those deemed negative. The most popular responses may indicate a wider viewership for public TV programs like John Forsythe's "World of Survival" rather than accurate perceptions about the manager's corporation and its image, but I doubt it. In case you're interested, however, lions were the most popular symbol.

The Central Purpose

Successfully merging a corporation's values with those of its individual managers is the basis for developing a successful enterprise. This is why in our best companies teamwork is no longer just a nice idea but is absolutely essential for the sake of competitive advantage. Most dynamic and vital to operating success is the corporation and its managers coming together over what constitutes its central purpose, its reason for being. How corporations perceive their managers, what they expect from them in terms of lifestyle as well as workstyle, and the parallel perceptions by managers of their organizations are all ingredients in a rich stew. Nonetheless, despite the varieties of background and qualifications, there exists one seasoning that provides the dominant flavor: the capacity for individuals in sufficient mass to uncover, internalize, translate, and communicate the corporation's core value system to staff, labor forces, and the corporation's various publics. Yet individuals can't come to this point alone. They can do so only through collaborations within and between their teams.

Among the ranks of management can be found executives who best authenticate their corporation's spirit and image. They are the clear embodiment of the corporation's central purpose. Top executives in a corporation are individuals whose own values for the most part comply with and complement those critical to the organization. If this were not true, they would have been winnowed out before they rose to the top. These executives more than others learned to adapt to and define their corporation's code of values to themselves and their associates.

They have to be good at demonstrating their mastery to a key person above them, too—the chief executive—if they are going to continue success. Surprising to many, the high priests of their corporate cultures, those topmost stewards anointed as chief executives, are the team players who for the most part don't write the music. Rather, they're the conductors who learned the score in earlier years by singing in the choir. And the most enduring, effective, powerful, influential ones realize that their present task is to make sure all sections sing their parts on key.

If the latter is true of your CEO, count yourself fortunate. It's likely you're part of a corporate culture that supports team values.

TAKE ACTION

1. Ask yourself, "Do I know our corporation's central purpose? Or am I a loner off somewhere hearing the wrong notes?"
2. Join the choir. This is where you'll learn the score.

---- *FAST TAKES* ----

on

Exploring Values

- Signs are messages that can be conveyed with raw blatancy or intriguing subtlety. They are ignored at your peril.

- Signs are more reliable messages than rhetoric.

- "In most rigorous and technically elegant structures, the weakest bit is still the softest and most familiar—people."

- We are woefully inadequate students of organizations. To develop our organizational savvy, we need the collaboration of our teammates.

- Your company's little agenda is remarkably resilient. It can serve you or wreck you.

- Bureaucracy, which is another word for hierarchy, gets a bad rap. Much of what gets called bureaucracy is something else.

- We can and will improve on the Japanese style of management; they rely too heavily on the mediocratizing process of consensus.

- Teamwork is not only a value itself, but an evaluator of values and an implementor of adopted values.

- Teamwork is humanity's nature. It is shared authenticity.

- All corporations manage themselves based on values. The issue is, are the values by which they are dominated "good" ones?

XII

SETTING GOALS AND TASKS

What To Do and How To Do It

If we believe that people want to feel their work is bigger than their jobs, and if we believe the ticket to belonging is contributing to the enterprise, then theme 2 is the proper one for this chapter on setting goals and standards: *The need to belong is a powerful human force that finds expression in teamwork.*

There are goals that sound right and there are goals that are authentic for you. The latter ones lead to your personal best and maximize your contribution: They make your purview much wider than your job description.

To be such a standard-setter, give thought to the following:

- Choosing goals that give birth to the will to win
- Choosing goals that give added meaning to current time and space
- Eliminating "chores" in favor of tasks that support your goals
- Taking on tasks nobody wants
- Conveying concern for detail

—— **59** ——

DISCOVERING YOUR THROUGH-LINE

During much of the 1970s, otherwise known (thanks to Tom Wolfe) as the "Me Decade," I was without conscious goals. This was my choice, and I was in step with the times.

In 1974, I published a book entitled *Work, Love and Friendship: Reflections on Executive Lifestyle*. In it appear these words: "Young adults today are much more in touch with the now. They wisely seek de-emphasis of goals and involvement *in* roles. They know that in a very real sense the future belongs to those who don't prepare for it."

The late Marshall McLuhan read this little volume and wrote, "It's a fun book, but immature." That stung. Ben Bradlee, a friend and editor of the *Washington Post*, told me in 1976 when we first met, "You're too young to have written a book of reflections." I was 39 when he looked me in the eye and said that.

Both men were right, though there's nothing about the book that embarrasses me. After all, I was merely recording my observations about life at the time, and I expect executives in their 30s reading it today would find much there that captures their attitudes. Now on the other side of 50, however, I know I was as wrong as I could be about goals. *We all need goals.* Not just goals that sound right, but authentic goals that give birth to the will to win.

Authentic Goals

Almost everything we are asked or expected to do by somebody, or are willing to entertain the thought of doing, is important by some standard. In other words, it has value on some level. Yet just because a particular action is worth consideration in certain quarters doesn't make it right for you, even though you see its merit.

No matter how narrow our corner of the world, life presents more alternatives than we can deal with. We must order our priorities and chart goals that support those priorities. If we don't, we will flounder and grow cynical.

Selecting goals that are right for us, though, can be a difficult task. They're not simply perched up there on the fence waiting to be picked off by us as we walk by. Even when we sit down to chart goals for ourselves and then try to reach them, we often find that they lack power for us and are easily discarded. We give up.

Distracting Gyrations

We get so embroiled with the demands made on us by others and ourselves that we neglect the real demand—self-knowledge. As I underscored in essay 48, we are so caught up in what we ought to be that we bury who we are. Each of us hardheadedly has to shut down all the gyrating machinery that fills our days and ask this simple question: What do I want to do with my life?

I embarked on this simple exercise in 1979 and had my answer after about 15 minutes of scribbling and pondering. When I said to myself, "C'mon, Allan, write down what you want to have as the ultimate *through-line* in your life," the answer popped up like hot bread from the toaster.

Here's what it was: "To make sure that in your work and community involvements, the 'right things' get talked and thought about." That's it. That's all.

Whereas I experienced my share of floundering and cynicism in the 1970s, this powerful thread constituted a long-range goal that gave shape to numerous short-range and intermediate ones since the time I brought it to the surface. It still does.

This didn't mean I had to leave my family, find a sweet young thing, and run off to Mexico to make sandals and massage my psyche. Rather, I saw that "victory" in life was available right where I was situated. Same family. Same job. Same teammates. Same community. This was good news as I embarked upon the 80s.

So now I write an occasional management column, books, and articles. I give speeches and conduct workshops. I delight in my team-effectiveness activities in organizations where I encourage corporate culture change toward ethical reflection, building self-esteem, and superior job performance. These varied activities center around this strong, simple through-line. And imagine, I get paid for it!

The same life-enhancing experience awaits you if you have the same blockage over goals that I did.

TAKE ACTION

1. Shut down the gyrating machinery. Stop worrying about who and what you *ought* to be and find out who you *are*.

2. Ask yourself (and take the time to answer): What do I want to do with my life? What will be my ultimate through-line? Do this and you'll see some building blocks fall into place.

—— 60 ——

WHAT STAR DO YOU FOLLOW?

Let me add on to the message of the previous essay. Alfred Adler, one of the pioneers of modern psychology, was a genius. He didn't believe in "drives." Rather, he believed that human beings became what they are because of the pull of the future. Two concepts central to his theory of personality are (1) style of life, and (2) the creative self.

Adler defined the style of life as an organized set of convictions about life of which the individual is at best only dimly aware. His point is quite simply that most of us go through life without being cognizant of the impact of this "organizing influence" on us.

He further argued that this core of convictions is constructed by each person in response to an all-encompassing goal set early in life. In short, the convictions are governed by the goal and exist for the sole purpose of serving the goal. Keep in mind that this dim perception is different from, say, a "life dream," in that such a dream is at the forefront of a person's thought processes.

The creative self is intertwined with the style of life in this way: My style of life is my own creation. I must admit that my physical endowment and many of my earliest experiences are not of my choosing; but neither can I overlook the fact that I *make use* of these as bricks and mortar to shape (create) the way I live thereafter. I'm in charge, whether or not I want to accept this responsibility.

Demosthenes was born with or soon developed a severe speech impairment. He could have accepted this as fate. Instead, he overcame his handicap by speaking alone for hours on end with stones in his mouth and went on to become one of history's most compelling orators.

Others may be born with great gifts yet squander them. Why is this? Adler would have said this is the creative self at work, meaning that such waste and its justification is an invention of people's own minds. Nobody forces them to think these things; they generate them on their own. My creative self, in other words, is the "life-making me," even when the life I make is self-destructive.

The Goal

If Adler is right, and I believe he is, and all of us are governed by an all-encompassing goal of our own selection that is not truly known by us, doesn't it make sense that we should give considerable effort to figure out what it is and whether it is constructive or destructive?

I imagine your answer is yes, but I'm quick to warn that this is a tricky challenge with no guarantees that we can get it exactly right. Still, it's worth a stab and I don't see how any harm can come of it.

Start by examining the major actions you've taken and decisions you've made throughout your life. Put aside all rhetoric—the "shoulds," "oughts," "tries," and "wishes"—and concentrate only on what you've actually done. If you're patient and contemplative enough about this, you'll begin to get an inkling of what star you've been following.

Your family or close friends can be helpful to you too in this process. Ask them what they would guess to be your life theme, the "drift" of your existence. People are more intuitive than they think, and their guess might prompt a "recognition reflex" in you.

I'm sure, for instance, that had we been fourth-century B.C. class-mates of Demosthenes in Greece, we would not have been far off in assuming that his encompassing goal—what governed most of his actions—was being heard. He sought, it seems, to move people with his ideas and words.

The Observer

About 15 years ago, I went through this kind of introspective exercise. It was the same exercise that I put my friend from Boston through—the one I described in essay 48. In so doing I discovered my encompassing goal was to be an observer. I concluded as well that this wasn't constructive. Life was rewarding from too far away. I was too much the little boy with his nose pressed up against Macy's window at Christmas.

I made changes, entered the store, and made my purchases. I converted the observer to the sometimes observed, and your reading this book is a partial consequence of that initiative. The through-line declaration I described in the previous chapter came about roughly three years after this event.

You may, of course, find all this gibberish and nonsense, and if you do, that's just fine. After all, you may be absolutely right.

But I doubt that and therefore urge you to give very serious consideration to this proposition: Your intermediate goals—those I recommended that you deliberately choose—can add authenticity to current time and space only if they are in support of a life goal that is constructive. If you have such a governing goal, you'll be able to enrich your life and the people around you in ways you never dreamed possible.

––––––––––––––––––– *TAKE ACTION* –––––––––––––––––––

1. Get nervy; pretend you're dead, looking down from some-where, reading your obituary. Assume you'd lived exactly the life you wanted to live, no exceptions. How would that obituary read?

2. Write it out in every particular. Now read it over several times to look for clues on what you want out of life that you're not yet obtaining. Get down to business!

—— 61 ——

CROWDING OUT CHORES

I'm active in my church. It's a large downtown church with more than 3,200 members and a staff of seven ministers. As you might expect, it's a busy place. There are the usual services of worship for the regulars and out-of-town visitors, but it also has some unusual outreach programs for the homeless, inmates of our county jail, and patients of our county hospital who sometimes feel like inmates; tutoring programs for children in nearby projects; daily activities for older adults; imaginative foreign missions projects; an annual arts festival; and much, much more.

The numerous activities of the church are ever before me because I chair the church's lay committee on communication and public affairs. Our committee's job is to publicize the church's various programs and ministries to its own membership and the larger urban community of which we are a part. The committee is great fun because it's made up of a bunch of working fools with good hearts. We take pleasure in delivering the "Good News."

But what's this? Earthly chores intrude upon heavenly pursuits? I arrived home one night four weeks ago to find a letter and packet from one of our ministers. She began her letter with these words: "I want to make your job as a volunteer leader at the church easier." How did I know that this letter with this opening line wasn't going to do that at all? Just psychic, I guess.

After some further explanatory matter, the Reverend Ms. Kapp continued: "Enclosed you will find copies of a volunteer opportunities survey and directions for completing it. We would appreciate it if you could define the job descriptions of the volunteer opportunities you coordinate by filling out one survey for each of those opportunities."

A Worthy Purpose

I got angry as I read this letter, even though I realized the purpose for these job descriptions is worthy. The church will use them to compile a directory of every volunteer job that exists in all its activities. The directory is a good idea. It will inform all who seek volunteer efforts of any kind. It will make our church work better and serve better.

Nonetheless, this struck me as a chore, and I found it repugnant. The four job descriptions I was expected to attend to were (1) media liaison, (2) photographer, (3) special events liaison, and (4) graphics coordinator. Pretty mundane stuff. What was I to do?

I first considered calling Deborah Kapp and just telling her I was too busy, and that yes, as her letter admitted, this was a lot to ask. That seemed pompous, though, and I rejected it. After all, other people chairing committees were going to find a way to get this done. Who am I to think I'm above it?

What I did was stick the packet in my briefcase thinking some time might present itself in my travels or on an airplane when I could put a couple of hours together and just get the job over with. That hasn't worked out; it's still in my briefcase, more than four weeks have elapsed, I have passed the deadline for returning the job descriptions, and am now writing about the project rather than completing it. What irony!

Or Is It?

It's not ironic at all, now that I think about it. The writing I'm doing right now that you're reading comes first. In fact, I've written four of these essays since I received the request for the job descriptions. It's easy to see, then, where my true goals rest, and however immodest it is to say so, I've been true to my first calling.

You would be right to ask, "But Allan, have you really eliminated the chore?" My answer to you has to be no in the literal sense. After all, it's still there, undone. But I did eliminate it *at the time* in that it has not interfered with what I insist comes first. In addition, I have played hob with the deadline that was somebody else's, not one that I was consulted about and committed to. To my mind, this allows me to claim a decent job of self-management and upholding my authenticity in this case.

A postscript is in order. You know already that I believe in the chore. It has value. Otherwise, I *would* have called Deborah Kapp and told her to count me out. Moreover, she is a savvy staff person who probably set an early deadline—knowing the nature of volunteer compliance—as a means of getting the project started. The real deadline is later.

The committee I chair meets this Wednesday night. My plan is this: As it turns out, I'll have a couple of hours between now and then to draft the job descriptions. I'll have the committee review them and make revisions. I could have had each of four persons actually write one description. That's what the delegator would do, right? I agree, but the members have worked awfully hard lately. I owe them this.

TAKE ACTION

1. A good offense is the best defense. Crowd out chores with what deserves your first attention.

2. Nature abhors a vacuum. So does the organization. In the absence of worthwhile activity, an organization will make chores, some of them virtually useless. Remember one of Parkinson's laws: Work expands to fill the available time. Keep "time" scarce with commitment to your goals.

— 62 —

TOOL BINS AND WORK YARDS

Let me tell a variation on a story so old that I can bank on most readers never having heard it.

The parents of ten-year-old twin sons wanted to confirm for themselves that one of their sons was a pessimist and the other an optimist. It was puzzling to them that two children born at the same time and raised in the same house could be so different. (They weren't familiar with Adler's "style of life" and "creative self"!)

It was early Christmas morning and the parents had set about an unusual plan. They lavished presents on the pessimist. He was given an electric train that ran merrily around the Christmas tree as he peered desultorily at it through his yet sleep-filled eyes. He was given beautifully wrapped bounty after bounty of sports equipment, clothes, and even a chemistry set. He phlegmatically expressed "thank you" as he unwrapped each one while keeping a dour expression pasted on his face. Meanwhile, his brother looked on, not agitated, but wondering why nothing had yet come his way.

As if noticing the latter's consternation, the father said to him, "Oh, son, there's nothing under the tree for you, but if you go to the basement, you'll find something different down there." The neglected twin ran off downstairs alone while the parents stayed on to keep company with the one who was still rummaging through the largesse.

Down below, the father had emptied out his hobbyist's tool bin and filled it full of hay that he'd had delivered from a local riding stable. In short order, sounds of industry and whoops of joy vaulted through the floorboards, puncturing the lethargy of existence around the Christmas tree. All three got up to see what was going on in the basement.

When they reached the bottom of the stairs, they saw the other twin thrashing around in the tool bin, furiously tossing its contents out the door onto the basement floor. When the boy looked up and saw their incredulous faces, he shouted, "Well, with all this hay, there's gotta be a pony in here somewhere!"

Optimist as Learner

You might be inclined to say, "Nice story as far as it goes, but what happens when the little fellow gets all the way to the bottom of the pile and learns there's no pony?" The answer is, of course, that he's going to be disappointed, perhaps even severely so.

Yet I've noticed that optimists get over their disappointments quickly, even when they're severe. I think this is because optimists are learners. While on the way to learning there's no pony, they somehow learn other things as well. They learn something about

213

expectations. They learn something about enthusiasm—about when it might be appropriate and when not. They learn about self-reliance. They learn about discovery. They learn about trust. They learn about tossing hay and they learn about putting it back. The pessimist drones on and on in his nothingness, while the optimist is a learner who makes sure *nothing never happens*.

The Learning Experience

You can see how any team is strengthened by the presence of an optimist who has learned on a few occasions that despite all the hay, there's still no pony. Every team needs its devil's advocates and its nay-sayers to save it from Pollyannaism, but it also needs those people who take the team out front by turning straw to gold.

The people most capable of turning straw to gold are those who have learned to do so by willingly taking on tasks others don't want to do or think they're too good for. They're the ones who head for the basement when others idly mutter that their American Flyer train should have been a Lionel. Or that it was painted black when it should have been red.

Just think how often we've all been part of conversations in which we speak admiringly of someone who took on a hopeless or thankless task and pulled it off or gave it a new dignity. Think about how that person has impressed herself upon us. Then think about what she learned in the process. Think about how she has developed her competence. How she added to her bedrock of self-assurance. How she's now more confident of facing even more difficult tasks ahead with a poise and authenticity we can only wish for.

"Life wears a visionary face," wrote Emerson. "Colleges and books only copy the language that the field and work yard made." The language of which Emerson wrote, the language that gives life its visionary face, is language created by the learner who sees value in the hidden corners of the field and work yard.

───────────────── *TAKE ACTION* ─────────────────

1. See that piece of drudgery everyone is avoiding or pretending doesn't exist? It needs to be done. Do it, then look for another. But don't ignore the advice of the preceding essay. There's more than

enough drudgery to go around. Make sure you see purpose in the task you choose. Make it fit your goals.

2. Even with all the hay, there's often no pony. Still, don't neglect your spirit. Remember these words from Martin Luther King, Jr.: "Even if I know certainly the world would end tomorrow, I would plant an apple tree today."

——— 63 ———

A ZERO-DEFECTS MENTALITY

Somewhere along the line in American business, we got lost. We knew where we wanted to end up, but we forgot how to get there. What I mean by this is that we sought to be profitable in our corporations while neglecting a concern for detail on our jobs. This has shown up in our poor quality of products and services, a subject I touched on briefly in essay 55.

Seeking profits is like seeking happiness. Simply wanting them won't produce them. They're by-products. They're not goals, but outcomes. One of the key elements in the production of profits is attention to detail. All achievers are committed to details and convey this to all their associates, particularly to their teammates.

Understanding the Business

A concern for detail fosters the understanding of your business. John Mienik, a friend and former client, is a premier expert in the burgeoning direct mail industry. For several years he was president of Publishers Clearing House. PCH is the Long Island company that pioneered the business of selling magazine subscriptions by mail.

For many years prior to being president, Mienik was vice president–marketing of this highly successful organization, and the idea man behind its expansion. Further, according to estimates of industry observers, PCH profits were up markedly while he was president and have been off since he stepped down to form his own consulting business. The company has slipped from its number-one position and been overtaken by its chief rival, American Family Publishers, 50% of which is owned by Time, Inc.

A demanding type, Mienik inspired his subordinates by his own performance and made clear that he would accept no less than their personal best. Part of that *best* was dotting every *i* and crossing every *t* in their jobs. "Forget the big picture," he would exclaim. "This is a detail business."

No subordinate would dare make recommendations or advance proposals in meetings unless they and their execution had been thought through in minute terms. In fact, a proposal to submit a proposal was not uncommon. What came of this was an executive team as knowledgeable about its business (what made it work or not work in a nitty-gritty way) as any I have seen.

A Builder of Attitude

A concern for the little detail is the big idea. It's part of the big picture. Nothing makes this more clear than the rallying cry of the earliest days of our extraordinary space program. Remember it? "Zero Defects." The scandal of the O rings in the Challenger disaster in January 1986 only proves how far the space program slid after its earliest years. Today, we may hope that NASA and the program are heading back to their former level of performance.

The rallying cry of zero defects conveyed our total commitment to assure safety and the preservation of human life. No value of ours is more representative of the big picture. If we were going to send people into space and risk their lives in a frontier operation, we would insist that there be no margin of error in any production over which we had control.

By holding themselves accountable to zero defects, the people in charge of the space program—those making products for it and those performing the countless services of this enterprise—steeped themselves in an attitude that produced mastery. While most of us aren't called upon for life-and-death matters in our work, if we are to achieve mastery, we must be no less concerned with detail than those heroes of a generation ago.

TAKE ACTION

1. Do, and don't know. List some tasks you believe in deeply but have thought beneath you because you were looking at the big picture. Do them or see that they get done. Itemize what you don't need to know that you thought you did.

2. Know, and don't do. Acknowledge what you must *learn* to be superior at your job. Learn it. Don't do what you're doing that subordinates or other associates can do better.

FAST TAKES

on

Setting Goals and Tasks

- The Me Decade folks were dead wrong. We all need goals.

- Your through-line is a powerful thread of authenticity running through your life. It's an overarching, long-range goal that can give shape to numerous short-range, immediate ones.

- Your "style of life" is your own creation. Your "creative self" is your "life-making you." *You make your own life!*

- There's often a big difference between announced deadlines and real deadlines.

- Optimists get over disappointments quickly. They do so because they are learners from every experience, even difficult ones.

- Optimists make sure *nothing never happens.*

- Seeking profits is like seeking happiness. Simply wanting them won't produce them. They're by-products. They're not goals but outcomes.

- A concern for the little detail is the big idea.

XIII

BEING TENACIOUS

The High-Octane Test

There's probably no behavior more difficult to model than tenacity. So often, the only margin of victory for an individual is stamina for hanging in there when others give up the struggle.

The same is true for teams, and the team whose members have taken cues from each other when the going gets rough is a consistent winner. Each member at the appropriate time brings her or his authentic strengths to bear when the other members might be flagging.

This chapter calls upon theme 6 to urge you to hold up your end on your team: *A team catalyst is an individual who takes upon himself or herself the responsibility for modeling actions and attitudes that support shared competence.*

To share in modeling tenacity, give thought to the following:

- Not feeling sorry for yourself
- Not getting bored easily
- Being willing to "take a pounding"

- Being the tortoise rather than the hare
- Addressing drudgery in your life and work

—— **64** ——

THE MARTYR'S SELF-SET TRAP

One day last week I realized I was feeling sorry for myself and understood all over again how debilitating a process this is. It took a comment from an associate to make me aware of how I'd been stewing in my own juices.

Late this fall, I conducted a team-effectiveness workshop for the chief executive and top management group of a privately held company. This is a good-sized operation as such closely held firms go, and it is the leading manufacturer in its industrial niche.

Near the conclusion of the workshop, I led the group through a rather intricate and novel discussion of vision. I told them what I thought the implications of this definition of vision could mean for them. I described how it could help them articulate and modify their corporate culture—something they're committed to doing.

Apparently, the group found the workshop in general, and my presentation on vision in particular, useful. The chief executive cornered me afterward and wanted to know if I could consult with them on helping to develop some changes in their corporate culture. I was delighted at this prospect, of course, and replied that yes I could. He said he would be in touch with me early in the spring.

The Letdown

Having known for years, as do all consultants worth their salt, that a good part of my job is salesmanship, I didn't wait to hear from my client but called him in early March. He took my call and was glad to hear from me. He told me, however, that he was about to go on vacation for a couple of weeks and would call me on his return.

Now let me interrupt my narrative at this point to underscore that I think the world of this man. He's an absolutely first-rate chief executive. I have known him for years, have worked with him on previous projects, watched him rescue this company from the brink of bankruptcy, and admire the way he works with people. In short, I think he's a champion.

I let a couple of months go by and called him again. He told me then that he and his key staff were thinking through the best way to approach corporate culture change and were considering other firms, along with mine, to see which one might work best for them. I said, "I understand that," and after a few niceties, we ended our conversation with him saying he'd get back to me when they decided what to do.

I Understand!

I said I understood and thought I did, but I really didn't. And because of my involvement in another client assignment, I simply let this slide to a level where it just sort of gnawed at me for a few days. Then one day last week I told this story to an associate and she, good supporter that she always is, exclaimed, "Well, if it were me, my feelings would be terribly hurt."

Though I'm grateful for my associate's support and appreciate her for that and many other reasons, her comment didn't have quite the effect she intended. Rather, her words triggered the realization that I'd been feeling sorry for myself. I'd been playing the martyr—hardly a role authentic for me.

Alistair Cooke once said, "A professional is someone who sometimes does his best work when he least feels like it." The professional in me said, "I understand," and I'm glad I said it. Moreover, the professional in me asserted itself in my workmanship on other projects when I was distressed by the turn of events on this one.

No promises had been made to me. The executives in this company liked the workshop, but all the chief executive did was ask me a question: "Can you help us?" Obviously, he's asked that question of a few others—as well he should! This is a big undertaking for this company. They need to be careful and they should be convinced they've chosen the best possible consultant.

The debilitating part of my martyring is that I was down when I hadn't even lost. That's a good way to snatch defeat from the jaws of victory. You're prompted to be rash and do dumb things. As it is, I just sent off a note to the chief executive that may make my services seem irresistible. So I may yet pick up all the marbles on this choice assignment.

TAKE ACTION

1. Whenever you're feeling sorry for yourself, break into your thinking by asking if you were expecting a free ride. That will get you down every time; there are no free rides. Your team will move forward only by your carrying your own weight.

2. Don't berate yourself for such martyring. We all do it. Just recognize it for the self-pampering that it is, and get on with the real tasks of your life and work.

—— 65 ——

THE NECESSITY FOR PULLING POWER

Item from the "Television Page" of the *Chicago Tribune*, September 17, 1988:

"Robert MacNeil, the Canadian half of PBS's 'MacNeil/Lehrer News Hour,' returns to his roots Saturday night as narrator of the four-part documentary 'Canada: True North' (10:30 P.M. on WTTW-Ch. 11).

"MacNeil said the series, which will run Saturdays through October 8, is designed to point up the differences rather than the similarities between Canadians and Americans.

" 'Canadians are not only annoyed, bemused, angered and frustrated at the ignorance of Americans as to the difference but also that they are so indifferent to their ignorance,' he said. 'Canada is invisible to the psyche of most Americans.'

"Noting one difference, series producer David Grubin, the only American on the production team, said the finished product had to be 'Americanized.'

" 'We had to speed it up,' he said. 'Canadian producers are not interested in the rapid-fire, blatant documentary style Americans are used to.' "

As I had returned from a two-day business trip to Toronto earlier this week, this short piece caught my eye. I spent hours with Canadian business executives in meetings and have to agree that they show a little more ease and grace in the manner in which they conduct their affairs than we Americans do.

The irony of this news item, however, is that David Grubin, the only American on the production team, carried the big stick. (Ah yes, some days we count the votes, and other days we weigh them.) The Canadian story, then, is going to be told the American way. In other words, in a hurry.

Keep It Moving

Frankly, I don't believe pace has anything to do with nationality. I think it has more to do with a concentration of people and technology. Canada is a larger country than the U.S. but has a tenth of our population. The ubiquity and frequency of people-to-people contacts in the States virtually demand that they be more brief and less primary.

The result of all this, however, is that without realizing it, we have come to be accustomed—even dependent—on a constant barrage of stimuli that is in many ways mindless. I know for a fact, for example, that each day I am being exposed to more information and am reading more than I ever read as a student, but I am thinking less in any holistic way.

Much of this exposure comes on the run and doesn't stick. The views or opinions I adopt are fragmentary and easily rejected when I am exposed to some "new research" that often turns out to be little more than a fad—the new "truth" that quickly becomes old and easily discarded. I occasionally find myself going back to some article or chapter in a book that I remember as having had quality about it. As I reread, I'm dumbfounded with how much of the material strikes me as new. It's as if I never read it before.

We watch and the images fade. We listen and the words drift away. We read, but we don't retain. We speak, but we don't remember what we said. We promise, but circumstances intervene. We travel light. The topsoil is very shallow, and precious little takes root.

Some say this is what it means to manage from now through the 90s.

Ha!

Fascinating, isn't it, that a new word emerged in just the past few years? *Burnout.*

Don't Be Bored

Much of our activity is just that: activity. Activity without substance. As I listen to many people, they say they engage in an unceasing round of such activity to avoid boredom. An expression I hear frequently is, "I get bored easily." The way people say it, I can tell they're proud. They think this is a display of intelligence.

More often, it is a display of a lack of commitment, lack of goal. People with authentic goals that force them to stretch themselves aren't bored. And the goals provide pulling power for investing themselves in something as well as a mechanism for sorting out the barrage of stimuli. What supports the goal gets included. What doesn't is discarded or ignored.

Another word, though not a new one, has emerged with new meaning right alongside burnout: *energy.* That's fascinating, too, because energy is the means for thriving in our age of activity. A goal is an expression of desire that in turn is the fuel for fortitude.

A client of mine is a guy named Jim. He's CEO of a large engineered-products company. One of his key officers said to me this week: "The great thing about Jim is that he sticks with something long enough to make it work."

I can assure you that Jim isn't bored. I can also assure you that he's CEO today partially because he wasn't bored with his yesterdays.

TAKE ACTION

1. Don't be bored easily. That means you're not engaged in something purposeful, something with a longer time frame attached to it. To be bored easily is to bore others easily. It is to lack energy and sap it from your teammates.

2. You've heard all your life, right, that we use only the tiniest fraction of our brains? So the stepped-up pace of our existence isn't truly beyond us. Bring focus to yours and you'll have the energy.

—— 66 ——

A SERIES OF SMALL COMPROMISES

I had a quick soup and sandwich this week with a man who knows his business. He's Dr. Morris Aderman, a management psychologist and a professor at the Illinois Institute of Technology in Chicago.

Management psychologists, like lawyers, accountants, account executives, insurance brokers, investment bankers, and consultants, are to be found on every street corner in the business district. Anyone who chooses to call on members of these groups for their services has to find a way to separate the wheat from the chaff. If you're interested in management psychologists, I'll save you some trouble. Morrie is wheat.

I enjoy Morrie's company, too, because he's such a good guy. He's got a great sense of humor, couldn't be pretentious if his life depended on it, has a born storyteller's gift and the Brooklyn accent to go with it. He can keep a group of executives in stitches all day long while he teaches them something they didn't know they learned until later.

Over our sandwich, though, I caught him using one of those psychologist's words and had to stop him in his speed-of-light pursuit of a topic to get him to explain it. The word was *infavoidance*. "Oh," he said, rolling his eyes and shrugging his shoulders. "It means what it means because there's no other word in our language that means what it means. It's jargon, and that's too bad. Infavoidance means fear of failure, that's all."

Redirected Laser

He could see that I was interested in this topic, so he switched his laser onto it. He said that the fear of failure is often accompanied by an oversensitivity to criticism and lack of endurance, even in people who are self-reliant and have high self-esteem.

I laughed and said that I wished he would stop talking about me. He laughed back without missing a beat and said, "Yeah, you might get a little expedient sometimes (referring to my lack of endurance) in the short run, but if you fail, you'll find a way to overcome it. You won't run from it."

I've reflected several times on that exchange with Morrie, and now here I am writing about it. It occurs to me that oversensitivity to criticism is the real culprit and a far more pervasive negative influence in our lives than we (certainly I) have attributed to it. I know that in my own experience, when I ask if *I will risk taking a pounding*—facing possible harsh criticism for my performance— I get the shudders. Yet I also know that if I intend to keep growing, if I'm going to have some depth my teammates can draw from, I have to be receptive to that possibility.

Risk

The operative word for most of us in the fright-inducing statement of the last paragraph is *pounding*, whereas things would go better if the word that caught our eye is *risk*. This noun that I have converted to a verb—risk—is not an invitation to disaster. After all, when we embark on what we consider bold, authentic action, there's no guarantee that we will fail, but only that we *might* fail. The other side of the coin, of course, is that we just as well might succeed.

I have learned that when I fear taking a pounding on some project, I usually have exaggerated the "pounding" I'm going to take if I do fail. Then I slip my mind into distortion overdrive and really do a number on myself. Because of my exaggerated fear, I begin to curtail my ambitions; you know, cut the risk so that if I fail I'll do so on a less grand scale and the pounding will be less. What I've done, ironically, is increased my risk of failure.

Avoidance of risk and lack of endurance become the naughty handmaidens of oversensitivity. First, we avoid what we really, authentically, down-in-our-gut desire in our work and lives because we think we'll shatter if somebody says something bad about our actions. Second, we facilitate our avoidance by giving up. We scale back our efforts. We get expedient and make excuses. We dishearten our cause by muttering something like, "Oh well, they won't like this, so why give it my best?" Then we fatefully trudge ahead with lack of spirit, give a mediocre performance, and assure our failure.

True enough, we gain a measure of safety this way. The pounding is less than if we'd failed going all out. Nobody says, "That was garbage!" In fact, nobody says much of anything.

In a recent issue of the *Harvard Business Review*, Tracy O'Rourke, CEO of Allen-Bradley Company, described the bold, intricate move his company made into computer-integrated manufacturing. This involved a $20 million investment, tons of endurance, and willingness to risk a royal pounding. It could have been a colossal failure. Instead, it turned out a smash because O'Rourke and his team went for the top of the line.

Said he: "Bad quality is nothing but a series of small compromises."

TAKE ACTION

1. Live with the possibility that you're oversensitive to criticism. If you're not, great. If you are, see how it controls you and compromises your contribution to your team.

2. Increase your endurance by doing what you believe in. Your performance won't be perfect and you'll probably draw some criticism. So what? Learn from it.

NOTE: O'Rourke has since been named chairman and chief executive of Varian Associates, Inc.

—— 67 ——

WEARIN' 'EM DOWN

I was driving home from a day's consulting work with a client located in one of Chicago's suburbs. I punched on the radio for some music to keep me company as I inched along in the bumper-to-bumper rush-hour traffic.

I was listening to a rock station and paid attention when the DJ announced that next up was a track from Queen's new album. I hadn't heard from Queen and their lead singer Freddie Mercury in at least a couple of years, so I turned up the volume as the song began. This is what I heard:

> "I want it all,
> I want it all,
> I want it aaalll . . . and
> I want it nowwwww . . ."

God help him!

Earlier this week, I had lunch with a friend who started his own consulting business seven years ago. We've stayed in touch periodically and I know that he has struggled to make his practice thrive. He works hard to get clients and keep them. He has hired a couple of people who haven't worked out. He has worried over cash flow and his ability to pay bills. He has wondered if he is in the right field. Time and again, he has suffered deep discouragement. He has doubted his wisdom in leaving a safe, secure job as a public relations executive with a major utility.

Still, he kept his head down and gutted it through. His business has acquired some stability and it's clear he's going to make it. He has learned an awful lot and tested himself in ways that would terrify most people who wonder aloud about being entrepreneurs. He's much stronger now, and his doubts about the wisdom of launching his own ship have vanished.

God love him!

The Hare

Freddie Mercury, or, to be fair, the person in the song he represents, has no staying power. He is propped up only by titillations. He is like a plant that takes root in shallow soil, sprouts fast, then wilts in the heat of day.

There's an abundance of the "I want it all and I want it now" folks in the executive suite, but I'm pleased to report that their numbers are shrinking dramatically. The "taking" mentality is now looked on as bad form since effective teamwork has emerged as the necessity of our time.

The tip-off for any job interviewer that she's dealing with a taker is when the interviewee wants to know first off what the job pays. Never mind, he thinks, the job's requirements and if he's appropriate to them, what the person is like who'll be his boss, what the company's plans are and what stands in their way. Nor be concerned with the company's stature in the community, what its commitment to ethical standards might be, or if its employees are proud to be associated with it. Rather, find out right away what it pays, what are the vacation policy and benefits, and when the next promotion and pay raise can be expected. If those goodies are in line, then be willing to continue the discussion.

The Tortoise

Abraham Lincoln said, "I'm a slow walker, but I never walk backwards." Never was a president more tested than he, never was a president more a giver to his country than he, never did a president overcome deep doubts more than he, never did a president pay a higher price than he, and never has a president been more revered than he.

Hanging in there with a belief or commitment doesn't require actual martyrdom as it did in Lincoln's case, but it does demand suffering in some sense. You might be the object of derision. "Come on Bert, give it up. You're beginning to look stupid for sticking with that division. Spin it off and put your money somewhere else."

As a team member, you may become the object of anger. Exhausted over grappling with a complex set of options, the team expediently accepts a questionable assumption and moves toward a faulty course of action. You puncture this self-deception and group-think and insist that you all get a good night's sleep and come back at it tomorrow. You prevail, but as the team breaks up the meeting, most everyone is glowering at you.

Rance Crain is president of Crain Communications, publisher of *Advertising Age, Automotive News*, several city business weeklies, and numerous other trade magazines. This company is highly successful, but not because their publications have made quick starts. Many spent years bathing in red ink. "We do well because we don't give up," says Rance. "Competitors underrate us this way, without realizing that our philosophy is a simple one: 'Wear 'em down.' "

TAKE ACTION

1. Don't embarrass yourself by being a hare. Don't look for the magic formulas, fast answers, inside tips, and easy way out. They don't exist.

2. Some people are impatient watching professional basketball. They think nothing counts until the last few minutes. If you're one of them, next time the score is a point apart with a minute to go in the game, watch for poise and stamina to make the difference. They do so nine times out of ten.

—— 68 ——

DRUDGERY, DRILL, AND DISCOURAGEMENT

The view was a stunner, even that day when the fog rolled in, making the sun seem delinquent at its job. I wondered then how executives perched high above San Francisco Bay in their office buildings got anything done. The sheer beauty struck me as too distracting.

Yet I knew such distraction didn't trouble the man hosting me on a Thursday afternoon as we sat in his office at the foot of California Street, overlooking the Embarcadero and Bay. He was approaching the end of his professional executive career and was in a philosophical mood.

He's Fernando Gumucio, an old friend and the president of Del Monte Corporation. He'd had this job about a year, having reached it through a steady rise up the sales and marketing ranks. He'd been with the company 27 years. He was born in Bolivia and speaks with a charming accent. Getting to the top of a big company was no picnic, but he'd done it with grace. I've never known an executive with more personal warmth and as well-developed a sense of humor.

He had me sample an upgraded product the company had high hopes for. I've never liked it, but had to agree they've brought it around. The bantering surrounding this taste test gave way to a more serious discussion in which Gumucio spoke his mind on managing.

Champion of an Idea

He underscored what in American business we're beginning to convert from lip service into performance, namely, that "back to basics" is today's method of corporate and individual achievement. He said that the prestige-school MBAs tend to stand on their educational pedigree and "big picture" everything to death. Meanwhile the grunt work goes undone. After ten years of their grand scheme, analysis paralysis has cost Del Monte dearly. As you might expect, these types did a fast fade in his organization.

Then he repeated the unofficial slogan of Del Monte under his direction—"Be a champion of an idea"—and proudly told me a story.

A young man from the production department ran into him in the corridor one day and said that if he meant it about being a champion of an idea, he had one for a new product, never mind that he had no experience in marketing.

Gumucio assured him that didn't matter, but if he was to see his idea to completion, he would have to put up with discouragement and obstacles. "If you believe in it," he said, "go for it. Only you can make it happen."

Said Gumucio: "No one knows now if it's truly workable, but this new product idea, after hard campaigning by the production executive, has won support from the marketing department. Whether it flies or not, the effort behind it is what I consider heroic, and I want to offer support for that kind of thing around here."

Life and Work

Gumucio knows about obstacles. He also knows about constructive drudgery. Remember, he'd been digging in for 27 years! He knows, too, as shown by his warmth, humor, and sense of balance, that separation of work from life itself is artificial. While quality performance at work depends on carrying out constructive drudgery, the same applies to being a good spouse, parent, or friend. Undeniably, the lessons of one sphere are applicable to the others. As you now know, that's the premise of many of these essays. That's why their examples are often outside the world of business. Art, then, isn't the only entity imitating life. So does work.

Soon after our visit, Gumucio, at age 52, announced his early retirement. After more than a generation with Del Monte culminating in his being CEO, he walked away. In a telephone conversation, he told me that he sought a second career in which, as he said "I can give something back to the country that has been so good to me." He offered that might entail government service or the agricultural side of the biogenetics industry. "I've got the energy!" he said.

Life imitating work.

TAKE ACTION

1. Ask yourself: "Do I believe that if I find what's right for me, things will come easily?"

2. If you do, stomp on that belief. Such an outlook will discourage you unduly and make you a compromised contributor. An authentic commitment is easier only in the sense that you truly believe in it.

FAST TAKES

on

Being Tenacious

- "A professional is someone who sometimes does his best work when he least feels like it."
- Being down when you haven't even lost is a good way to snatch defeat from the jaws of victory.
- People with authentic stretch goals aren't bored.
- Risk is not an invitation to disaster. We might actually succeed!
- "Bad quality is nothing but a series of small compromises."
- Hanging in there demands suffering in some sense.
- Back to basics is today's method of corporate and individual achievement.
- "Only you can make it happen."

XIV

BEING OF
GOOD HUMOR

A Very Serious Subject

I define humor as the capacity to accept the comical in ourselves without hurting our own feelings. This means the enriching, leavening influence in our lives that serves as ballast for us is one that accentuates our commonality by reminding us of our human limitations. In a word, our mortality.

The bonding we call teamwork is intensely dependent on the legitimately laughable antics that periodically characterize all associates who share time and tasks. Now and then, we all can be expected to be absurd. And to forgive ourselves for it.

Because this chapter calls attention to the spiritual essence of teamwork, theme 5 is highlighted: *Belief in men and women as social beings is a lofty one and is best authenticated with down-to-earth performance.*

Humor is social, yet as earthly as anything can be. To cultivate your humor, give thought to the following:

- Feeling glad more than mad, sad, or afraid

234

- Shunning idealized roles for yourself
- Taking humor seriously
- Contemplating a wisdom greater than your own

—— 69 ——

GLAD IS WHAT GLAD DOES

My office is in the Wrigley Building on Michigan Avenue. It sits directly on the north bank of the Chicago River and faces east, looking out to Lake Michigan. I live a mile and a half north and walk to and from work on days when I'm in town.

About halfway home, Michigan Avenue converts to Lake Shore Drive, the high-rise buildings change from commercial to residential, and one's eye falls upon patches of rich lawns, shrubs, and flower beds in place of omnipresent concrete.

At the end of a summer work day, with the sun settled behind the protective barrier of its high-rise apartments, Lake Shore Drive is for me, and for many others I believe, a path with great restorative powers.

I had particular proof of this one day last week. Those patches of rich lawn I mentioned are typically watered by a variety of sprinkler systems and mechanical devices at about the same time we cliff-dwelling foot-commuters are heading for our cabins in the sky.

The problem with these marvelous moisture rejuvenators is that they create an annoyance by spraying past the borders of the lawn in their care onto the sidewalk and fastidious types like me who like to keep their clothes well pressed and shoes spotlessly polished. This is a real pet peeve of mine.

Seeing one of these water missiles ahead on the day under discussion, I veered left to avoid its sweep. But on my right, a woman of dispatch in her late 20s passed me and headed straight for it. And when she reached it, she simply stopped in her tracks and let it shower her with its bounty.

As I passed her, I chuckled to myself—an inner laugh of innocent envy, if there can be such a thing—while she stood there in her

Nikes, her Sony Walkman clamped to her ears, oblivious to all, having the best time imaginable.

Because she walked faster than I did, she passed me twice more and repeated the process when we came to a watering way station. By then, several other people had noticed her and were enjoying her freedom vicariously.

I had no idea, of course, what the woman's plans for the evening were, but it was obvious that she was going to embark upon them in a good-natured, stress-free frame of mind. Clearly, here was someone who was glad more than she was mad, sad, or afraid.

What's to Lose?

Now, I have to be honest. The dress she wore looked washable. My suit, were I to follow her lead and abandon my streetside inhibitions, would have to be drycleaned. Likewise, the leather of my shoes would be less forgiving of their laundering than the canvas of her bouncy running shoes.

Moreover, from head to toe, she sent out consistent signals that would let any onlooker know that grooming and glamour were far from her highest priorities. So if I might just trivialize Kris Kristofferson's work for a moment, the words of one of his songs, "Freedom's just another word for nothin' left to lose," may have some application here.

In fact they do. This woman's particular actions on this evening's walk home were much less costly to her in many ways than they would be to me if I were to do the same.

Interpreting the Lesson

My point, then, is not that I should mimic this spirited woman, nor should you. After all, we're different people in countless specific ways. Rather, it is that her behavior sets off healthful stirrings in us; we'd do well to find ways to lower some of our own costs so we can spot and head straight for those unlikely oases in each of our own lives.

By their nature, committed team members end up in many high-stakes arenas. At any given time, therefore, they may have much to lose by their actions. It would be silly and not at all desirable to wish these circumstances away. I say this because there is exhilaration for them in being put to the test in some way and learning that they not only survive but excel in some endeavor.

The way through all this, it seems to me, is to maintain the balance between engagement and retreat. Team members need the "wild times" too, when there is no cost to their actions and they can be at ease. Such times revitalize them, help them reestablish their sense of self-worth, just in case they were beginning to doubt it. That's what the woman in sneakers has to teach.

TAKE ACTION

1.   No-cost retreat can be so in more ways than one. It needn't be lengthy and you needn't go far away. On the contrary, withdraw momentarily and often. Make it a routine. Weave such balances into your daily life. They help renew contact with your own authenticity.

2.   There are other project-type outlets as well. For you, you might go crazy—or glide—on a dance floor. You might have a passion for barbershop singing. You might be a cutup only-male in an otherwise all-women's lunch-hour exercise class. Whatever, it doesn't matter. Find ways to be glad. In so doing, you'll gladden those around you.

—— 70 ——

THE DISTINCTION OF ADEQUACY

A scholar and writer I hold in high professional regard is Peter Berger, a sociologist and professor at Boston University. I've read almost all of his numerous books but find myself going back repeatedly to an early gem of his, published in 1963. It's *Invitation to Sociology: A Humanistic Perspective.*

This is a book of deep insights laced with rich humor. He has a way of presenting social data that produces inner smiles. For example, when he describes the dating and mating ritual, he notes that "the lightning shafts of Cupid fall within rather rigidly defined class lines." This doesn't call for guffaws, just the recognition that he has a clever way with the subject of social stratification.

At another point, he mentions the clergy and, as an aside, tweaks seminary students who "progressively lose their sense of humor as they approach ordination." Berger's right about this, I'm sure. I remember a story from another source that told of the courtly minister who made a pastoral call on a family one evening after dinner. He remarked to the mother what a good time they all seemed to have together. One of the younger children overheard his comment and blurted out, "We do, we do. And we have even more fun when you're not here!"

Roles Given, Roles Chosen

The two squibs I pulled from Berger show that we all are subject to considerations of class and professional roles. Some of these can be extraordinarily formal, such as requirements of physical examination required of a young woman who marries the Prince of Wales, or demands of duties and dress of a priest conducting high mass.

Other roles we choose for ourselves in the practice of our profession, say, are quite arbitrary. In other words, they're not imposed on us. Rather, they're matters of our own volition. The fact that we may have taken on such behaviors earlier in life, and they have become deeply ingrained as habit, makes them no less the product of our own initiative.

A "morally superior" Jimmy Swaggart, a charismatic presence if ever there was one, chose to see himself as a direct arm of God—with special powers—and acted out that choice as a frequent judge of the actions of others.

This was, of course, an idealized role in the extreme, and when he was unable to live up to what most would consider even the barest minimum standards of conduct for the clergy, he was totally discredited and fell into deep depression.

Executives who choose to be "the best" in their spheres may likewise be setting themselves up for a fall. That fall won't be as deep or publicly embarrassing as Jimmy Swaggart's, but undeniably it will be demeaning, devitalizing, and depressing.

I find that "the best" always turns out to be a phantom. Best at what? Best to whom? Best for sure? Best for how long? I contend these are unanswerable questions. Tell me, who is the greatest soprano ever? Greatest clarinetist, chemist, actress, heart surgeon, basketball player, marketing manager, or CEO? We seek to be our *personal* best, which is the authenticity we owe ourselves and our teammates, but the quest to be *the* best is an assignment in self-torture.

Rifles and Watermelons

A woman dear to me is Adaline Starr. For decades she's been on the faculty of the Alfred Adler Institute in Chicago. She was an instructor in psychodrama when I took extensive postgraduate studies there during the 70s. I learned heaps from her.

Adaline was firm, yet spoke softly with a smile. One day I remember her standing before a small circle of us in class, pounding her right fist into the palm of her left hand, fixing her eyes on each of us in turn and imploring, "When are we going to learn that adequate means ADEQUATE?"

No one strikes us as more humorless, out-of-balance, and a general drag than the person who is overly ambitious. Please understand me. There is hardly anybody more concerned than I with the ideas of acting on our strengths and refining our gifts. To not do so is, to me, a sin. But I'm talking about rifle shots, not grapeshot. There's a time and place to seek and express mastery—to be front and center with distinction—and there's a time to carry watermelons at the company picnic.

Just yesterday, I met with a doctor to review his results on a questionnaire I've developed. He runs a department in one of the top hospitals in the country. This questionnaire measures the same 20 key dimensions of team-style management that are treated in this book. He looked at his results and saw that he was strong in some, not so strong in others. When we finished, he said simply, "It's the profile of your average performer." I said, "Yeah, with the emphasis on *performer*; isn't that neat?" He replied, "Yeah, it is." We both grinned, we shook hands, and he walked away with a bounce in his step—a man who knows not to impose idealized roles on himself.

─────────────── *TAKE ACTION* ───────────────

1. Know when you're supposed to be a star, and be one.
2. Know when you're supposed to be adequate, and be adequate.

───── **71** ─────

FOUND BY COMEDY

I began work on this essay by thinking back to the last thing that happened to me, or that I thought about, saw, read, or heard that was funny.

What do you think came out of that inquiry? It was stunning to me that I couldn't think of anything. "Think again," I said to myself. "There must have been any number of occurrences in your life in the last week alone that were funny." Nope, not a one. Void. A big zero of the mind.

Now I'm getting concerned. I pull out my calendar of appointments to see if I can jog loose any recollection of humor in the events of my life in just the past week.

It turns out from my day-by-day survey of the calendar to have been a very good week overall. There was some bad news, but not unexpected, on the health of a close relative. A neighbor confided a personal problem to me that we both know will give him a lot of grief. But other than these, the week was chock full of good things at work and even gave cause for two small celebrations over milestones passed by two close friends of mine. Still nothing, though, that made me laugh out loud for real.

Into His Own

Now another thought enters my mind. I remember reading a short article on Leslie Nielsen in the features section of the newspaper early this week. The piece noted that this veteran actor has come into his own with comedy roles and is currently starring in "The Naked Gun," a movie that is drawing big crowds.

Then, yesterday morning, just before starting a meeting with a client, she asked, "Do you remember Leslie Nielsen, the one who was so funny in 'Airplane?' " I said that I did. "Well, he was on Johnny Carson earlier this week. He's starring in some movie that's a smash. He's getting raves and I guess people are surprised at how good he is. He says he's relishing the role. He says he loves comedy acting. He looked and sounded great. It was a good interview— really got my attention."

Now I think back on Leslie Nielsen. I first recall him playing the male lead opposite Debbie Reynolds in the movie "Tammy." Then there were other bit parts for him in movies that were thoroughly forgettable. Then I remember him on television when he played the mainly absent movie studio head in the melodramatic series "Bracken's World." Always, I noticed him. Always, I liked him, this handsome, nicely graying journeyman, and, obviously, his name has stuck with me. Yet, and here I may be remaking history based on what I now know about him, his characters always seemed to be supercilious, pompous, overbearing. I can't help wondering if he didn't sense the absurdities in his roles and play them to the hilt, hoping we'd catch on.

The Leslie Nielsen in "Airplane" was not that different from his previous roles, except there, he went over the edge and was a riot! I gather he's a riot in "The Naked Gun" as well. He's truly a man found by comedy.

Bereft of Humor?

Would you find yourself bereft of humor, as I am, if you reviewed the past week in your life? I'm not talking about jokes now. I'm talking about enjoying a good laugh at your own expense. I'm talking about a smile that breaks across your face, or even a belly laugh that erupts within you when you see the absurdity of your own actions or those of others that just as easily could have been yours. After all, humor is nothing more than acknowledging the comical in ourselves. For my part, I can see that I take too many things too seriously and humor not seriously enough.

You're aware by now that I think *the* idea for all organizations in the 1990s is the team. Corporations that don't think team and interteam linkage can't prosper. People who form the interpersonal network known as the company must learn the techniques for generating the best ideas from each other as well as pulling together rather than getting in each other's way. This requires bonding, yet how can bonding take place in the absence of humor, real human comedy?

When speaking of the embattled John Tower, whom the Senate rightfully rejected for President Bush's cabinet, Jay Leno can say, as he did, that he looks like Yoda with a bad haircut, and that may be clever. But it's not humor. On the other hand, if I can laugh and say to my teammates that I'm the guy who made a presentation to the board of directors yesterday with my fly open, I'll have taken a big step closer to bonding.

Just like Leslie Nielsen, I'll have stepped out from pomposity and been found by comedy.

TAKE ACTION

1. Go through the eye-opening experience I did. See how much humor was a part of your life this week.

2. If in fact it was a good share of your life, rejoice again. If it wasn't, pledge to poke small fun at some of your own imperfections.

—— 72 ——

HELP FROM THE HILLS

A few weeks ago I met with Bill Wiggenhorn, Motorola's vice president of training and education. We had a sandwich together; then he took me on a tour of the company's knockout Galvin Center. This center is named for Paul and Robert Galvin, respectively founder and current chairman of the executive committee. The company brings executives from around the world to this center for advanced training.

That training these days is focused around the "cause" of quality and total customer satisfaction. It's working. Recently, Motorola was a winner of the first Malcolm Baldrige Quality Award. Their semiconductor defects, once measured in parts per thousand, are now measured in parts per million and even parts per billion.

Wiggenhorn heads up this whole training effort, one that he began in 1981. His responsibilities and charter show how critically his tasks are viewed throughout the company. He chairs an advisory board to his function that is made up of the heads of Motorola's eight major businesses. Bob Galvin also sits on that board and attends virtually every meeting.

It was with great interest, then, that I opened the latest issue of *U.S. News and World Report* and saw a two-page spread by Motorola that began with the title "The Power of Belief: #1 in a series."

The ad reads in part, "The company that is satisfied with its progress will soon find its customers are not. It is this belief that has spurred Motorola to a 100-fold improvement in quality since 1981." Then it continues with Motorola's simple formula for progress:

- First, banish complacency.
- Second, set heroic goals that *compel* new thinking.
- Finally, "raise the bar" as you near each goal. Set it out of reach all over again.

The ad closes with the tag line "Building On Beliefs."

A Religious Message

What dazzles me about this message from Motorola is how religious it is. Oh, I realize that the advertising agency who helped craft it and the marketing department at the company who approved it would probably disagree. True enough, there is here no reference to any deity. Nor is any written authority cited by way of a canon such as Koran, Talmud, or Bible. There's no recitation of doctrine from ages-old religious music, poetry, or creeds. No artwork with religious themes is on display. There is even no individual quoted or held up as a model who in turn might be construed as a person with strong religious sentiments. Bob Galvin himself, for instance, who was a trustee of Notre Dame University from 1960 to 1987, isn't mentioned.

Yet consider that the ad begins and ends with the word "belief" as centerpiece, and that Motorola's arrestingly effective three-part formula for progress is committed to values that can't in any meaningful way be separated from religious tradition.

That there are religious foundations to our corporate undertakings (Motorola, is merely one of many such examples) shouldn't surprise us. After all, *Fortune* reported in a survey published in the April 28, 1986, issue that 91% of CEOs of the 500 largest industrial and service corporations enact their duties while laying claim to values nurtured in their earlier church experiences and religious upbringings. We can assume as well that such values aren't characteristic of CEOs alone. In short, when it comes to values that shape the bulk of corporate decision making, religion has critical mass.

The Spiritual Essence of Teamwork

The words that creep into our language tell us an awful lot about our leanings, even though we most often don't stop to think of the source of these words and what they signal beyond their literal meaning. For example, think of "mission," a religious word if ever one existed. There isn't a company today with any sophistication that doesn't base its strategy on a hard-thought, clearly presented mission statement. The mission statement, moreover, cannot come about with any validity or pulling power unless it, in turn, arises out of the corporation's values.

The reason the Motorola ad calls attention to no individual is that the simple, three-part formula for progress is totally dependent on teamwork for its implementation. No star, however gifted, can carry the day. The "heroic goals" Motorola asks for draw their imagery from religious martyrdom and connote the highest form of "selfless" risk taking and an authenticity that comes from the Creator's children linking hands to be fully themselves, fully human, and fully accomplished. It's fascinating that the *Random House College Dictionary* defines achievement as "accomplishment as by superior ability, special effort or great *valor*" (italics mine).

The achievement Motorola people inspire from each other on their teams is spawned by a wisdom greater than their own. Let us follow their example. Let us look forward by looking up. The Psalmist wrote:

> I lift up my eyes to the hills.
> From whence does my help come?
> My help comes from the Lord,
>   who made heaven and earth.

In the midst of making sturdy demands on ourselves, it's good to remember that "looking up" healthfully calls attention to our own limitations and our own mortality. In the preceding essay I defined humor as acknowledging the comical (mortal) in ourselves. Intriguingly, humor and high standards make wonderful partners. The humor that comes most naturally to us when we are cognizant and appreciative of a wisdom greater than our own is also the vehicle for staying lighthearted about our deadly serious mission.

TAKE ACTION

1. Recognize that teamwork is communion and our teammates are communicants.

2. Realize that caring and commitment and mirth all have to come from somewhere. They come from the hills. Claim them. They are your birthright!

FAST TAKES

on
Being of Good Humor

- We need to maintain the balance between engagement and no-cost retreat.
- Pressure-packed, hard-charging team members need "wild times" too.
- "The best" always turns out to be a phantom. Adequacy may well be what's most authentic for you at a given time and place.
- To be overly ambitious is to be a drag—to yourself and others.
- Would you find yourself bereft of humor if you reviewed the past week in your life?
- Humor is nothing more than acknowledging the comical in ourselves.
- Bonding can't take place in the absence of humor.
- Humor comes most naturally to us when we are cognizant and appreciative of a wisdom greater than our own.

XV

BEING LUCKY

The Courtship of Dame Fortune

If you believe you make your own luck, you see your work as bigger than your job. You're proactive and use your position as a lever. Someone else might be reactive and use it as a chair. You know, just sit in it . . . a solitary *occupant* . . . proud of the title stenciled on its back . . . that reward alone being quite sufficient.

No one can deny the element of raw chance that exists in our lives. Yet how resourceful we are in dealing with good fortune or bad, and the impact we have on actually influencing the hand we're dealt, is in the end determined by the degree we're linked to others. Therefore, theme 2 is important throughout this chapter: *The need to belong is a powerful human force that finds expression in teamwork.*

Lucky is as lucky does. Dame Fortune visits those who act on their authentic need to belong. To be lucky, give thought to the following:

- Not being a "yes, but" executive

- Sharing an attitude of expectancy with your team
- Being a helper who spawns help in return
- Rejecting the notion of *can't*
- Supporting your teammates with your vitality

—— 73 ——

LITTLE PATTERNS, LITTLE IMPLICATIONS

We all have little patterns in our lives that are ridiculous; that is, they just don't stand up to reason. Nonetheless, they persist as a way of ordering our existence. They are ridiculous because when other people learn what they are, they're almost struck dumb at their impact on us.

Let me give you an example. As you now know, I'm a Chicagoan who travels on business a great deal. When I do, I usually fly out of O'Hare Airport, perennially the busiest in the world.

But we Chicagoans have a second airport, Midway, nowhere nearly as busy, but getting steadily more active from spillover from a cramped O'Hare. Yesterday, my plans called for me to fly out of Midway at 7:00 A.M. for three meetings in another Midwestern city, then fly back at the end of the day.

Because I would be gone only for the day, I decided to drive and park my car near the airport. "Near," I say, because I had learned from a friend that there was a parking lot a half-block away that was considerably less expensive than the $14 I usually pay for valet parking on the airport grounds.

Well, do you know that when it came time to find that lot and drive into it, I was *afraid* to? Oh, it was dark out all right, and I couldn't see exactly where the entrance was, and it had snowed some during the night, and the cars in the lot were all covered over, and it was now minus two degrees, and I could just hear my engine giving about three growls before expiring after a 12-hour bout with Chicago's wind.

Yes, my friend's tip was a good one, *but* there were all these problems! Now think about this statement: *Yes*, my friend's tip was

248

a good one, *and* I was afraid! The second clause doesn't cancel the validity of the previous one as it does in the first sentence. Keep in mind, too, that I was afraid of the whole experience before arriving on the scene. All the way to the airport, at the back of my mind I was dreading this uneventful event. This sort of thing is a pattern with me.

The Unfamiliar

The forceful element in my fear was the unfamiliar. I'm not all that acquainted with Midway, and even less so with its environs. So when encountering the negatives I rattled off to you, I found they weren't any kind of a revelation or surprise, but, rather merely confirmed what I expected (wanted, really) to find. I had my excuses for not coping with the unfamiliar. I turned my car around and pulled into the airport's friendly turf. There I dropped off the car with the attendant in front of my airline entrance and relievedly paid the 14 bucks.

Exaggerated Perceptions

You may wonder if I'm being hard on myself. After all, my recital of the negatives were pretty convincing. I doubt, however, that you would have found them so had you been there. You or someone else would have just pulled into the lot, that's all. It wouldn't have been as dark for you. The cars in the lot would have been "dusted" with snow, not "covered," and you would have found the entrance without difficulty. Fact: The lot for valet parking is open-air as well, and when I returned to Chicago, my car, having stood out for 12 hours, started up with a snap. No, I'm not being hard on myself. I'm telling this little story on me because it's funny, actually, and instructive. It's an example of how negative thinking sets us up for failure. I had found the bad news I was looking for.

——————————————— *TAKE ACTION* ———————————————

1.   Avoid saying, "Yes, but." It cancels initiative to yourself or your teammates. Frequently it is nothing more than negative thinking and commonplace fear of the unfamiliar.

2. Rather, more often say, "Yes, and." For example: "*Yes*, your idea is a good one *and* let's run with it. Let's run with it even though it scares me!" That's the spirit of a real teammate.

—— 74 ——
EXPECTANCY AND STOICISM

My mother was a shy, strong-willed woman. Not many people knew her. She grew up in the little farming and mining town of Pittsburg, Illinois. She was a middle child among her seven siblings, and together they were evenly divided between four noisy and four quiet ones. She was one of the latter.

The sign beside the two-lane highway leading into Pittsburg declared in 1953 (the last time I was there) that it numbered just over 800 people. They must have counted the chickens! Pittsburg was coal country and was located 60 miles from the western Kentucky border. The rural regions of which it was a part had an outlook and language that could be called nothing other than "Deep South."

There had been hardship in Pittsburg. Virtually no extended family had been spared a death from some mining accident, while those who lived off small farms did so at just above dirt-poor levels. Pittsburg's main social event of the year was a summer ice cream supper sponsored by the Pleasant Grove Methodist Church.

My mother married a young miner who had come to Pittsburg from Jasper, Alabama. He had a restless spirit and came looking for work. It wasn't long before he had his eye on Chicago, however, and persuaded my mother in the mid-1920s to make the move north. There, for almost 30 years as a sheet metal worker for the electro-motive division of General Motors, my father was the provider he wanted to be for his wife and four children.

The Stoic

I sometimes think my mother had a lot to do with my becoming an incurable optimist. This is because the stoical side of her was always apparent, and she was ever prepared with a short chop for her eager, youngest child.

"Don't get your hopes up," she'd tell me routinely. Or, when she thought I was truly getting out of line, she'd stare me down fiercely and say, "Don't get too big for your britches!"

It used to make me angry, those limits she put on me, and I was determined not to let them stick. I would. I could. I will. I'll get there. I'll find out. I'll talk him into it. I'll go. I'll do it. I'll make the team. I'll be elected. Fighter. Biter. Dynamiter. All the way.

Yet, my mother's stoicism—a defense developed in reaction to a life of frequent disappointment in her early years in Pittsburg— sometimes went into reverse in the service of my expectations. The summer between my junior and senior years in high school, I wanted a job for spending money and college savings in the worst way. All my incessant pavement pounding, door knocking, and phone calling wasn't working, and I was horribly discouraged.

She knew this and felt bad for me. She was never that demonstrative, but I could see it in her eyes. Whereas she earlier had been telling me, "Don't get your hopes up," she now began to switch to a cliché I had never heard from her. "Stick with it," she said. "It's always darkest before dawn." Then she made a simple suggestion. "Call back all the people you called on earlier. Things may have changed, and they'll be impressed by your stick-to-it-iveness."

I did, and in a half-day I got a job as an assembler of aluminum storm windows in a local shop at the then-unheard-of wage for a high-schooler of $1.35 per hour.

The Lodge

I'll shift forward now, from reminiscences of my stoical mother to Yuppie Barsville on Chicago's near-north-side Division Street. As you'll see, it's not a difficult transition. To be found on this byway is the most famous saloon in America, Butch McGuire's. Butch's is all the rage, and has been for a generation. But right across the street from Butch's is my favorite bar in the whole world: the Lodge. I like it a lot because in its own way it creates a feeling of belonging and lifts one's spirits.

The Lodge is a hard-drinking establishment, to be sure, with a down-home quality to it (Pittsburg revisited?). Its patrons aren't quite as upscale as Butch's lawyers, accountants, and ad agency fast-trackers. Here, the people include some blue-collar types along with ambivalent careerists who aren't sure the high, hard corporate climb is worth it. They like to party.

The Lodge has the best jukebox anywhere, and when certain songs come on, the customers—full of fun and jammed to the rafters—all sing along. The song that generates the most exuberance in this wonderful place is Frank Sinatra's oldie, "High Hopes," and the words that rope in everybody together are these:

> Just what makes that little old ant
> Think he'll move that rubber tree plant?
> Anyone knows an ant, CAN'T
> Move a rubber tree plant. . .
> But he's got high-igh hopes
> He's got high-igh hopes
> He's got high apple pie in the sky hopes
> So if you're gettin' low,
> 'Stead of lettin' go
> Just remember that ant
> Oops, there goes another rubber tree plant
> Oops, there goes another rubber tree plant
> Oops, there goes another rubber tree plant.
> ker-PLOP!

Even these ambivalent careerists, some of whom may be like people you work with and don't know exactly what they want their work and lives to be, know the value of expectancy.

TAKE ACTION

1. Raise your expectations. Do this and you'll raise your performance along with that of your teammates. Lady Luck will flirt with you all.

2.   Realize that the combination of high hopes and tempered stoicism can be a powerful antidote to discouragement. Winston Churchill, who knew ups and downs as well as anyone, gave this advice to his listeners in his very last words in his final speech in public life: "Never give up. Never, never, give up."

—— **75** ——

LET GEORGE DO IT

I've never had the opportunity to meet George Shultz, our Secretary of State during most of the Reagan years. Yet I have exchanged correspondence with him on a couple of occasions and found that even in those brief, distant encounters, the greatness of the man shone through.

Like most Americans, my knowledge of George Shultz is limited to what I've read in the papers and magazines and seen of and about him on television, and an anecdote or two I've heard from people who know him or have met him somewhere along the line.

For me, he is quite simply the most honorable, distinguished, competent appointed public servant of my adult life. Everything I've read about him or seen in him on the merciless video box we all watch suggests that he's honest, perceptive, loyal, dedicated, shrewd, judicious, good-natured, strong-willed, blunt, articulate, brainy, poised, tenacious, decisive, persuasive, compassionate, objective, optimistic, energetic, and pragmatic and that he takes the long view. Though no one could be more faithful to his formidable office, he strikes me as a man who sees his role as no more than a small link in a chain of events that he prays is pulling us to a better, safer world.

A Helping Person

George Shultz has been a kind of Mr. Fix-It. He's a stabilizer, someone who accomplishes much in difficult times, in complex constellations, and who keeps his ethics intact. He was an untarnished mainstay in the Nixon administration. In the five years he spent in that first sojourn to Washington, he occupied three cabinet positions.

In the Reagan administration, he came to the rescue of State when the charismatic, voluble Alexander Haig made one power-grab too many, and the president who hated to fire anybody gave Haig the pink slip. Shultz stepped in and brought new clarity at Foggy Bottom.

George Shultz is *the* model for what it means to be an effective executive—including CEO—in the information age. This is to say he's a facilitator and coach. (More on this in chapter 19.) First of all, he's an astute selector and recruiter of associates. Second, he's an invisible initiator. Unlike the always out-front Haig, he steps back and insists that his talented associates act on their unique strengths and refine their gifts. Third, he's a leader in communication. He ensures that quality ideas (valid, useful information) bubble up from whatever he's part of. Fourth, despite his high position, he's a *follower* by being a helping hand in doing the work that emerges from his collaborations with his associates. No one has been more tireless.

People Help Helpers

People like George Shultz understand their jobs, which is a lot more than can be said for many executives whether in government, corporate life, or the not-for-profit arena. Shultz types see themselves as helpers, not people who always have to be right or always have things done their way or go their way. *They are authentic!*

This refreshing departure from grandiosity means that they believe in generating the contributions of all participants in a project. And they lend their abilities and know-how to empower them to make those contributions. This is how they turn out to be Mr. or Ms. Fix-It. Time after time.

One way or another, all Mr. or Ms. Fix-Its turn to the people they work with and ask, "How can I help you?" They're enablers who are committed to the growth of their associates. They're not blamers or punishers. When things go wrong, they even own up to their own part in adding to the predicament, then work with their associates to find a way out of the mess.

Then, when the actions or attitudes of an associate are clearly out of line and harmful to the enterprise, the helper-boss confronts the associate with words something like these: "Listen, Phil, you know I could fire you for that. But I don't want to. You're too talented, and you have a lot to give. People around here know you're good! Tell me what's bugging you, so we can work together on a solution. You know better than I do things can't keep going the way they are. Your performance is dragging down the team. We've been missing deadlines. But it doesn't have to be that way and you know that too. So tell me what's going on."

Such words may not be eloquent and may even indicate some self-consciousness on the part of the boss, but they're wonderful words nonetheless. They show unequivocally that the boss cares about the subordinate, believes in the contribution he has to make, and is committed to his development. The boss could fire him easily but has the courage to get at the root of the problem face to face.

Funny, isn't it, how the helper—the fix-it boss—is often so lucky? Funny, isn't it, how such people usually get the job done despite the odds? Funny, isn't it, how people line up to help the helper?

TAKE ACTION

1. Add to your management vocabulary. Start using words like "enabling," "coaching," "helping," "supporting," "growing," and "trusting." Use these words to describe what kind of manager you're becoming.

2. See yourself as a facilitator-coach. This will make you a helper who gets the help you need.

—— **76** ——

NO I WON'T AND YES WE CAN!

In essay 42, I wrote about my older brother-in-law, Lloyd Robertson, who was an inspiration and guide to me in my growing-up years. I described him as a patient man with enormous goodwill and indicated that his regular refrain was "There's no such word as can't."

That declaration has stuck with me to this day. It's my brother-in-law, therefore, who is responsible for my asking you about the "can'ts" in your life today. Do you reject the notion of can't? You know the right answer!

It's the simpleminded person who looks at a simple statement and calls it shallow. Alfred North Whitehead, perhaps the most outstanding philosopher of our age, averred, "It requires a very unusual mind to make an analysis of the obvious." Such is the case with saying no to the notion of can't. It's an impressive, complicated feat demanding depth of perception to convert a can't to a can or will.

For an example, let's look at something on a grand scale that is not yet in existence—former president Reagan's Strategic Defense Initiative. Forgetting partisan politics for the moment and whether you believe SDI is feasible or even a good idea, think about how far that idea has come given the initial nay-saying and derision it received when the president first announced his intentions in 1983. For ever larger numbers of people it has gone from a laugh, to a no-way, to an ummm, to a maybe. And for many, it's an "Oh, yeah . . . only a matter of time."

No I Won't

Saying no to the notion of can't will inevitably draw scoffs from those who find this orientation too wedded to the power-of-positive-thinking rosy-scenario set. One way to put them straight is to let them know you have no difficulty with the notion of *won't.*

To say "I won't" demonstrates that you're a person of discrimination and know who you are. You in fact do know your authentic limitations and also what is fruitful for you to undertake. You may, for example, have a nice singing voice but are out of practice. Someone asks you to sing at a benefit. You know that doing the job right would take hours of drill and rehearsal. You say, "I won't" because though performing would be nice, the market research project you're heading up has an early deadline and requires much after-hours work. Doing this job with distinction means more to you at this point in your life than singing, so you say no. It clearly isn't that you can't sing, but that you won't sing. Saying that to yourself and finding a gentler way to say so to the person who invited you may still risk offense, but in this small way you'll have owned who you are, taken charge of your life. There's nothing pollyanna about that.

You're not Superman or Wonder Woman: "I can't leap tall buildings in a single bound" sounds *legitimate*. "I can't tell Nick he has bad breath" sounds *whiny*. "I won't have time to prepare for the benefit, so my answer, I'm sorry to say, is no" sounds *strong*.

Yes We Can

If we're to succeed in our work, we have to meet many of our responsibilities with unstinting individual effort. Such is the case with thinking, planning, report-writing, preparing for presentations, and the like. Yet increasingly, our work is collaborative. The shrinking world of communication, global markets, and our organizations as social institutions unto themselves all combine to form a hitherto unknown complexity. No one person, including the CEO, is smart enough to figure it all out and know what must be done.

To thrive, we must be affirmative, and we must be affirmative together. We must spawn initiatives, about which we collectively declare, "Yes we can!"

Far too often, one company looks at another to conclude what it ought to be doing. This closes down options and produces a leveling effect—a drift toward mediocrity—in an entire industry. This, of course, prompts foreign competitors, who aren't limited by monkey see, monkey do, to come into our markets and clean our clocks. While we're saying, "We can't do that," they're saying, "Yes we can!"

Fear not. We're regaining our can-do spirit in this country. But it takes a while. Years elapse between the time a company says "yes we can" amid the can'ts and flat-footedness of the nay-sayers and when that affirmation comes to full fruition.

A generation ago, we said no to our own Mr. Deming's notion of team commitment to quality. Japan said yes. Then we said no to our own cars, but yes to those produced in Japan. We're awake now, however. I like the signs I see.

—————————— *TAKE ACTION* ——————————

1. Next time you say, "I can't," stop and listen for a whine in your voice. See if you shouldn't be saying, "I won't."

2. Work, work, work with your associates at developing the "Yes we can!" in your company. That's the way to thrive. That's the way to be lucky.

—— **77** ——

LEAVE YOUR BLAHS IN THE CAR

Yesterday, I attended the quarterly meeting of the Midwest Human Resource Planners Group. These are day-long affairs, and they're usually quite good. Yesterday's session was especially good.

One presentation that contributed to this quality day was made by two executives of Allstate Insurance, along with a consultant from DiBianca-Berkman Group who works with Allstate. All three have been collaborators on a leadership development program designed for Allstate's 195 officers.

This leadership program has now been in effect for four years. We in the audience were left with no doubt that this trio is pleased with the program's results. They bubbled over with enthusiasm for what they've accomplished and what they yet have before them. It was catching.

One of the Allstate executives, Ed Dixon, was particularly captivating, not because he was so eloquent, but because he had vitality oozing from every pore. He combined humor with a conviction for what he does for a living that launches from the balls of his feet, whirls around his gut and brain, then vaults from his mouth while he keeps a twinkle in his eye. All this without an offensive rah-rah style.

"We're going to say some outrageous things," he promised, when it was his turn to talk in the trio's introduction to their presentation. And true enough, they did. But mostly, *he* did.

You Can't Mean It!

This 20-year veteran of Allstate is currently vice president of auto marketing, an area loaded with opportunity, he said, because "*nobody* likes auto insurers." But until three months ago, he was vice president of human resources, and it was in this job that he apparently developed quite a reputation for saying outrageous things.

He told us that when Allstate began the leadership program, he knew the ideas he was going to espouse would wreak havoc among his fellow officers, so he had his business card printed with an acronym on the back and gave it to all of them. When they had a problem with him, he asked that they just walk up to him and hand him his card with the backside face up.

The acronym was EYCRMTS. He said this stood for "Ed, you can't really mean this stuff." "Yeah . . . 'stuff'," he told us. "If you want to, you can make the S stand for stuff." This brought the house down.

I don't have the space here to recount all of Ed's "outrageous statements," or the "leadership principles" on which the Allstate program is based, but let me pass along from this authentic man a bit of his conviction I referred to earlier. Then I'll follow that up with an idea of his that deserves our full attention.

The twinkle in Ed's eye held firm, but we knew it was backed by steel when he said, "By the year 2000, we're going to be the insurer of choice. We're going to do this by being the employer of choice." Look out, State Farm!

The Forgotten Half

The idea of Ed's I'd like us to think about concerns coaching. I want us to think about it because it pertains to supporting our teammates with our vitality. It also deserves our attention because in advancing this idea—and the way he advanced it, namely in his highly empowering way—he walked his talk. He was an example to us. He strengthened us. He made us see things in a fresh way.

"Everybody talks about coaching these days," he said. "But they forget about half of it. They forget about upward coaching." He then proceeded to tell us that for years he kept looking for the brain trust in his company. He assumed it was in the upper ranks. He kept waiting for all these great ideas to come down so he and his associates could go to work carrying them out. But they never came down, at least not in a pure sense. What came down had to go up first. Bingo!

CEOs get credit for the ideas they are identified with. But the ideas aren't theirs. They're alternatives they choose between, Ed reminded us, that are generated and presented by whom? "You!" he said, answering his own question, pointing his finger at us. We can't just sit around waiting for pronouncements from the brain trust. He was telling us we're the brain trust. Our bosses need our ideas. They need our support. They need our guidance. They need our vitality.

The fascinating aspect of watching Ed in action yesterday was that while he was urging us to send *our* vitality upward, we were experiencing the benefits of him sending out *his* to us sideways.

What stands out in bold relief is that vitality is the engine of coaching whether its direction is down, up, or across. So it turns out that most of us have forgotten not half, but two-thirds of coaching.

And Ed Dixon, even if he can't get his fractions right, is a helluva guy to emulate.

TAKE ACTION

1. Be outrageous. Dare to believe the good fortune of you and your teammates is dependent on your good spirit.

2. Heed the advice of John Spoelhof, president of the Prince Company of Holland, Michigan. In his comments to Prince management assembled at a recent meeting, he had this to say: "We need *you*, here, fully, every day. When you walk in, leave your blahs in the car."

FAST TAKES

on
Being Lucky

- We often find the bad news we're looking for.
- Desire + expectation = hope.
- Hope + tempered stoicism = luck.
- You don't always have to be right. Things don't have to be done your way or go your way.
- Funny, isn't it, how the helper is often so lucky?
- You can declare your authenticity by saying "I won't." This saves your energies for occasions where you can make your breaks.
- We can help make our breaks by coaching upward and sideways as well as downward.
- Vitality is the engine of coaching—and of good fortune.

DELIVERING

*Our grand business is not to see
what lies dimly in the distance,
but to do what lies clearly at hand.*

THOMAS CARLYLE

XVI

PRACTICING QUALITY

The Trust Others Hold in You

The theme for this chapter on practicing quality is number 1: *Today's management style of necessity is one of quickened response.* Please recall from my earliest comments in "Disclaimers and Proclamations" at this book's beginning that *quicken* is a shading on authenticity and refers to more than just speed. Other definitions for the word, to repeat, include "to give or restore vigor"; "to animate, revive, restore life to"; and "to become alive, receive life."

We live in a time when our corporations, if they are to thrive, need nothing less than such an infusion of vitality. Another word for it, of course, is quality. Not just quality products and services, but the quality that comes before that—the quality of teamwork.

To practice quality, give thought to the following:

- Visualizing the persons you serve within your company as customers
- Serving people rather than systems
- Being punctual
- Counting commitments and deadlines as a trust

—— 78 ——

PRODUCING QUALITY, BEING QUALITY

Yesterday, I met with Larry Perlman, president and CEO of Control Data Corporation. I wanted very much to spend some time with this man who began his career as a lawyer and has since proved himself an outstanding general management executive.

In two short years before becoming president and COO he turned around CDC's troubled data storage division. He did this in a competitive environment that includes such awe-inspiring Japanese names as Hitachi, Fujitsu, and Mitsubishi. Now he and CDC's management cadre give early signs they're going to assure the survival of this once-great company that has been in dire straits since 1986.

Perlman is a warm, bright, tough-minded dynamo and a superb communicator. He seeks free expression of ideas from his executives and gives them the latitude to make their own decisions in their areas of responsibilities. At the same time, he has exacting standards for performance and doesn't suffer fools gladly.

The outstanding reputation of Control Data from its inception was based on the quality and dependability of its products. Therefore, much of Perlman's thoughts and efforts go straight to making sure his people are re-committed to producing quality and to *being* quality themselves. As they say, it's lookin' good. Perlman himself would probably limit his comments to, "It's looking promising."

Being Quality

We hear executives described in many ways: "He's an ambitious executive." "She's got a lot of moxie." "He's one of the smartest guys I've ever met." "She's creative." "He's a politician." "She's timid." "He's overbearing." "He's dependable." "She's a good motivator." I could go on writing this kind of stuff for several pages.

Every once in a while, though, a person catches us up short with a tone of voice, vocal pacing, and sense of conviction when describing an associate he or she deems special. The words go something like this: "Bill? Oh, well, now. That guy is somethin' else. He's a *quality* executive."

Being quality means you contribute much more of what you have to give than your peers do. You are a practitioner of authenticity. That's why you stand out. And to whom is it as a quality executive that you make this contribution? Why, to your teammates on the job, of course! Sound ridiculously simple? Then why in heaven's name are there so few contributors? Why do quality executives stand out so much? Why are they so easy to identify? Why is it so effortless to reach agreement on who they are? Why do executive recruiters begin to hear the same few names over and over when they bear down on wanting to know the "deans" of an industry?

Quality Means Team

Being quality, then, is to make a contribution. And to contribute is to give to, serve, or please a recipient. Givers and receivers who link up regularly and make a point of switching the giver and receiver roles on an equal basis constitute a team.

Most executives in a corporation have no contact with the ultimate customer or end user. But they have constant contact with teammates and other associates who are counting on them to deliver the goods just the same. If we don't live up to our commitments to that person next to us in the management process, we aren't quality and our company won't deliver quality on the outside.

John Roach, CEO of Tandy, said in a recent cover story in *Success* magazine that he wasn't looking over his shoulder at IBM. Rather, he was looking over his shoulder at themselves.

With the same idea in mind, Larry Perlman seeks to inspire his hard-charging people with this challenge: "We are the competition."

--------------------------- *TAKE ACTION* ---------------------------

1. Don't limit your thoughts of producing quality to a product or service. Think of yourself. Ask: Am I quality? How can I be quality?

2. Name three or four "customers" in your workplace you have not served well. Stop to think how that has hurt your corporation's production of quality. Work at fixing those relationships.

------ **79** ------

YOU MAY ASK YOURSELF

As a human resources practitioner, I attend numerous group meetings. These meetings are of all kinds. Some are of short duration and scheduled over breakfast, lunch, or dinner. Their central feature is usually a speaker of some expertise who addresses a subject of interest to the audience.

Some of these meetings are longer, held over a period of days. They are conferences or conventions with an array of subjects and speakers and activities. These can be huge affairs with thousands in attendance who are all members of some professional association, or of more moderate size, made up of, say, the key management of a corporation.

Others of these meetings are small-group workshops or seminars where a handful of people become intensely involved in a topic or skill-building activity ranging in time from a half-day to a week or more.

I'm periodically found at some of these meetings as one of the supplicants, there for purposes of fellowship and my own professional growth. More often, I'm there to make my living—as a workshop leader or meeting speaker. In any event, having been in attendance at such meetings for years, I have become something of an expert evaluator of hotels, where easily 90 percent of these meetings take place.

Who's Serving What?

Most hotels do a poor job of accommodating and facilitating meetings. This is in part because they're more concerned with serving their systems rather than people, *their* needs rather than those of the customer.

I remember giving a keynote speech first thing in the morning to a large group of bankers at a "premier" hotel in San Francisco. The speech went well enough, and the audience was responsive, but this was the case only because we all had leapt over a significant psychological hurdle.

The large room in which the meeting was held had been a ballroom the night before, and its "contemporary" color scheme was predominantly and stultifyingly black! Can you imagine the aura of a room, filled first thing with just-risen, morning-after revelers enjoying a business trip to America's greatest tourist town, with walls a floor-to-ceiling funereal black?

The hotel's decor (system) was served, but the people were not.

The chances are good, too, that you've attended a meeting—large or small—in some hotel where you were unable to concentrate fully. The reason this was so, you'll recall, is that sounds of music or voices spilled into your meeting room from the room next door. It turns out that those movable partitions used to convert one large hall into several smaller spaces that are billed as soundproofed are anything but.

The hotel's need for flexibility (system) was served, but people were not.

Now consider something as simple as the typical hotel's meeting-room chair. It is anything but comfortable. It is in most cases an ugly, stainless-steel-and-Naugahyde contraption that is sure to take the crease out of anyone's slacks while adding wrinkles all its own. Its redeeming virtues are that it is virtually indestructible and easily picked up, transported, stacked, and stored—all conveniences for the hotel, not the hotel's customers.

Who's Serving Whom?

The examples I've given from hotel life that portray people serving systems rather than systems serving people all happen to be physical, tangible. They have to do with objects. But there are systems routinely put into play in our organizations that are intangible, yet have

269

great potency—much of it negative. They go by such labels as "policies," "procedures," "rules," "directives," "guidelines," "recommendations," and the like. And many such systems end up requiring service far more than providing it. Some call this bureaucracy, but that's seldom correct.

More often, systems we employ that get in the way of providing service to the rightful receivers are nothing more than habits, predilections, and practices. Have you been on an airplane lately? Have you boarded the plane and opened several overhead bins looking for a place to put your bag only to find most of them already occupied by the luggage of flight attendants who came on board before you?

Have you ever gone to use the restroom near the end of your flight only to discover a flight attendant logging major-league time in it reapplying makeup or otherwise sprucing up for a fast getaway when the plane lands?

One of our most refreshing, bizarre, and talented rock groups is "Talking Heads." One of this group's most thought-provoking songs, "Once in a Lifetime," makes repeated use of the refrain, "You may ask yourself . . ." followed by options that the listener, smug with materialistic well-being, is urged to ponder. Well, in turn, we may ask ourselves, "Do we serve systems more than people?"

TAKE ACTION

1. Take a mental stroll through your work to see what "systems" are at work there. Discard those that have taken on a life of their own—that is, systems that you're serving rather than those that serve you.

2. Be a contributor to your organization by urging a similar scanning by you and your team. Ask yourselves about some of the company's practices. Are they self-serving or serving the rightful receivers?

—— 80 ——

A COOK'S TOUR OF TARDINESS

Let me admit right up front that tardiness is a behavior I detest. I can chuckle when someone else in good-natured despair describes an associate who has trouble showing up on time. But I find that when I'm on the receiving end of a lack of punctuality, I consider it anything but a laughing matter. To my mind, punctuality is a component of being quality.

Perhaps I just grew up this way. My father was a stickler for punctuality and so was my mother. The latter, a strong-willed but shy and soft-spoken soul, as I've already told you, once shocked me with her vehemence on this subject. I was in junior high school and had a morning paper route. I delivered the *Chicago Tribune* to 150 households. That was far too many papers to be carried on a bike, so I covered my route on foot, pushing a three-wheeled cart.

Halfway through my route one morning, one of the cart's large side wheels "froze" from lack of lubrication and wouldn't budge another inch. I called in to my boss at the newspaper agency for help and cooled my heels for half an hour until he came. My boss arrived in his truck and unloaded a working cart. We threw the papers into the new cart and I scampered off as fast as I could to finish the route.

We both knew I'd probably be late for school, so he doubled back to meet me near the end of my route, helped me pitch the remaining papers onto the customers' porches, loaded the cart onto the back of his truck, and rushed me home.

My mother was standing on our front steps, waiting, in a rage. She swatted me on my backside as I tried to squeeze by her like a dog with its tail between his legs. Through clenched teeth, she exclaimed, "Get upstairs, get your books, and get to school!" As I bounded the steps up to my bedroom, I could hear her giving my boss the tongue-lashing of his life. The last words I heard as he ran for cover were, "This just won't do!! And it better not happen again!!!"

Mrs. Cook's Wisdom

I ran the three blocks to school, dashed to the desk of my homeroom teacher, Mrs. Cook, and gave her the excuse my mother had written. The room was now empty because my fellow students had gone to their first class. In the stillness as Mrs. Cook read the note, I heard the large pendulum clock on the side wall tick-tocking away. It read 9:05.

Mrs. Cook, a thin, frail, pale-faced woman who wore lots of blue dresses and an abundance of rouge, then looked up and spoke to me: "Allan, I know you get up early and work hard on your paper route. I think that's admirable. If you were an hour late, that would be excusable. But you were only five minutes late. You could have done something to avoid that. This will have to go as an unexcused tardiness."

You might think I was as appalled by Mrs. Cook's statement as I was shocked by my mother's outburst. But I wasn't, actually. Mrs. Cook was not sneaky or sly. She had announced her views on tardiness when she first became our homeroom teacher, and I'd heard her say much the same thing to other kids who arrived to school late by a whisker.

No, the truth is that I thought then and still think Mrs. Cook was dead right. I feigned surprise and disappointment, to be sure, but I agreed with her. For example, I knew the cart was going bad. If I had called for help when I first discovered this, I could have pushed the cart on a squeaky wheel for a few blocks more and delivered more papers while my boss dropped what he was doing, rounded up a replacement cart, and got it to me. That would have saved the half-hour downtime. I could have washed up, had breakfast, walked to school, and been sitting at my desk when the 9:00 A.M. bell rang. Instead, I showed up the little urchin with my lower lip pushed out.

In Our Control

How different is the experience of this 12-year-old from the tardy executive in the adult work world? Not one whit. Punctuality is one thing in this life over which we have control. No demon makes us stay in bed in the morning. No malevolent force keeps us from anticipating traffic, leaving our offices promptly, and hailing a cab to make it to a luncheon in time. A plane may sit on a runway for an hour or weather may delay its takeoff, but if we miss a scheduled departure, who but we are to blame?

——— *TAKE ACTION* ———

1. Realize that when you habitually keep teammates or other associates waiting, this behavior serves some dim, inauthentic purpose for you. Ask yourself the hard question: What purpose does this serve?

2. Then ask the follow-up toughie: Is this behavior serving me well? It's likely your answer will be no.

——— 81 ———

SACRED COWS AND THE TRULY SACRED

Over lunch last week with a fellow consultant, I came into contact with the concept of "Work-Out."

I want you to know about Work-Out even though what you're about to read on it is fourth-hand. You'll get it from me. I got it from my colleague. He got it from a client of his. His client got it from a friend of his who works at the corporate headquarters of General Electric.

Work-Out goes something like this: We American corporations got too layered and bloated to be responsive to foreign competition. So we delayered and downsized. Fewer people were left to do the work of the firm. People had to work more hours, but not as many as you might think due to increased productivity from advances in information technology and robots.

Nonetheless, many sophisticated companies, G.E. among them, think we're not yet lean and mean enough to excel on a global scale.

Hence, still more people have to come off the corporate payroll. The edict has been met with an outcry: "Hold it! Enough! Our executives are commonly working 50 or 60 hour weeks and are coming in on weekends! They can't even do what they're supposed to do now!"

The reply to this, as spoken at G.E., is what is known as Work-Out. Work-Out says, "OK, we understand that. We also think that means, however, that much of what you're doing isn't crucial to the enterprise and has to go. Get rid of the excess baggage you've accumulated. Sort it out. *Work it out.*"*

Just in Time

Imagine the response when the executive retorts to the official Work-Out explanation by saying, "I hear you, boss. I'll take care of it. But you need to know that distribution project you've got me working on is gonna be the first thing to go!"

Obviously, there must be a lot of negotiation between executive teams, their bosses, and their boss's bosses to make Work-Out work. Ultimately, that negotiation takes its cues from a clear sense of corporate-wide priorities that are in turn based on a crisp, compelling corporate mission. Though my remarks may convey the thought that Work-Out is merely another example of jargon and corporate faddism, let me assure you this is not the case. Work-Out is a good word picture for an operating necessity of our day.

Metaphors are word pictures, too, and a good metaphor for Work-Out is "just in time." Just in time refers to the type of manufacturing in which raw material and components for production aren't stored in the manufacturer's warehouse but are provided by the suppliers shortly before they're needed (just in time). This cost-efficient, quality-enhancing process based on tight interteam linkage between supplier and manufacturer was mastered by the Japanese and caught us flat-footed.

When I first heard about JIT several years ago, I was incredulous. Now true enough, I'm not a manufacturing executive, but

---

*CEO Jack Welch was interviewed in the September–October, 1989, issue of the *Harvard Business Review*. In that interview, he briefly discusses Work-Out.

I've tramped through enough plants in 25 years of consulting to know the extraordinary degree of coordination necessary to make a plant hum. To put a business at such risk as to be dependent on a supplier over whom you don't have absolute control was unthinkable. Though many of our manufacturing executives used to feel the same way, now they don't. Nor do I. JIT is a Work-Out. Warehousing was something we thought we had to manage, but we discovered that someone else could do it better, reducing our costs.

The JITs in Your Work

Be sure to count the commitments and deadlines you've agreed to as a trust. Lock in on this by making sure you and your team members are aware of the JITs in your joint work. Working together to make the unthinkable thinkable is Work-Out in action, and it virtually clears the way for you to be good to your word. It does so by getting rid of such blinders as, "But we have always done this" and "But we have always done it this way."

Work-Out is separating the sacred cows from the truly sacred. Let me hasten to admit that this isn't easy. Nor, I'll also admit, is this alone a new challenge. People always have had to set priorities to perform well. But in this time when we probably have gone a little overboard in flattening out our organizations, we have no choice but to reach agreement among our associates as to what constitutes first things first. The right slogan has become "More than ever, second things never." And "Do it now" is more likely to be replaced with "Don't do it at all!"

TAKE ACTION

1. Think through Work-Out with your team members. Aligning yourself with revised corporate priorities is not an activity for isolation.

2. Given the increased demands on you and your time, realize that Work-Out enhances your capacity to deliver the goods—quality goods at that—and to do so when promised.

FAST TAKES

on
Practicing Quality

- Givers and receivers who link up regularly and make a point of switching the roles on an equal basis constitute a team practicing authenticity.

- If we don't live up to our commitments to that person next to us in the management process, we aren't quality and our company won't deliver quality to the outside.

- It's easy to go astray serving systems rather than people—our own needs rather than those of our customers.

- Not all (or even most) systems are physical and tangible. They often go by such labels as "policies," "procedures," "rules," "directives," "guidelines," "recommendations," and the like.

- Systems often end up requiring service more than providing it.

- Punctuality is a component of being quality.

- Working together to make the unthinkable thinkable is Work-Out in action, and it helps clear the way for you to make good on your commitments to your teammates.

- Worthwhile new slogans: (1) "More than ever, second things never." And instead of "Do it now," (2) "Don't do it at all!"

XVII

BEING PERCEPTIVE

Peering Behind the Facade

Theme 1 makes a fast return by being as pertinent to this chapter on perception as it was to the preceding one: *Today's management style of necessity is one of quickened response.* The essays that follow will demonstrate again that such quickening is authenticity demonstrated through the power of the team.

Theme 7 as well has a major bearing on the subject at hand: *Exercising vision is developing an understanding of where you are and where you're headed—both as an individual and as an organization.* These essays on perception feed such an understanding.

To help quicken your team and understand where you are and where you're headed, give thought to the following:

- Your corporation's forms not being compatible with its functions
- Not relying on cause/effect inquiries
- Relying instead on "the parts anticipate the whole" inquiries

277

- Exposing your subordinates to "anticipate the whole" inquiries
- Eliminating dissonance in your department by squarely facing your trade-offs

—— **82** ——

SULLIVAN'S LEGACY

It was a thing to behold, a real beauty. It sat back a hundred yards from the river that ran through the village. Perched atop a rich grassy knoll, this new building stood out from all sides in plain view, folding in magnificently with its natural setting. True enough, its contemporary architecture drew gasps from a few, but for all the rest, this was a proud emblem of a progressive community.

The structure I cite was the cultural arts center of a town numbering 50,000 inhabitants located 50 miles from one of our nation's largest cities. When it was dedicated, with municipal leaders looking on contentedly, reporters from the big city's radio and TV stations and papers were there to capture it as a model of community spirit and achievement.

That was five years ago, and today the cultural arts center is no more. Plans for its full usage never materialized. Despite energetic attempts by a dedicated few to feature concerts, lectures, and showings, its programs were largely ignored. It closed within two years.

A year ago, however, after undergoing mainly internal modifications, the building reopened and is now thriving—as an older adults center. The concert hall is in use at least three times a week for lectures and programs arranged in conjunction with a league of the town's 16 churches, two synagogues, and university extension. The dark lighting was replaced by bright so people can play cards and games together, read in their own small library, and work enthusiastically at crafts and hobbies. Dark, textured wall coverings were replaced with pastel colors and vivid murals.

Out on the grassy knoll, when I saw it on an early fall afternoon, four men played shuffleboard on two concrete strips. Women and men sat in clusters in lawn chairs talking in full view of the curved sweep of river. The river itself was a sun-filtered, silver-blue slice cut through a populace of trees turning a robust gold, rust, and red.

This town didn't want a cultural arts center; it wanted an older adults center! "Old" forms were abandoned in favor of new forms that served the community function.

Function

The lesson from this town can be applied neatly to that community known as your corporation. Well-meaning persons can win support for or railroad through some initiative that is not at all appropriate to the enterprise. Though these people may sound good and draw praise from outsiders such as business journalists and financial analysts, such wrong-headed thrusts can prove disastrous. At the very least, such efforts often distract from the company's true function.

Forms

Louis Sullivan, Frank Lloyd Wright's mentor, in 1896 gave us the brilliant insight, "Form ever follows function." His view was that function always has the final say. Forms incompatible with function create dissonance, confusion, clutter, and disease, but they inevitably give way to function. This is plain to see in the experience of our town.

Today, I can't help but wonder if all our downsizing, spin-offs, and LBO formations in corporations are true function being expressed at the expense of fat payrolls, unneeded layers, bloated wage scales, and conglomerating that were abuses by forms in the recent past.

I suspect so. If I'm right, we owe a different kind of examination to such movements.

TAKE ACTION

1. Review causes you've backed in your company that mystified you by their failure, even though you thought they had widespread support. Could this have been form following function?

279

2. Keep such events in mind in all so-called strategy discussions you're party to along with your teammates. This will keep your joint actions authentic, more in line with true company need.

—— 83 ——

THINGS AREN'T WHAT THEY SEEM

- "I thought they'd love it; they hated it."
- "I thought they'd hate it; they loved it."
- "What caused this?"
- "What's the root cause?"
- "Let's find the first cause."
- "What brought this about?"
- "Let's get to the bottom of this."
- "How come we did the right thing, and the wrong thing resulted?"
- "Last time we tried this and it worked. This time we did it the exact same way and it didn't!"
- "Last time we tried this and it didn't work. Then we changed our approach and it still didn't work. Then we came back and tried it the way we did the first time and it did."
- "I thought for sure we could make it happen, but we didn't."
- "I thought for sure our approach would never work, but it did."
- "We thought these were the effects of the problem. We took away the problem, but the effects were still there."
- "We thought this was the problem, but we couldn't do anything about it at the time. So we did nothing. Then what bothered us went away, but the problem stayed. I guess the problem wasn't the problem."
- "We thought this would be the effect, but just the opposite occurred."

- "We thought we had it figured out."
- "After floundering around as a group with the best brains in the business, there it was, the solution staring us in the face. It took us three years to see it!"

Puzzlement and Shock

We hear it said almost daily that we live in a world turned upside-down. Things have gone berserk. The old rules are out and we don't know what the new rules (assuming they exist) are.

Change is a constant. Today women not only work, but they marry later and delay having children while they move toward top positions in their vocations. Divorce is common. The nuclear family is shot. Sexual restraints are loosened. Today's television would have been rated X 15 years ago. Casual sex abounds and live-in arrangements among yuppies are the norm. AIDS terrifies us while stress itself is the rampant disease of our time. People care only about themselves and are rude to each other. On top of all this, America is in economic decline. The Asian Tigers, led by Japan, put us to shame. Even Europe's businesses are showing signs of life while we languish. The corporate reorganizations taking place via merger-mania and LBOs are nothing more than rearranging deck chairs on the *Titanic*.

Things are out of control! What's going on! What's the cause of all this!

George Will likes to tell a short story that goes something like this: In 1905 in Dayton, Ohio, there were two cars, and on July 11 of that year, they collided.

I have to believe the citizens of Dayton felt the same way over three quarters of a century ago that we do today. Two horseless carriages colliding meant the town had fallen prey to frenzied living.

Lost in America

I cite these laments of our current "lostness" in America to portray our sense of futility in trying to figure things out. We persist in explaining life by relying on cause-and-effect thinking, but this clearly does not give us the answers we seek.

For example, economists on both sides of the political spectrum argue the causes of the federal deficit. The sum of the parts of their arguments don't equal the whole of our existence—or, in other words, reality as we understand it.

Protectionists and free traders argue the causes of our trade deficit. Again, we can assume both groups are wrong. To repeat, the sum of the parts of their arguments don't equal the whole of our existence—or, in other words, reality as we understand it.

In short, cause-and-effect thinking doesn't get it.

──────────────── *TAKE ACTION* ────────────────

1. Consider the possibility that there's a better way than cause-and-effect thinking to figure things out.

2. Have you and your team stay tuned. I'll have more to offer on this subject in the next essay.

────── **84** ──────

THREE HERETICAL PROPOSITIONS

You'll recall that in the preceding essay on the pitfalls of cause-and-effect thinking, I wrote a paragraph on the standard laments we hear of our society gone berserk. I concluded that paragraph with these words: "On top of all this, America is in economic decline. The Asian Tigers, led by Japan, put us to shame. Even Europe's businesses are showing signs of life while we languish. The corporate reorganizations taking place via mergermania and LBOs are nothing more than rearranging deck chairs on the *Titanic.*"

Now think about the following paragraph from a letter I received this week from a client of mine. He's president of a company that's the largest and one of the finest in its industry. If I were to name it, you'd recognize it. The company has just been reorganized through a leveraged buy-out (LBO).

"It appears the management style of our LBO framework is going to emphasize even more the decentralization of functions into the two operating segments. The need for teamwork at the top corporate level may not be so pronounced. The need for teamwork within the two segments will be very pressing, particularly in the decision-making process for capital allocations. For the first time in the business history of a lot of us, capital programs will be restrained by the availability of cash, as opposed to the absolute value of each program. Put another way, we will have to turn down good programs. This will be hard for us to deal with, but the better understanding we all have of the process—in other words, the better the teamwork—the easier this will go."

Cause/Effect

We believe, don't we, that (1) for very action there is a reaction? We believe, don't we, that (2) the parts of some whole cause the whole itself? We believe, don't we, that (3) today's effects come about from yesterday's causes? In other words, we believe, don't we, that the past (history), whether in real time occurring aeons or seconds ago, is the cause of the present?

Consider for a moment three heretical propositions:

- What we think of as causes are most often effects.
- The parts emerge in anticipation of the whole.
- The future causes the present.

If there is anything to these propositions, and I hope to show that there is, then only question 1 reflects the actual state of affairs.

History of the Future

Ironically, my client made reference to history in his letter: "For the first time in the business history of a lot of us, capital programs will be restrained. . . ." Are we to assume this restraining of capital is a *result* of high debt *caused* by the company going private and having to buy out its public shareholders?

No, we are not. This particular LBO is a very, very, very small effect, not a cause, of a much larger whole. And though that whole is something not fully understood by any of us, we nonetheless sense it. We anticipate it in our collective gut, and the fact that we anticipate it means that it lies somewhere in the future.

I'm suggesting that the best way to study the history of an organization, a country, or a life is to explore how the events of the past were an expression of the beliefs and senses of what lies ahead. Study causes as the effects they are, as omens good or bad that tell us where we're heading. By studying history this way, you'll be studying the history of an expected future. What did the people of an earlier time show by their collective actions that they believed was before them? Those actions were parts that emerged in anticipation of an unarticulated—yet sensed—whole.

Without fully knowing it, my client was saying in his reference to history that never before had business life required him to respond to the anticipated future in this particular way. These anticipations signal a shift with implications for us all. Later, when he looks back on today, he'll realize the future caused the present!

TAKE ACTION

1.   Wait until after hours, then put your feet up and let your mind float, float, float. Get absurd! Set a leisurely pace and ask yourself what's occurring in your life and work at present that may be the result of a not fully understood—but sensed—future. Review the actions you and your team-members are taking currently. In what ways might they be parts emerging in response to an anticipated whole?

2.   Stay tuned. I'll have more on this in the next essay.

—— 85 ——

THE FUTURE'S FIX ON THE PRESENT

The director of communication and corporate relations is holding a full-day meeting with her staff of five in a small conference room. She has assembled them so they can come up with the solution to a persistent problem that has befuddled them all.

She poses the problem: "We've got a terrific charter in this company, but we're being ignored by too many people we can help." She goes on to outline several instances in which her department's ability to get the word out in the most effective way was shunned by several departments in favor of doing nothing or taking a backseat to well-intentioned but inept do-it-yourselfers. This occurred both at headquarters where her department is located and at several divisions scattered throughout the country.

She had given her team homework. In a memo to each of them a week before the meeting, she drafted the problem and asked them to come prepared to offer their best thoughts on the following:

- When are we ignored?
- Where are we ignored?
- On what kind of project? New product introduction? AIDS benefit package? Donation to the county park foundation? The city orchestral association? The CEO's heart attack? The new quality improvement program?
- By whom are we ignored? Everybody? A random few? Always the same people?
- What are the possible causes? Our image and perceived competence? Viewed as irrelevant? Unimportant? Unnecessary? Worse, a needless cost? Lack of support from the VP-administration? Lack of support from the CEO?

The Survey

The director asks the participants to offer their views on all these questions. One by one, they present their thoughts and briefly write them on a flip chart. After they finish, they post their work on the walls around the room. Next, they're ready to look for patterns among the abundance of ideas that have been surveyed and to prioritize them for their importance. Which ideas, they want to know, are the ones we should work on?

The pattern-seeking and prioritizing is a time-consuming but fascinating process. It requires give and take, a lot of energy, authentic free-flow of opinion, willingness to ask absurd questions and make leaps of faith, and honesty to admit what isn't known.

Suddenly, something unusual happens. One of the team says, "Let's stop looking for causes to this problem. We've just been going round and round the last hour and getting nowhere. We've heard some of these causes before and they just don't explain what's happening; not to me, anyway. And others are competing causes, so even if they sound right, we know some of them, if not all, are wrong."

Function Revisited

The teammate continues: "I've been sitting here thinking that despite our best intentions and efforts to be helpful, this problem of being ignored is amazingly persistent. It just won't go away. And I'm now finding myself asking instead, what gives this problem its life? How does it persist? Since it won't go away through normal actions, I want to know what function it serves!"

You can hear a pin drop. Nobody knows what to do immediately, but the team senses their fellow member is on to something.

The director breaks the silence with her voice rising. "I think I get it. If a person, or idea, or a product, or a problem persists, if it is retained, then no matter how much it baffles us, it's serving some function in the system. That function may be good or bad, but since it continues to 'live,' that means it will ensure some sort of future that is desired—legitimate or not. Fantastic!"

This energetic team has just discovered the heretical proposition I put forth in the last essay: *The parts emerge in anticipation of the whole.* They may not yet (or ever) be successful, but they now know what they're up against. For now, their company's dominant perspective is that of a future in which this team's efforts are not sought. That future perspective (whole) is anticipated in the company's rejection (parts) of the team's contribution.

At this point the team's task is to overcome the resistance to its work from the rest of the organization. That resistance can be overcome only by an imaginative presentation of an alternate whole—a desired future that will show the current barriers to be self-destructive. As I've written, strong cultures can kill.

―――――――――――――― *TAKE ACTION* ――――――――――――――

1. Emulate this team's thought processes in your work.
2. Remember, too, that while you're a team member on a peer level, you're a team leader with your subordinates. Direct your team's efforts like the leader in this essay and you will likely experience success too.

―― **86** ――

YOU CAN'T HAVE IT BOTH WAYS

Have you caught yourself getting annoyed with people who do either/or thinking? By that I mean thinking that something or somebody has to be one extreme or another but not a little of both or somewhere in between. You gain a clue to my disposition on this subject by seeing that I prefer shadings. Note how I soften the extremes in the two choices I've given you in answer to the 100 questions listed in appendix A.

Be that as it may, we might hear someone ask:

- "Do you intend to just stand around and mope, or are you going to attack that with a vengeance?"
- "Are you going to speak up or sit there silent as the sphinx?"
- "Are we going to be a company that's there first with the most or allow ourselves to dribble off into oblivion?"

- "Are we leaving this morning or will we still be here at sundown?"
- "Is she beautiful or ugly?"
- "Is he fast or slow?"
- "Is it simple or complicated?"
- "Is it long or short?"
- "Is it near or far?"
- "Can we count on you, or will you skip out?"
- "Do you love it or hate it?"
- "Is it black or white?"
- "Is it right or wrong?"
- "Is it your way or my way?"
- "Is it win or lose?"

A Fork in the Road

Yet my distaste for either/or thinking, and yours as well if you share my view, must not keep us from facing our trade-offs. For example, when it becomes clear to us that our business has reached a fork in the road, we are fooling ourselves if we think we can go both ways. Better to follow the example of Robert Frost:

> Two roads diverged in a wood, and I—
> I took the one less traveled by,
> And that has made all the difference.

There are at least two ways to learn from Frost's lines. One is to see them as allegory and understand what is unique about our enterprise, and thereby benefit from taking the road less traveled. The second is merely to be decisive as Frost was, to reach the fork and choose—perhaps even the more traveled road—but choose nonetheless, and be on our way believing it is the right direction for us at this point.

I almost sensed the need to call upon another giant from the past—Emerson—to help defend my seeming inconsistency of rejecting either/or thinking and asking that we be decisive at the fork in the road. After all, you'll recall, it was Emerson who wrote that "a foolish consistency is the hobgoblin of little minds."

But I don't need Emerson and here's why. Either/or thinking is usually a false manipulation of ideas and a rhetorical device to place judgment on or coerce someone. It's taking conditions that aren't so and attempting to make them appear as if they are. Example: "Can we count on you, Adam, or are you going to skip out?" The authentic answer shows this manipulation is quite different from a trade-off: "Oh, I'll be there, Vern, you can count on that, but I'll vote my conscience, not yours!"

A Golden Egg Goes Rotten

Some years ago, I was consultant to a privately held company that was owned 50–50 by a divorced couple. The husband had founded the business 25 years earlier, and it was a dream. It had a niche. He created something out of nothing and filled a need nobody had been able to see or articulate. When he did, customers flocked to him. The company prospered beyond his wildest expectations. His profit margins were staggering.

He and his wife became wealthy. They divorced, however, and he lost interest in the business. He pursued some personal goals in not-for-profit foundation work. His wife was not active in the business but sat on the board. They still own it 50–50 but he brought in nonfamily management, and his participation was limited to collecting dividends.

The business has suffered, though, because imitators were drawn to this niche like filings to a magnet. Meanwhile, the board, dominated by the wife, insisted that the company deal with a fork in the road by going both ways. The directors remained adamant that the bulk of investment and management resources be devoted to greater refinements of the original market that was eroding yearly. Simultaneously, management was also expected to develop new products. No new products captured the board's fancy, however, because they couldn't match the margins of the original business.

The dissonance created by this company not perceiving a major trade-off squarely has left management inert and severely demoralized. It is probably too late to save it. Unwilling to see she was hanging onto a hopeless cause, the good madam thought she could have her cake and eat it, too.

TAKE ACTION

1. Look at your department. Ponder it. Be perceptive, then abide by those perceptions. If you're as strong as a bull, you still can't swim like a dolphin. If you can soar like an eagle, you still can't blaze a trail through a jungle.

2. Be what you are. Know your trade-offs. Commit to one road. Gallop on down. Don't permit you and your teammates to divide your efforts.

FAST TAKES

on
Being Perceptive

- "Form ever follows function." Function has the first and final say.

- Cause-and-effect thinking often doesn't provide satisfactory answers; what we think of as causes are most often effects.

- The parts emerge in anticipation of the whole.

- The future causes the present.

- Function may be good or bad, but if it continues to live that means it ensures some sort of future that is desired—legitimate or not.

- Resistance to initiatives can be overcome only by an effective presentation of an alternate whole—a desired future that shows current barriers to be self-destructive.

- Anyone who hopes to change corporate culture must keep the central ideas of this chapter clearly in mind.

- Our perceptions must lead to a clear articulation of the trade-offs we face. This is one of the most important ways for a company to be true to itself; in a word, authentic.

XVIII

REFINING YOUR GIFTS

No Pain, No Gain

The theme for this chapter on refining your gifts is number 4: *The authentic state of humanity is union, and, ironically, this state enhances one's uniqueness.*

In chapter X, I urged you to reclaim your unique strengths. By using the word *reclaim*, I conveyed that those strengths you have that can bind you to your teammates are there for the taking. They're available right now! All you have to do is reach down below a layer of inhibition for what you've discarded and take them back.

In this chapter, however, the emphasis is longer term. The message I'm proclaiming here is that the gifts (different from strengths) that also make you unique and potentially bind you to your teammates require extra time and labor on your part.

To refine your gifts, give thought to the following:

- Not expecting the world to be your cheerleader
- Not allowing failure to be devastating
- Working long hours in areas that encompass your desires
- Using your gifts to make an impact you're proud of

—— 87 ——

THE POWER OF A COMPLIMENT

I give speeches. Recently I addressed a group of executives at a trade association luncheon. My subject was, "Just What *Exactly* Does Ethics Have to Do With Us?" That's a topic I warm to and I gather it showed.

The point of this essay doesn't allow for false modesty. Afterward, a member of the audience I respect and have worked with came up to me and said, "I love to listen to you talk." You can imagine how pleased I was.

At home, we're having some decorating done. We're fortunate to have a particularly good crew at work doing the painting and papering. Yesterday, after viewing the work of one of the craftsmen who wallpapered two bathrooms, I told him he'd done a beautiful job. He gratefully said thank you, but his face said much, much more. I'd made his day.

Compliments are, of course, a form of cheerleading. That being the case, you might expect we'd make more use of them. In fact, we're quite sparing of them. In other speeches I've given, I've observed how executives respond when they hear me say something like this: "Somewhere around age 36 or 37 up to about 52 or 53, executives stop getting compliments. Have you noticed that? Is that true of your experience?"

At first their faces become a question mark. Then they cock their heads and give almost a collective "Hmmm . . ." Then many of them start nodding aggressively.

A Fascinating Range

That particular age range fascinates me for two reasons. First, in past years part of my consulting activity included conducting top executive searches. This range accounted for 95% of the searches I did. Only occasionally would a search for a CEO or other special situation result in a placement who was older than 53. Moreover, by and large, people younger than 37 aren't experienced enough for top management.

Second, these are also the years that roughly correspond to those given the most intensive study by Yale psychologist Daniel Levinson in his groundbreaking book *Seasons of a Man's Life*. (I'm pleased to report he's about to publish a follow-up companion study, *Seasons of a Woman's Life*.)

Therefore, I can't help but wonder if a lack of compliments, the competition for top executive positions, and the mid-life crisis all have something to do with each other.

In my book *Inside Corporate America*, I queried 1,086 executives from 13 major corporations on a wide range of subjects. When it came to advancement, these respondents indicated that their corporations preferred to promote executives into top management positions who were aged 41 to 45. Closest to that in preference was 35 to 40. Then came 46 to 50. The range 50 to 55 trailed off quite a bit.

It's intriguing that Levinson labels the years from the late 30s to the early 40s as BOOM, or "becoming one's own man." The tasks of BOOM, he says, are to find one's own voice as a senior member of one's enterprise and to prune the dependent ties to bosses, mentors, critics, and a spouse.

A Precarious Time

The 40s then, are a time when dreams come to fruition and thrive, or show they're a little brown around the edges and ought, in some cases at least, to be discarded. The latter is most often a painful experience while the former is anything but placid. Even when dreams come true, they are seldom a sure thing, and their uncertainty can keep you self-absorbed and neglectful of extending social amenities—such as compliments—to others. Further, when their fondest wishes are realized, many executives are left singing the song Peggy Lee made popular around 20 years ago: "Is that all there is?"

So what's the bottom line on all this? My most practical if not wholly gratifying response is that no matter how worthwhile some project you're involved in is, no matter how conscientious and competent you are in carrying out your tasks, don't expect compliments for your work. Be prepared to go for it on its intrinsic terms. The chances are that nobody's going to be in the wings cheering you on with smiles and big applause.

––––––––––––––––––––––– *TAKE ACTION* –––––––––––––––––––––––

1. Rediscover the power of compliments, authentically given. You know how much you appreciate them. Now make a point of giving them. You'll mark yourself as a rare bird.

2. The team is where you'll find an exception to the state of affairs I've been describing in this essay. Make sure you're on it. The promising development of team effectiveness in our corporations is the best antidote and hope for the self-absorption and isolation that have run rampant. On the team, compliments are part of the language.

–––––– **88** ––––––

THE RIVER OF SEOUL

Carl Lewis, U.S. star of the 1984 Olympics in Los Angeles, hoped to repeat his feats in 1988. In the worst way, he especially wanted to win the 100-meter sprint and defeat his archrival, Canada's Ben Johnson.

It went the other way. Or so it seemed. On September 23, 1988, in Seoul, South Korea, Ben Johnson became the greatest sprinter in history by smashing Carl Lewis's world record. Johnson's 9.79 seconds might even have been better had he not looked over at Lewis just before reaching the finish line and thrown up his arms in defiant celebration.

Lewis came in second, setting an American record for this event. Though he was not always a gracious winner, he was magnificently poised in defeat. He said, "I ran the best I could, and now it's on to the next race." Then he added, "I don't agree that everyone who finishes second in the Olympics is disappointed. The Olympics is about performing the best you can, and I did."

Time Is a River

In his *Meditations*, second-century stoic philosopher and Roman Emperor Marcus Aurelius wrote: "Time is a sort of river of passing events, and strong is its current; no sooner is a thing brought to sight than it is swept by and another takes its place, and this too will be swept away."

I'm not suggesting that Carl Lewis is steeped in stoic philosophy, or that he likely was musing over the ideas of Aurelius on the eve of the great race. On the other hand, any such person so willing to test and stretch his limits is someone who must learn how to live triumphantly with pain—both physical and emotional. Carl Lewis seems to have done this. He has come of age.

On to the next race.

The river is a good metaphor, and Carl Lewis is a good example for us all. Events can loom overlarge in our minds, and successes, perhaps even more than failures, are evanescent. I know that the intensity of my joy at victory is less than that of my sorrow in defeat.

For this reason, I believe, champions have great difficulty repeating their mastery year to year. The challenger, who has lost one, has a stronger memory and is more mobilized for the rematch. Lewis, you may remember, beat Johnson earlier in the year in Zurich. So I don't truly believe Lewis ran the best he could. Rather, he ran the best he could under the circumstances on that particular day. This was Johnson's race to win and we thought he won it. Our hats were off to him.

The Cycle

Heraclitus was a Greek philosopher who lived almost 600 years before Marcus Aurelius. He too wrote about the river. His pithy thought was this: "You never step into the same river twice."

296

Having won four gold medals in the 1984 Olympics, Lewis may have begun training for 1988 with the thought that his activity was all about winning four more—an unprecedented feat. I suspect, however, that though this may have been a stated goal for him, he realized down deep that you never step into the same river twice.

The loss to Johnson dashed his hopes for four gold medals, and his poised reaction to this loss led me to think his training was all about winning in life. Time will tell. What's certain is that his body never again will be able to endure such rigors. He's found himself in a new arena, even though in the same place.

The old wisdom teaches there is a time to be born and a time to die, a time to laugh and a time to weep, and so on. There is also, as we all know when we're honest with ourselves, a time to win and a time to lose.

What I'm concerned with here has nothing to do with nice guys finishing last. Rather, it has everything to do with absorbing losses without bitterness, learning from them, and getting on with overcoming those losses. Many of our losses are not at the hand of someone else. They are defeats we bring on ourselves for reasons such as poor attitude, fear of taking risks, inadequate preparation, or choking-off our authenticity.

We won't always get it right, of course. We won't always be up to the challenge. Distractions will now and then intrude and we'll compromise our performance. That's okay. I'm telling you, that's okay!

What's not okay is staying down after a loss. We mustn't be so grand as to think we're impervious to failure. The first person to forgive when you've been knocked down is yourself. Other people of good will have already forgiven you—if it was even an issue. Get up and realize your teammates are waiting for you.

TAKE ACTION

1. Lifelong learning counts more than anything. Keep before you the notion that you never step into the same river twice.

2. Remember this: Lifelong learners lose less.

NOTE: Two days after I wrote this essay, Ben Johnson, as the whole world knows, was stripped of his gold medal by the International Olympic Committee because he failed his drug test. Lewis was then awarded the gold for that event, giving him two for the games and the chance to keep his dream. But he failed when he was beaten in the 200 meters by Joe DeLoach, his younger training partner.

Chicago Tribune sportswriter Phil Hersh wrote that Joe DeLoach burst into prominence when he became Carl Lewis's training partner in Houston and that he obviously has learned from the master. Said DeLoach: "Carl has been the inspiration for me all season. I've trained harder than ever before." Said teammate Lewis: "I'm glad I recruited him for the University of Houston and America."

The point of this essay remains the same.

―― **89** ――

THE ARENA OF PAIN

Today, I'm thinking about:

- The professor poring over journals late into the night, painstakingly reviewing research that has been completed in areas that have new interest for him. He's preparing a paper he will deliver to colleagues at his learned society's annual meeting next month.
- The copywriter, beat, clicking off the light to his office at 9:00 P.M., leaving just enough time to get to the station to catch the last train home. He's stumped for now. He can't find the right words as a closer for a full-page ad that will run in several major magazines.
- The medical researcher working on a cure day after day, early in, late out, meticulous, unrelenting . . . because she believes . . . and cares.

- The teacher spending extra time with students who aren't getting it, weekend excursions to museums, libraries, exhibits, taking pictures, collecting—all in the interest of increasing her knowledge and making her classes more stimulating.
- The priest, minister, or rabbi who studies hard in preparation for the classes he teaches and the sermons he preaches. He's always on call for hospital and home visitations for sickness and crises that aren't subject to advance scheduling. In attendance at evening meetings and morning breakfasts, he makes himself available to the flock who work during normal hours.
- The manufacturing manager, up at 5:30 A.M., into the plant no later than 7:00, making the rounds before his special presentation to the management committee in the conference room at 8:00. He hangs around the office until 6:00 P.M. finishing off the paperwork he wasn't able to get to during the day. He walks to his car, whistling.

Naming Your Desires

It seems to me that the people who know their desires are the fortunate ones. Any question about their devoting long hours to areas that encompass their desires is academic. That's a given. They just give the time, and in so doing they're a model of authenticity for the rest of us.

It turns out such a question is a little bit tricky, though. Yet I don't intend for it to be. Anyone who can identify true desire in her or his life will find it impossible not to spend long hours at it. Those endeavors passionately call us, and we go to them, most often without hesitation.

This isn't to say we aren't ambivalent about our desires on occasion. Naming a desire, if we get it right, requires a labor of love, and while such toil ultimately brings deep satisfaction, it is labor nonetheless. Just like that copywriter who revels in his work and for whom the words won't always come, we'll know discouragement and now and then heartbreak itself.

The obstetrician who arrives at the hospital at midnight may deliver a stillborn child before dawn. The manufacturing manager may catch a trusted employee in a large-scale pilferage scheme. The priest may say last rites to three teenagers in the ditch along Interstate 80, shattered remnants of a broken vodka bottle strewn throughout their wrecked car. The energetic teacher may not ever get through to Billy who acts up and constantly wreaks havoc in her class. Knowing and naming the desire in our lives, then, not only subjects us to failure, it assures it.

Agony and Ecstasy

"One man's meat is another man's poison," goes the old saying. When we look at a woman toiling long hours without the benefits we think should accrue to such effort, we're inclined to say, "Why don't you just give it up, Carol? Can't you see that you're not getting anywhere?" We do this without realizing how much this is a labor of love to Carol and that she has the emotional resilience to keep after whatever it is she's engaged in that means so much to her. We're often tempted to say these things to Carol because she herself has voiced frustration with the activity. We should learn that she's only letting off steam before going right back to the arena of her pain.

If we're disciplined enough to have reflected deeply and named the desire in our lives, we have learned that such desire is our magnificent obsession. Though it eventually causes pain and failure for us, just as it does for Carol, it also promises ecstasy. Without agony there can be no ecstasy.

Desire will always create failure for us because it calls on us to stretch. When we extend ourselves this way, we'll always be a little awkward—unfamiliar with the turf and what's required to perform well in the new setting. Desire seeks mastery, but mastery can't come without trial and error.

TAKE ACTION

1. Don't worry about the hours. Worry, rather, about whether you're working on your heart's desire and contributing to your team's efforts. Such contribution distinguishes authentic desire from workaholism.

2. Name your desire and work on it, and you won't short-change those who love you and seek your company. Rather, you'll inspire them. You'll be teeming with life and they'll benefit from receiving it. You'll benefit from giving it.

—— **90** ——

THE CASE FOR ARROGANCE

I was in New York last week and ran into Spencer Stuart at the corner of 54th and 5th. I'd also run into him a year ago in an elevator of the Wrigley Building, the building in Chicago where I have my office.

Before these chance meetings, I hadn't seen him since 1968, when I left his firm and its management committee at the ripe old age of 31 to strike out on my own. To my mind, Spencer Stuart was always the unparalleled star of the executive search profession. He was a man of big ideas and he believed in himself. When I left Spencer Stuart & Associates, it was the largest search firm in existence and had pioneered offering its clients a global presence.

What struck me about Spence in these two recent random encounters is how little he has changed physically and mentally in the intervening 20 years. Spry is not the word for this man who's now over 70. The most accurate word is powerful. He walks with the vigor and erectness I'd always seen in him. His gestures are alive and purposeful. His face is unlined and full of color. His voice is vibrant and his brain still brims with ideas. He remains a man with a mission. *He is authentic.*

He sold his firm to his partners 10 or 15 years ago and left the search business. Then he sold his house in Connecticut, which he and his wife replaced with two others—one each in Palm Springs, California, and Reno, Nevada. From these, he commutes weekly to New York where he runs an investment business. He also sits on six company boards.

Arrogance

I learned a lot from Spence, and thinking about him now reminds me of just how much. I used to be asked two questions after giving up a bright future with this bustling firm to hang up my shingle. The first was simply, "Why did you leave?" The second was, "What did you learn there?"

The answer to the first question was that I didn't want to limit my life's work to executive search. The answer to the second, which I invariably offered laughingly, was, "Arrogance!"

Let me explain. Most people don't know that before Spence started his firm, for a short stint he was a 20-percent partner with Heidrick & Struggles, a large search firm with rich traditions. He insisted after a time that Gardner Heidrick and John Struggles make him a full one-third partner and add his name to the masthead. When they refused, he opened up his own shop, and before too many years streaked past them. To know Spence is to know that where he cannot have an impact, he's history.

The spirit of arrogance—of insisting on making an impact in whatever one is involved in—was filtered throughout Spencer Stuart & Associates when I was there, a spirit that I took to naturally.

Big-Minded

Spence was an intimidating presence who was big-minded. He saw things other people didn't see. And he could be harsh with staff who were little-minded—those unprepared to make bold moves based on opportunities they wouldn't fathom or expectations he had that they found frightening or preposterous.

Many of my associates also thought him humorless, though I didn't find him that way at all. I found him an avid learner with a ferocious intent to build his business. This intensity put some people off, and they didn't see that he could enjoy a good laugh, even at his own expense.

Spence on the ski slopes, at a cocktail party, or on an airplane was Spence at work building the business: meeting people, asking questions, introducing himself, and, without fail, offering opinions.

He knew clients and staff alike snickered at him for the way he would "work a room" in the interest of generating business. Let them laugh, he would think. His income and net worth were at least double that of any of the chortling bystanders.

At management committee meetings, Spence would work tirelessly at raising our standards. "Present candidates who are better than the clients ask for," he would say. "Let them know what a quality guy (they were all guys in those days) looks like. Don't just complete the job; solve the problem. Do it with distinction!"

He urged us not to think of ourselves as merely recruiters with our noses pinned to some set of specs. We should be consultants, he would intone, who help clients think through structure and larger organizational issues as well. "Be there to listen," he'd remind us, "and don't tell the client all your problems—that's not why you were hired."

The arrogance of Spence boiled down to a message, admittedly sometimes delivered pompously, that we were to use our gifts to make an uncompromised impact on clients and ourselves and thereby make ourselves proud.

Your team, whether you serve it as leader or member, can use such arrogance from you.

TAKE ACTION

1. Don't make the typical executive's mistake. See yourself as gifted.

2. Gifted is as gifted does. Make that uncompromised impact. Refine those gifts you've identified. Use them.

FAST TAKES

on
Refining Your Gifts

- We mustn't expect compliments, but we'll mark ourselves as rare by giving them.

- Winners learn how to live triumphantly with pain.

- For some, perhaps you, the intensity of joy in victory is less than that of sorrow in defeat.

- There is a time to win and a time to lose.

- The first person to forgive when you've been knocked down is yourself.

- People who know their desires are the fortunate ones. They have articulated their authenticity.

- Knowing and naming the desire in our lives not only subjects us to failure, it assures it. Without agony, there can be no ecstasy.

- Desire seeks mastery, but mastery can't come without trial and error.

XIX

BEING A FACILITATOR

Helping Others Act on Their Unique Strengths and Refine Their Gifts

The theme that stands out as central to this chapter on facilitation is number 3: *Consensus seeking is a time-wasting, leveling influence that impedes distinctive performance.* You've been exposed to my views on consensus in several places, but in essay 95 I make my strongest statement on its de-authenticating effects.

Whenever the designation "facilitator" arises in management circles, many people think of it as a code word for someone engaged in "touchy-feely" methods. They see a "facilitated" group as one in which people sit around a circle eating up a lot of time, talking psychological mumbo-jumbo, answering questions nobody important is asking, and generally languishing in indecision.

Being a skilled facilitator, however, is making certain that just the opposite of all that takes place. Facilitation helps to declare uniqueness and act on it. Uniqueness of team members. Uniqueness of options. Uniqueness of results.

To be a facilitator, give thought to the following:

- Ensuring that you're a team contributor

- Shunning the "not invented here" syndrome
- Not hogging credit that should go to subordinates and peers
- Encouraging your teammates to act on their unique strengths
- Pledging allegiance to your team

—— **91** ——

THE ROOTS OF TEAMWORK

My task as a team-effectiveness consultant is to facilitate a bonding between a group of executives who are either new to each other, want to increase their level of linkage, or are engaged in outright conflict.

This past week I began such a new assignment. I'm to design a team-effectiveness retreat that I'll conduct at an off-premises conference center for the CEO and nine top executives of one of America's best-known, oldest companies.

Some say I won't succeed because this is a management group in total disarray from conflict and politicking. I know for a fact, too, that I wasn't the first or even second choice as a consultant. Others were contacted by the company's head of human resources and begged off because this was far too risky.

Moreover, as I spent three days this week interviewing these senior executives, they could agree on only one issue, namely, they are not a team!

So I may indeed be wasting my time and should pay attention to some of the executives themselves who told me nicely enough that I have an impossible task.

But I doubt it.

Whose Task, Really?

First of all, making this disparate group into a team isn't really my task at all, but theirs. *They* have to figure out how they can work together. I'll merely help them think through the process.

306

Second, almost everybody likes to be on a team and revels in the sense of belonging, of making a contribution and being respected for it, of getting close to people in a climate where failure is met with empathy and victories with shared celebration.

Just think of all those Budweiser and Miller beer ads we see on television that capture camaraderie. Recall those Hewlett-Packard "What if . . ." computer ads that capture the sense of joint effort and commitment. Ponder those Army ads that intone, "Be . . . all that you can be . . ." while showing young people accomplishing impressive feats in a team way. These ads tug at us because we all crave that kind of union. And so do these ten executives who comprise the top management of the company.

Design

I'm coming to think of design as one of the cosmic concepts. You know, like function, relativity, and such. It's much broader than the merely physical, such as the design of cars, buildings, clothing, or furniture. Design also applies to behavior. It is central to thinking about human systems and personal action.

Because this management group is made up of people who—just like you and me—*want* to belong to a team, their not being a team means they are part of a human system that is poorly designed.

I don't mean the structure described by their organizational chart. Rather, I'm concerned that the CEO design a different decision-making style for himself that stops his executives from currying his favor, as they now do, instead of tending to their responsibilities. In addition, I'd like to see his executives design their work styles so that they are sharers rather than hoarders of their time, who they are, and what they know.

If I can get these ten people to do this, they'll have designed a system that is called *team*. Likewise, if you'll think of the concept of design as how it can impact your work with your associates in a positive way, you'll be taking the first steps toward becoming a genuine facilitator. The facilitator is, after all, today's preeminent management model. You-as-facilitator is how you demonstrate your mastery of team style.

─────── *TAKE ACTION* ───────

1. Get on board as a team contributor. Design your work style for team style. Be a sharer.

2. If you haven't done so yet, acknowledge your desire for union.

─── **92** ───

WHO OWNS AN IDEA?

Earlier this week, I had occasion to be talking with a senior editor of one of our major business magazines. I was near completion of an article I was writing on management style changes CEOs should consider and wanted his thoughts on one part.

This was a role reversal and I was enjoying it. So was he. Ordinarily, people like him call people like me for stories or "think pieces," as they call them, that they're working on.

He offered some rich insights as I expected he would on a perspective on ethics I wanted to pursue. My view was that CEOs create cynicism in their ranks by talking a good game on ethics, but limit their real thinking on the subject to approving what rhetoric is used for the bronze plaque mounted in the headquarters lobby. He agreed and cited recently retired Johnson & Johnson CEO James Burke as an exception to this practice. Then he suggested I talk with an executive we both know who used to work for him. I did. (See the results of that conversation in essay number 100.)

Our discussion almost concluded, I was about to close it off with this editor. Then he said, "You know this piece you're working on? When you finish, send a copy to Art Farnham [fictitious name]. He's one of our top writers and is contributing heavily to an upcoming issue I'm in charge of with a theme similar to the one in your piece."

"Shouldn't I just send it to you, then?" I asked. "Oh, sure," he said, "I'll need one too. Even though he does a lot of our writing, he gets most of his ideas from me."

The Collaborated Idea

After we hung up, I ran through the tail end of our conversation and began to chuckle to myself. My inner mirth was not at the expense of this editor I know to be gifted, but came from my realizing how often I like to claim the birth of ideas that aren't mine.

The onrush of team management in our corporations today results in countless situations that prove that an idea's coming of age is rarely an individual enterprise. True enough, a light bulb may go on for someone who contemplates a problem in search of a solution. But light bulbs will go on for colleagues as well who are also thinking about the same problem. When they get together to hash it out in a meeting, they are likely to end up with attempted solutions that are different from what anyone had in mind individually. They will still in all probability be competing options, but in some ways different from how they started out. What person in such a group can legitimately lay claim to the birth of the final idea that is adopted?

A Progenitor's Obsession

Yet many remain obsessed with being the pure progenitor of an idea. If they can't put their own label on it, no matter how good and useful it is, they reject it. They may not be able to discard it outright, risking consternation from credible onlookers, but they'll prove resourceful at sabotage while paying lip service to its merit.

On the other hand, some are good-natured and forthright about "trademarking" their ideas. The executive vice president of one of our soft-drink makers hosted me in his office many years ago when he was a young turk climbing the corporate ladder. I was an observer to his first meeting with his advertising agency's account executive on a brand my friend had just taken over.

My host's boss, Jim Beasley (also a fictitious name), had taken a bigger job in another company, and my host had been moved up into his position. The account executive, also young, was saying, "The brand is doing real well. Look at these numbers—all of them

309

up, way up. I imagine you'll just want to stick with the current campaign. No sense breaking up a good thing."

My newly promoted friend then stood up, grinning from ear to ear, and began pacing around the room. "Oh, no," he exclaimed, still grinning, obviously having a good time, and now stretching out both his arms like eagles' wings for emphasis, "that would never do! This campaign has Beasley's name all over it! We have to come up with a much better campaign! One that has *my* name on it!"

We can enjoy the outlandish, petty rebellion of my swashbuckling host, realizing that nobody got hurt by it—except the creators of the first campaign who saw their effectiveness squashed through no fault of their own. But even they know such client whims go with the territory, and they might enjoy having to create a new one. Moreover, the brand did continue to grow with the new campaign (whether it was "much better" was open to question) and my friend came out smelling like a rose.

On most occasions, however, we'll do well to remember we're not well served by the "not invented here" syndrome, whether perpetrator or victim.

TAKE ACTION

1. Don't be petty. Revel in good ideas, whether they're yours or not.

2. Realize your idea, no matter how good, probably won't come of age until it's debated. When it does it won't be wholly yours.

— 93 —

SUCCESS FROM AN ORPHANED PARENT

Scarcely a week goes by that I'm not standing before a group making some sort of presentation. That presentation may be as short as a 45-minute speech to a large group, or as long as a four-day workshop I'll conduct with a chief executive and seven or eight direct reports.

Not long ago, I was asked to give a speech to the key management of the Prince Company. Prince is a Holland, Michigan, first-rate supplier to the Detroit Big Three and other major car makers around the world.

I flew into Holland the night before my speech. I had dinner with Prince's vice president of corporate planning, Brian Kopp, and director of human resources, Mark Van Faasen. We'd never met, but the three of us got on quickly and well.

During our conversation, Brian got to talking about a professor of his at the University of Michigan whom he admired. He told Mark and me how this professor believed to his very core that he was in the classroom to make sure that he passed along what mattered most to him. You can be sure that "what mattered most" to a professor known throughout the world for his distinguished research and writing was a transforming experience for grateful students.

A Needed Reminder

Perhaps Brian was sending me a message. Because we hadn't met previously, he might have been letting me know subtly that he hoped I wasn't here just trying to impress or entertain. Rather, he might have been saying, "Tell us what you've learned along the way. Help us to be better at what we do. Give us something to think about, something we can use." It doesn't matter whether he was dropping a hint or his story simply came up spontaneously in the flow of conversation. In either event, I was deeply impressed with what he values and took the story as a worthwhile reminder on authenticity.

The reminder is this: Whatever you're doing or called upon to do, know what you're there for. In my case, when I'm called upon for speeches or workshops, if I remember I'm there to teach what I know, believe, and have experienced, my work is a success. If I get overly concerned with cosmetics, with looking good rather than being good, with being clever and trying to impress, my efforts are likely to fail.

Pass It On

When I've done my job right, people feel empowered. This is true even in a workshop where, say, we have been directing our discussion to how the CEO's style impedes what he or she wants to accomplish through subordinates. I do what I do best, then, when I direct attention away from myself by teaching what I know that others can use. My job is to pass it on and then rejoice in seeing others benefit from what they have learned and applied.

The same is true for you. You run something, right? You've got a job to do. You're responsible for getting results in some area, and that always means working hand in hand with others, whether subordinates or peers. A standard to impose on yourself as you carry out your tasks is not to hog credit that should go to your subordinates and peers.

When placed in charge of some department or project, realize that you're there to be a facilitator. This means you teach what you know, and insist that those with whom you've linked hands teach the rest of you what they know as well. Your work effort becomes a circle in which "pass it on" emerges as a supreme value. What is passed on, first of all, is information in the form of study, reflection, opinion, belief, and experience. What is passed on, too, is credit.

Now, I'm not trying to fool anybody or deny the fact that we all, one way or another, seek recognition. But why not let that recognition come in the form of someone saying, "Sally, you run a terrific team. I love being a part of it." Or, "Vince, I've grown a ton while working with you. I just want to say thanks."

TAKE ACTION

1. Don't always have to be right. Don't always have to be smart. Don't always be the one who "figured it out," "made the call," "saw it coming," "knew it wouldn't work," "knew it would work," etc., etc., etc.

2. Direct attention away from yourself by teaching what you know to others who can put it to use. Give credit to them for applying what they've learned. Success has many parents, it is said, whereas failure is an orphan. Be an orphaned parent of success.

—— 94 ——

RESOLVING AN UNHOLY ALLIANCE

The image that springs to mind as I consider the subject of this essay is two people with expressionless faces sitting alone side by side in a stark white room. They're looking straight ahead. Profile to profile, there's no positive flow between them.

Each is aware of the other, so there's no lack of contact, but that contact is charged with tension. Let's say a third person, a man they both know, walks into the room. Immediately the tension drops between the two as they stand, greet, and relievedly direct their energies to the new party they have in common.

If this group were to remain a threesome for any length of time, however, the third party, whether fully aware of it or not, would become unable to absorb the unnatural attention directed his way, and tension in the room would again begin to rise.

But let's suppose instead that the room steadily fills up in about ten minutes, so that there are eight or ten people present. In this case, the original two are likely to separate and mingle with persons elsewhere to get as far away from each other as the four walls of the room will allow.

From Image to Boardroom

Though the foregoing is only an exaggerated image in my mind, I have extracted it straight from reality. Something like this goes on in our companies every day when our management teams gather. This is true whether the team is the board of directors, top management, a product design group, a global task force on a distribution problem, the public affairs department, the internal audit staff, or, yes, even a quality circle.

It's important to remember that all teams are groups, but not all groups are teams. As I've written in appendix B, what we call "the management team" is most often a case of mistaken identity.

The original two people of the image are people we know well. We can give them names: George and Ted. Bill and Gloria. Sue and

313

Craig. Carole and Denise. They know who they are, too, and they're uncomfortable as hell with the situation but don't know how to get out of it, fix it. Mostly, they just wish the other person in this unholy alliance would disappear.

Yet here's the shocker. This unholy alliance exists at our pleasure. The rest of us in the group tolerate it and, in some cases, even enjoy it. We enjoy it because these two people take the heat for strained or distant relationships we all feel within the group. We may not have acknowledged this fully to ourselves, but these two people in obvious conflict become the subtle outlet for how everyone in the group feels about someone else.

You may think I'm stretching things a tad here, but try as you may, you'll have a hard time convincing me otherwise.

Focus on Contribution

Like individuals, groups don't always function at their best. They have their ups and downs and we have to accept that. Nonetheless, it's in our best interest to make our groups into teams. The best way to do this is to acknowledge the conflict that exists between people in the group and insist on appreciation of each person's contribution to the team as a whole.

It's difficult to continue to dislike someone when you look her in the eye and say, for example, "Kay, your bluntness scares me. I'm always dreading you're going to turn it on me. Yet I have to agree you saved us a lot of time this morning when we were floundering over my proposal. You took issue with my conclusions, and that made me mad. But you saw the value of my research and put into words exactly what I was struggling with and couldn't put my finger on. You got us on the right track."

What's happened here? Nick has told Kay that Kay scares him. By admitting this weakness, Nick has slain a ghost and displayed his own strength. Nick has also admitted his grudging respect—even envy—for Kay's insight and directness. He's acknowledged Kay's contribution to the team while the rest of the team is left with little choice but to agree with him. Nick will no longer be as afraid of Kay's bluntness as he was, and will in fact become more

314

blunt himself. He's gained respect from the team for saying what others in the team feel as well.

Kay, for her part, has been given a compliment authentically. She's been encouraged in front of the whole team to act further on a unique strength of hers. She's also learned, however, that she probably needs to lighten up a little. She got a straight message from Nick, whom she hasn't liked, and now will feel less of a need to "go after" him. She sees him in a new light. "Maybe I don't like him," she thinks, "but the guy does first-rate research."

Nick and Kay's exchange shows us all kinds of possibilities we tend to avoid in our work groups.

TAKE ACTION

1. Work at making your group a team. Be like Nick. Face up to that person with whom you're in conflict. Don't worry about the quiver in your voice. Speak your mind to Kay before the team.

2. Be like Kay. Appreciate the respect you've been shown in such an exchange. Return the appreciation to your initiator.

— 95 —
THE TEAM MEMBER'S CREED

1. I believe in involvement
2. I believe in collaboration
3. I believe in soliciting opinions
4. I believe in asking questions
5. I believe in admitting what I don't know that I need to know
6. I believe in admitting mistakes and failures
7. I believe in asking for help
8. I believe in calling a spade a spade
9. I believe in the authority of everyone—at various times

10. I believe in authority as an act of trust, that I am called upon to delegate it upward and sideways as well as downward

11. I believe in the boss—that there is someone who sits at the head of the table for good reason.

12. I believe in lifelong learning; in coaching and being coached

13. I believe in a deeper wisdom than charisma

14. I believe in clarity of options and their consequences, not consensus

15. I believe in team vision

Any one of the above items of the team member's creed would make rich material for a chapter on facilitation all by itself. Even in this small space, however, I'd like to direct my comments to two of them: 10 and 11.

Authority as Trust

We hear the complaint often: "I've got the responsibility for this project, but not the authority!" It's real, this lack of formal authority, and when it's true of us in our work, we know we may well be out on a limb that can be sawed off behind us.

We typically think that authority moves downward. The complaints we voice usually have to do with our not being given authority by our superiors. We feel the heat and pain from fear of turning in compromised results, and wish the boss would loosen the reins and let us run.

We tend to be self-centered about authority, then. We think of it in most cases as being denied to us. We are all the more covetous of it, therefore, as it is parceled out sparingly. Abraham Maslow said, "Man lives by bread alone when there is no bread." We might say here that executives hoard authority so long as it is scarce.

Or *assumed* to be scarce. Actually, on another level, authority isn't scarce at all. It's all over the place. Nothing (nothing!) is ever done without authority. Every act requires it. Even when you do something you aren't "authorized" to do, you are *taking* authority.

You may be applauded ultimately or thrown in jail for your audacity, but when you act, you act with authority.

It's how authority is *shared*, though, that really deserves our attention. Most of us are unwilling to share it. The lack of authority we complain about at the hands of our bosses we are equally guilty of perpetrating on our subordinates. And what's truly ironic is the way we withhold authority from our peers and bosses. We have the power to keep them from doing what they ought to be doing, and we exercise it all the time. Miserly, petty potentates we are, if ever they existed.

This fundamental lack of trust in others occurs when we insist on being included in a decision or initiative where we're not needed. Or when we pout and lie down on the job when a decision doesn't go our way. Or when we take two weeks to process orders that the department next to ours has a right to expect from us in two days. Or when we criticize John's proposal just because we don't like John.

The Boss

Moreover, nowhere is this operational avarice expressed more clearly than in our antipathy for the boss. Few are more enthusiastic than I at the movement toward greater collaboration in our society and in management in particular. But amid this positive development, there is one gross self-deception afoot; *it's deadly and must be named for what it is and destroyed.*

It's that much of our preening over "collegiality," "democratic process," "consensus seeking," and "committee action" is a spiteful subterfuge to deny others, especially bosses, exercise of their necessary authority. This leads to mediocrity, paralysis, and finally organizational death.

True equality is the expression of authority. An atmosphere of equality is one in which authority is granted as a trust to those who can best exercise it at a given time. The team is a delicate balance, to be sure, but one that never degenerates to anarchy. The team thrives on competence, knowledge, experience, commitment, gifts, timing, insights, information, hunches, and more. All of these, each in its own time, weave their way among all members.

The team also moves forward on yeas and nays. For these, along with an abundance of other things, it looks to the boss.

TAKE ACTION

1.   Be reminded of what I wrote in the introduction: "You have to give up something to be on a team." What you give up is not your brain, your mouth, your caring, or even your ambition. Rather, you have to give up inauthentic roles and destructive self-images. You also have to give up a measure of authority. You have to share it.

2.   Share authority and you'll learn the meaning of trust. Without affirming and supporting the authority of others, there can be no team.

FAST TAKES

on

Being a Facilitator

- A group's task to make itself into a team isn't someone else's. It is its own.

- Almost everybody likes to be on a team. The team is the ideal opportunity for expressing your authenticity.

- Design is a cosmic concept that also applies to behavior. It is central to thinking about human systems and personal action.

- You-as-facilitator is how you demonstrate your mastery of team style.

- Whatever you're doing or called on to do, know what you're there for; whenever we're overly concerned with looking good rather than being good, we're likely to fail.

- Most often, "team" is a case of mistaken identity.

- "Unholy alliances" take the heat for the rest of us.

- Much of our preening over "collegiality," "democratic process," "consensus seeking," and "committee action" is a spiteful subterfuge to deny others, especially bosses, exercise of their necessary authority.

XX

VISIONING

A Chinese Proverb Says It All

The most pertinent theme for this concluding chapter on visioning is number 7: *Exercising vision is developing an understanding of where you are and where you're headed—both as an individual and as an organization.*

As I wrote earlier, virtually all seven themes are present in all chapters, and that's certainly true in this case. You'll see earlier ones revisited, such as the themes of quickened response and being a team catalyst. Yet a telling point presented in this chapter is that even vision itself—that greatest indicator of all of a corporation's health and authenticity—is dependent on teamwork for its enactment. It seems the right one with which to bring down the curtain on this book.

To exercise vision, give thought to the following:

- Seeing your team as an agent of alignment
- Not associating vision with charismatic people
- Associating vision with *authentic* people

- Not assuming vision precedes dramatic action
- Displaying performance that is a mixture of good judgment and good timing

—— 96 ——

THE TEAM'S THE THING!

Not long ago, I met with the chief executive and human resources officer of a company with annual sales of almost $7 billion. The three of us discussed alignment.

The chief executive complained that his top management hadn't coalesced around his vision and strategy. As a team-development consultant to him and his staff, my concern at the moment was with mechanics. I would interview the 15 members of the management committee, then design and direct an off-site workshop to enhance team alignment.

The chief executive wanted to include all 15 in the workshop. The vice president of human resources argued that only the chief executive and eight people who report to him should attend. She said because alignment was the central problem, and many sensitive issues would arise, the smaller group would be more effective. After some debate, the vice president won her case.

Alignment and span of control were two sides of the same coin in this ironic disagreement. Here was a chief executive who concurred reluctantly that 15 officers were too many to achieve resolution of alignment problems. How then can we expect to pass alignment through our managerial ranks when spans of control for bosses are that large or larger?

The decision by the chief executive is instructive to any boss who reflects on whom to include on a project of consequence. This is so whether the project is drafting a mission statement, laying off staff in the southeastern region, reviewing suppliers of powdered metal for plant number three, or improving day-to-day communications of, say, the product design department.

The Flat Organization

Today, projects take place in flatter organizations—so configured for reasons of cost reduction and adaptability in meeting customer needs. This radical flattening whereby whole layers of supposedly non-value-adding middle managers are taken out of a company has not been a garden of delight. We've enlarged our spans of control markedly, and there is confusion among executives over roles and exercise of authority. This plays hob with alignment.

Because your job as a boss is to be a team leader who facilitates options and decision thinking among subordinates, see how we make your job unworkable with too large a span of control. See how you are mistrusted by your gaggle of subordinates. Most of them suspect that peers are pulling strings behind the scenes and have your ear more than they do. To a person, they gripe that you're hoarding authority. Moreover, winning your approval for any undertaking is difficult because they seldom see you. When they do, you are harassed and distracted.

The latter is doubly discouraging because by the time they get to you they have spent inordinate blocks of time checking with everyone in their department to make sure they're not duplicating efforts. The subordinate engages in this reconnaissance to avoid the terror of showing up at the hard-won appointment with you with an idea that is redundant. For your part, you end up delivering to your own boss not information, but mere data. You don't have the time or structure to manage your subordinates in the exchange of ideas.

One astute subordinate said recently, "In the attempt to streamline, we created a problem. When you look at our large department, we're flatter. But if you look at us from the top, as through a microscope, we're like a wheel with tiny spokes pointing to the center. We're all on the periphery with only one or two people at the hub. Everything goes through them and we have bottlenecks. This was supposed to be more egalitarian, but we're more competitive with each other than ever."

322

Data with a Brain

Some observers suggest that before long a boss's span of control will expand to 70, 80, or more people. They say this is possible because of information technology. The highly educated specialist won't tolerate close supervision and will operate independently. The greater expertise and independence on the part of a boss's charges means, therefore, that the boss can direct the activities of a large number.

This point of view is misguided. Remember that information is data with a brain. Information is what comes of age after data have been subject to observations from experience, opinions, beliefs, philosophies, specialized knowledge at odds with other specialized knowledge, facts as understood, articulated trade-offs, and what's yet missing from the equation. Such coming of age won't occur in a bullpen of 70, no matter how expert. It occurs only in a team, which, to repeat, I define as a unit of five to nine people. The team thrashes out ideas and values with an appreciation for authority and who is expected to do what by when. The team, then, is the organizational atom—the locus of power—and if executives are going to foster alignment throughout their ranks, then the team is where they must start.

Both the preceding essay and this one propose a pledge of allegiance to the team. They propose, further, the necessity for the proper exercise of authority—of followership as well as leadership. Authority being *shared* determines whether a small aggregate becomes a team that works. Finally, shared authority also provides the linkage for *interteam* alignment throughout management. The team is great. Teams linked by an explicit purpose are greater still.

―――――――――――― *TAKE ACTION* ――――――――――――

1. Be a catalyst. Make sure your team plays a role in contributing to your corporation's vision. Do this by articulating your understanding of your corporation's central purpose.

2.   Aid in interteam alignment by thrashing out your understanding of central purpose with fellow teams. Vision isn't an unrealistic wish list. Rather, it's gaining company-wide clarity as to what you're (as a company) committed to and have the resources to address—not what you *ought* to be committed to. Later, you may or may not redirect your efforts to the ought. But for now, get clear on the *are*. Then you can judge it for its appropriateness and be more focused on your options.

--- **97** ---

SPARE ME THE CHARISMA!

A new client of mine runs a group of businesses for a large West Coast parent company. The annual sales of his group is in excess of $500 million, and his group is far and away the most profitable in the corporation.

I've known him for over 15 years. I first met him at lunch in 1974 when I tried to recruit him to become executive vice president of a small janitorial services firm. The janitorial services industry gave every indication that it was going to boom—which turned out to be the case—but he politely declined further interest.

We developed a fondness for each other, however, over that short luncheon we shared at the Wrigley Restaurant in Chicago's famous landmark building, and we've stayed in touch. When he introduced me to his top management team in a meeting recently, he said, "Allan's finally going to be able to recoup his costs of postage for keeping me on his mailing list all these years."

My fondness for my client—let's call him Rolfe—isn't due to his being entirely lovable. In fact, he can be aloof, moody, petty, and cantankerous. All this has been obvious to me, even from a distance, even though I've never worked with him.

Yet what's been equally obvious to me is how exceedingly able he is, and that beneath his sometimes cold, harsh exterior beats the heart of a man who cares deeply about his businesses and the people who work in them.

Working on Charisma

As I've made the rounds among his top executives, I've had confirmation of my impressions of Rolfe. I've learned that he's "decisive," "a take-charge guy," "absolutely brilliant—almost scary," "a strategist's strategist," "someone who's made us crisp, sharp, and alert around here," and "a guy who can go to the heart of a problem faster than anyone I've seen—he keeps us from foundering."

I've also learned that he can be "extremely difficult," "easy to respect, but hard to like," "cool on the shop floor and unfriendly to clerical staff," "unpredictable as to what he considers good and bad news," and "one who keeps you at a distance." And to top it all off, two of his officers used identical wording to provide me with what they consider a summarizing understatement: "Rolfe needs to work on the charisma."

Vision: Understanding the Here and Now

In my book *The Making of the Achiever*, I define vision not as some sort of distant clairvoyance, but vigilance in the here and now that tells us how what we are now is a sign of what we're going to be in the there and then. In my last book, *The Achiever's Profile*, I stated that vision is not some wishful description of "where we want to be and how we get there," but *understanding*. It's an understanding of where we are and where we're headed. If we can understand that—and it's not easy—then we can knowledgeably blow the bugle or the whistle on what we're about.

As I'll point out again in this book's closing essay, vision and charisma have come to be linked together in the political and corporate mind. Those who have vision, we say, are charismatic, and vice versa. No generalization could be more fraught with danger. My client Rolfe, who obviously doesn't measure up on the charisma scale, is nonetheless someone who understands where his businesses are headed and has demonstrated an awe-inspiring ability to blow both bugle and whistle at appropriate times.

Spare me the charisma, I'll take the vision. So will Daniel Boorstin, the distinguished social scientist, Pulitzer Prize-winning author, and our Librarian of Congress emeritus. The June 20, 1988, issue of *U.S. News & World Report* contained an editorial by him under the title "Beware of Charisma."

He writes: "Our politics, unlike that of France, Spain and Italy, has been less a search for the political hero than for the Representative Man who possesses common virtues to an uncommon degree. However prosaic, our leader is apt to be Dale Carnegie's man who wins friends and influences people: So we might describe Washington, Jackson, Lincoln, Theodore Roosevelt, FDR, Truman and Eisenhower.

"... But is there some common quality among those Representative Men who have been most successful as our leaders? I call it the need to be *authentic*—or as our dictionaries tell us, 'conforming to fact and therefore worthy of trust, reliance or belief.' While the charismatic has an uncanny outside source of strength, the authentic is strong because he is what he seems to be."

My client Rolfe will be just fine and so will any organization he manages. He's bypassed charisma and is putting his efforts where he needs to: on chipping away at a facade of his that obscures his authenticity. How do I know? Because the work he has brought me in to do with him and his executives is team effectiveness. This will be an empowering activity for both him and his people.

TAKE ACTION

1. Don't assume that the charismatic person you so admire is blessed with vision. Some of the most shallow people you meet are oozing with charisma.

2. Anybody who's committed to his or her involvements can be persuasive. Get involved in the here-and-now exercise of vision and you'll involve those around you. That's all the charisma you'll ever need.

—— 98 ——

BEING AN AUTHENTIC EXECUTIVE

I'd like to follow up with a further lesson from the editorial by Daniel Boorstin that I cited in the previous essay. Boorstin writes:

> The unanimous complaint about our presidential candidates is that they lack "charisma." People somehow yearn for another touch of the "Kennedy magic." They forget how short-lived it was and how much it now owes to the afterglow of martyrdom. They also forget that a historic achievement of our constitutional democracy was to free us from the bonds—and follies—of charisma. For millenniums, European peoples were victims of the divine right of kings. Even after that divinity was dissolved, charisma reappeared in the modern claims of a Duce, a Fuhrer and a party-anointed General Secretary.
>
> Few of the horrors of political life today cannot be traced back to the arrogance of someone who claimed or was credited with charisma.

Finally:

> The authentic is the man who somehow shows us that he is not trying to be something that he is not. He is credible. And he encourages us. For while we cannot and dare not all aim at charisma, we can all enjoy being ourselves, and so feel a warm affinity for the [authentic] leader by sharing his virtue.

Charisma Can't Stand Alone

I don't derive from Boorstin's words any thought that charisma is automatically bad. As a matter of fact, most of us—even discounting the afterglow of martyrdom—would still consider JFK charismatic. Likewise, FDR, one of our presidents he named as authentic, also strikes me as undeniably charismatic. As a young boy, I was captivated by his voice booming out of our family's Zenith radio console. We crowded around it in the living room, listening for hope during those World War II years when my older brother was fighting with the infantry somewhere in France and Germany. Hope is what we heard.

The same can be said for Ronald Reagan. He too combined charisma with authenticity. He left office after eight years as president with one of the highest popularity ratings ever. He had his Iran–Contra affair, as Kennedy had his Bay of Pigs, as Roosevelt drew immense fire for trying to pack the Supreme Court. All three survived their shortfalls in our hearts. FDR was elected four times. Had he lived, JFK would have been reelected. Had the law allowed, Ronald Reagan could have run and, I believe, won a third time, despite his age.

In a democracy, as Boorstin implies, such longevity cannot be sustained by charisma alone. While it can have its redeeming features, charisma must be combined with authenticity in a president, or we'll see through him for what he is—a depthless, vain, nonperformer or worse—and throw the rascal out.

Vision and Authenticity

Although charisma and vision can exist in the same person, they can easily, and usually do, exist apart. Many people who are what we call charismatic lack vision while many who lack such charisma may indeed exercise vision.

On the other hand, it seems unlikely that a person can exercise vision without at the same time being authentic. If vision is, as I've defined it, vigilance in the here and now that tells us how what we are now is a sign of what we're going to be in the there and then, there's no chance for its exercise by someone who doesn't know or won't be himself or herself. To put it another way, if I'm an executive who can't read or understand myself, how can I realistically perceive the events taking place in and around my company? How can I possibly set a course for the company (if I'm CEO) or the function or department I manage that is in the best interests of all concerned if I'm refusing to be who I am?

When Richard Nixon was banished from the White House, or when deposed CEO Sewell Avery was forcibly carried out of Montgomery Ward's offices by Federal marshals, what quality of vision do you think they'd been exercising that led them to that sorry state of affairs? This isn't to say that they earlier lacked vision or authenticity, but that as events unfolded, their moorings became wobbly and their actions turned erratic and self-destructive.

You can't stress too much, therefore, the impression of staying true to yourself. That's what helps keep the moorings firm. Nor can you overestimate the importance of seeking and applauding such authenticity in your boss. That's what helps keep our organizations integrated and moving in the right direction. The authenticity of the leader we respect, says Boorstin, is shown in those virtues we share. The sharing process is, of course, union, and it is with *that* leader we will encounter the exercise of vision.

TAKE ACTION

1. See charisma for what it is: a quality that may portend positive or dreadful circumstances. Look for more, both in yourself and in whom you may put your trust.

2. If someone close to you says, "You're not yourself," pay heed or things will get worse.

— 99 —

THE UNDERRATED ACHIEVER

I first learned about John Richman in 1977. He and I were among a handful of people interviewed for a multi-audio-cassette program. Our interviewer was Joe Cappo, now vice president and group publisher with Crain Communications. The cassette program was recorded as a companion to a college business text, *Management*, written by William F. Glueck and published by Holt, Rinehart and Winston.

At the time, Richman was senior vice president–administration of Kraft. While there were also executives on the tapes from such companies as Sears, Ford, and Kodak, I turned to Richman's interview first. I did so because I knew his large food company had recently undergone a massive reorganization that Richman was in charge of, and that Kraft had relocated its headquarters from New York to Chicago. These factors made him, for me, a man worth knowing.

I wrote him, then called. We made an appointment to meet at his office and have lunch. We got to know each other and he introduced me to key members of his staff. I've done some work for the company—not a lot—but we've made a point of staying in touch.

Master of Ambiguity

John Richman is a Harvard-trained lawyer. Perhaps he learned how to negotiate early in the game. I don't know. I do know this: There's nobody better anywhere for calmly holding the fort with his team amid large-scale changes and the ambiguity that accompanies them.

He's a bit shy, actually, and slightly ill at ease when meeting strangers. But he's confident of his ideas, has a will of iron, is phenomenally perceptive, combines the big picture with attention to detail, is able in the art of diplomacy, is known for human decency, and is a voracious reader of books—not escape novels but real books. The man knows things.

In the mid-70s, when Kraft CEO Bill Beers saw the need for this too-set-in-its-ways company to undergo change, he tapped John Richman to carry it out. Richman directed the task force that managed the Kraft reorganization, and he did it without the aid of consultants. That reorganization was an important link in the evolution of the company that continues to this day.

Richman has always been underrated by outsiders. When Beers retired and named him his successor, Wall Street and the press were shocked. They thought Kraft's top management ranks offered up better candidates.

Soon thereafter, Richman sought a merger partner and entered negotiations with Dart Industries of Los Angeles. The pundits and analysts predicted the charismatic Justin Dart, Dart's CEO and member of Ronald Reagan's "Kitchen Cabinet," would eat Richman alive. Moreover, the highly profitable Dart group of companies would make Kraft—with its flat margins—look sick. Richman emerged from those negotiations as CEO of Dart & Kraft, Inc. Justin Dart was chairman. Warren Batts, whom Richman had recruited from Mead Corporation, was named president. The new company was headquartered in Chicago, not Los Angeles.

A Rodney Dangerfield?

John Richman would probably laugh at my belief that his merger with Dart was meant to wake up the colossus of Kraft—to continue the evolution of this sleepy giant that he nurtured with his reorganization. Whether or not that was the strategy, that's what happened. Kraft people were indeed embarrassed that smaller Dart's profits exceeded theirs, and they got moving. Meanwhile, business reporters I knew routinely told me that when they visited Dart & Kraft to interview Richman and Batts on the prospects of the company, they came away thinking the wrong guy was CEO.

In 1982, Richman and Batts brought in the exceedingly capable Mike Miles to run Kraft and speed up its recovery. This he has done. Then in 1986, Batts and Richman announced the splitting of the company into its original parts. The part that was Dart became a separate public company called Premark with Batts as CEO. Kraft stayed Kraft with Richman as CEO.

Late in 1988, Philip Morris, which three years earlier had added monolithic General Foods to its stable, now did the same with Kraft. "Oh-oh," went the pundits and investment bankers. "There goes John Richman." Poor, quiet, underrated John.

Then Philip Morris announced in early 1989 that this huge food business they had assembled would be headquartered in Chicago and called Kraft General Foods Group. The 61-year-old Richman was named CEO "for the next year or so" until Mike Miles completed the consolidation.

And then there was John Richman in a full-page color photo in a recent *New York Times Magazine* article on this megamerger.

Now Philip Morris's vice chairman, he sat well apart from chairman and CEO Hamish Maxwell on the latter's long sofa in his sumptuous Park Avenue office. In front of Richman on the coffee table was a platter of cookies. He was smiling and reaching for one.

——————————— *TAKE ACTION* ———————————

1. See the lesson in this story. John Richman's abilities escape the popular eye. He is a man of vision and his accomplishments show that dramatic action need not accompany such vision. He is a man of authenticity.

2. John Richman couldn't save Kraft from a Croesus-rich suitor. Yet Kraft has emerged as the jewel in the Philip Morris crown. See how a quiet, steady hand makes the most of a bad situation. See what a difference that makes in favor of quality team effort.

Note: On September 28, 1989, Kraft General Foods announced that Mike Miles, president, would become chairman and chief executive effective immediately. This announcement came on the eve of the first anniversary of the megamerger. For his part, John Richman will join the prestigious New York City law firm of Wachtell, Lipton, Rosen & Katz. I'm eager to see what he does for an encore. At 62, he's got a lot of steam left.

—— **100** ——

ALTERNATIVES TO CHARISMA

Many of us have long been suspicious of charismatic people. It isn't that we don't see their value. And it's not that we haven't had our favorites among them along the way. For example, who could deny the demonstration of power and legitimacy wrought among a dispirited people by Martin Luther King, Jr.'s proclaiming, "I have a dream!" Or FDR's stiffening America's spine by claiming, "We have nothing to fear but fear itself."

Yet for every Martin Luther King, Jr., religion belches out more Jimmy Swaggarts. Instead of an FDR in a time of crisis, nations large and small produce Hitlers, Amins, and Noriegas.

Charisma is our elixir. We swallow it as a cure-all for what ails us. Nowhere is this more apparent than in our companies. It shows in the way we embellish with language. We say we want leaders for our corporations, not mere managers. The word "leaders" in this case is spoken with lilting voice and bright eyes, conveying that these are especially winsome creatures with endowments not quite of this world. A simplistic slogan has taken hold: "Managers do things right, but leaders do the right things." This is all nonsense. Anyone effective in work learns to do both, and do them at the right time to boot. A rich mixture of judgment and timing contributes more to effective leadership than does a captivating, swashbuckling presence.

When it comes to enhancing their leadership qualities, executives have better places than charisma to direct their attention and yearnings. I suggest three alternatives.

Managing Values

First of all, underscoring thoughts presented in chapter XI, they will be better leaders by giving their energies to the evaluation and management of corporate values.

When executives behold the corporation as the social institution it is—an interpersonal network committed to some mission in the service of customers, employees, shareholders, and publics—it's not surprising they think the management of values may be the ultimate description of their jobs. Some have become spokespersons on this point, while others, not as vocal, have just as energetically put such conviction into play in their companies.

Perhaps the most authentic and impressive model of doing both over the past decade is James Burke, the recently retired, uncharismatic CEO of Johnson & Johnson. Burke, you'll recall, received numerous kudos for managing J&J's response to the Tylenol poisonings. Yet as deserving of high praise as his actions were, that's not what was most remarkable about him.

Rather, he is to be emulated by peers and all ranks of executives who now follow for the way he involved himself in the day-by-day, year-by-year, layer-by-layer recognizing, evaluating, prioritizing, articulating, and infusing of J&J's moral values.

A gimlet-eyed friend of mine who worked with Burke talks about him this way: "What's typical today is for the CEO to send out a staff-drafted two-paragraph ethics statement to the managers. The managers are asked to read and sign it. They do this perfunctorily, and that's it.

"A guy like Burke knew that was ridiculous, that it's not enough, that there's no reinforcement without the CEO's involvement. By spending the time that he did on values, Burke signaled their importance to his people. He put action behind his words. There is no way that anyone who works as a manager in a company where the CEO takes the time on values that Burke did could ignore how important those values are."

This people-sensitive, customer-responsive, investment-spending, innovation-inducing, long-range-thinking CEO made us forget about charisma while giving ethics and values a good name! This wouldn't have been so if the J&J numbers weren't impressive. The fact is they are, and Burke claims that companies with credos they *follow* generate superior financial performance consistently.

Vision and Collaboration

A growing leader's second alternative to charisma is the exercise of vision. Ironically, there is a need to distinguish vision from charisma itself. As I pointed out in essay 97, this is because popular business thought erroneously rolls up charisma and vision into a tight little ball. A common notion is that vision is the exclusive province of a charismatic, clairvoyant corporate leader. Vision is routinely taken to mean gazing at a crystal ball rather than understanding where a corporation finds itself at present and where it's headed.

In its simplicity, a Chinese proverb shows us that the latter option is the wiser course and is vision in action. Consider this little gem: "Unless we change our direction, we are likely to end up where we are headed." Despite low scores on the "Mr. or Ms. Excitement" test, the executive able to take this earthy wisdom to heart—to develop a sense of the corporation's purpose and trajectory—will be a leader of distinction.

All effective leaders labor with their associates to gain an understanding of place and direction. That's a special seeing we are correct in calling vision, and requires that they be persons with a moral compass and the courage of their convictions. Leaders such as Burke, who win our lasting admiration and work to ensure our futures, are the courageous ones poised to blow the bugle out in front of some needed initiative. Or to blow the whistle to stop us dead in our tracks when they envision that we're misguided. The truth for them is that a desirable faraway tomorrow depends on the quality of decisions they make today.

A superior leader's third alternative to charisma is collaboration. He or she is committed to collaboration, knowing firsthand that it produces management team effectiveness and assures improved corporate performance. It does so by re-enlivening and tapping into the souls and minds of a company's executives who have gone flat because they've lost contact with their authenticity. Now, they see themselves anew as valued contributors. Collaboration is the way to generate the best ideas and options for running a business. The times demand it. Corporations that won't think team won't make it. We need every idea we can get.

The spirit of complex organizational life these days is collaborative. In our finest firms, much gets done daily without dazzle or hype by teams of people, people committed to their involvements, all pulling together. Words like "we" and "our" replace "I" and "my." The team—not the leader—becomes the star, while the latter serves primarily as the articulator and sponsor of the vision that emerges out of the team's collaboration. Several heads are better than one. If we didn't believe this before, we surely do now.

What better explanation than such team involvement can account for the achievements of a J&J and the rock-solid, determined ascendancy of a James Burke, who on the face of it might even be called colorless? The technology of the team is not in the typical executive's repertoire. But that technology, as explained in this book's introduction, isn't complicated and can be learned with practice. Indeed, it *must* be learned. There's no more appropriate quest than such team involvement for executives eager to be part of the solution rather than part of the problem. This, after all, is the prize of effective leadership.

─────────────── *TAKE ACTION* ───────────────

1. Stop worrying about whether you're "Mr. or Ms. Excitement." Rather, immerse yourself in what you believe in without apologies. You'll be amazed at how inspiring you'll be to your cause.

2. Don't concern yourself with decisions that have to be made on some far-distant tomorrow. Rather, give your best thoughts and authentic commitment to decisions you'll make *today* that will affect that far-distant tomorrow.

FAST TAKES

on

Visioning

- Vision depends on information. Information is data with a brain. Such information comes of age only in a team—which is a unit of five to nine people.

- The team is great. Teams interlinked by an explicit purpose are greater still.

- Vision is an understanding of where we are and where we're headed.

- Some of the most shallow people you meet are oozing with charisma. Charisma is no guarantor of vision.

- It's unlikely you can exercise vision without being authentic.

- Vision is a here-and-now challenge. A desirable, far-distant tomorrow depends on the quality of decisions we make today.

- Corporations that won't think team won't make it. We need every idea we can get.

- The team—not the leader—is the star. The latter serves primarily as the articulator and sponsor of the vision that emerges out of the team's collaboration in authenticity.

A Closing Word

and Recommended Reading

By way of a broad introduction and 100 short essays, you have been asked to give expression to your authenticity by (1) opening up to your prospective teammates, (2) reaching to new heights of performance, (3) maturing by virtue of increased self-understanding and commitment so that in turn (4) you and your teammates can be known for delivering the goods to your rightful receivers.

This all boils down to a quickened, new way of work. As with learning any new skills, we're clumsy at first and not at all sure of ourselves. But the key is practice by carrying out the action steps at the end of each essay. In fact, without such action steps, you can't meet the standards of the effective team style described in the introduction. By consciously giving hard thought to what you have to do to improve yourself as a team member—and then practicing what you think—you begin to come of age and get your legs.

Your confidence grows as you see the superior ideas that empowered teamwork throws off, the fresh spirit it generates in people, and the depth you'll sense in yourself and your teammates as you

338

learn to be direct and authentic in your collaborations. Check out your current and future team efforts by reviewing the Cox Team-Achievement Inventory in appendix D.

Keep this book around. Read and reread it. It should serve you well over time. One chapter or another may mean more to you later, when it parallels some experience of yours, than it does now. In addition, the message of these "fast-take" essays, because of their spare prose, may seem at times a bit obscure. A second reading may bring them home to you in a different light.

Finally, if the framework of team effectiveness as presented in the introduction and the dynamics of collaboration without consensus as shown in the rest of the book have prompted you to do further study, and I hope such is the case, let me recommend the following list to you. I do so with only the proviso on consensus seeking that I noted in "Disclaimers and Pronouncements."

Cox, Allan. *Inside Corporate America*. New York: St. Martin's Press, 1986.

Daniels, William R. *Group Power I*. San Diego: University Associates, 1986.

_____. *Group Power II*. San Diego: University Associates, 1990.

Francis, Dave, and Don Young. *Improving Work Groups*. San Diego: University Associates, 1979.

Hastings, Colin, Peter Bixby, and Rani Chaudhry-Lawton. *The Superteam Solution*. San Diego: University Associates, 1987.

Heirs, Ben. *The Decision Thinker*. New York: Dodd, Mead, 1986.

Schein, Edgar H. *Process Consultation*. Reading, Mass.: Addison-Wesley, 1969.

Schaeffer, Ruth G. *Building Global Teamwork for Growth and Survival*. New York: The Conference Board/Research Bulletin #228, 1989.

Starcevich, Matt M., and Steven J. Stowell. *The Coach*. Salt Lake City: The Center for Management and Organizational Effectiveness, 1987.

APPENDIX A

Team Style Questionnaire and Profile

Please mark one answer for each question.

Chapter I
BEING ACCESSIBLE: INVESTING IN OTHERS

1. Do you praise/thank your subordinates for their daily accomplishments?
    Usually/Often _____   Sometimes/Seldom _____

2. Are your smiles genuine?
    Usually/Often _____   Sometimes/Seldom _____

3. Do you enjoy going to lunch with your associates?
    Usually/Often _____   Sometimes/Seldom _____

4. Are you learning to be a coach?
    Usually/Often _____   Sometimes/Seldom _____

340

5. Do you save up criticisms of your subordinates' performance until a formal review?
Usually/Often _____ Sometimes/Seldom _____

Chapter II
LISTENING: MORE THAN BEING A BLOTTER

6. Do you look beyond the literal content of a teammate's comments to you—to their timing, location, and manner?
Usually/Often _____ Sometimes/Seldom _____

7. Do you risk speaking your opinions to an associate even though you don't know the associate's thoughts on the matter under discussion?
Usually/Often _____ Sometimes/Seldom _____

8. Do you give thought to converting your questions to statements to clarify your position?
Usually/Often _____ Sometimes/Seldom _____

9. Do you make yourself available for discussion with subordinates and peers?
Usually/Often _____ Sometimes/Seldom _____

10. Are you afraid to admit you don't understand something that your discussion partner is saying?
Usually/Often _____ Sometimes/Seldom _____

Chapter III
ENCOURAGING: THE ART OF EMPOWERMENT

11. Do you show enthusiasm over the long pull for a teammate's display of courage through your voice, facial expression, and gestures?
Usually/Often _____ Sometimes/Seldom _____

12. Do you avoid imposing on your subordinates your ideas of how a job should be done?
Usually/Often _____ Sometimes/Seldom _____

13. Do you encourage your boss?
Usually/Often _____ Sometimes/Seldom _____

14. Do you lobby for top management team effectiveness in your organization?
Usually/Often _____ Sometimes/Seldom _____

15. Do you encourage yourself to reclaim some neglected strength?
Usually/Often _____ Sometimes/Seldom _____

Chapter IV
BEING AFFIRMATIVE: THE DISCOVERY OF OPTIONS

16. Do you engage your teammates' strengths rather than focus on their limitations?
Usually/Often _____ Sometimes/Seldom _____

17. Do you avoid acknowledging discouragement when it comes?
Usually/Often _____ Sometimes/Seldom _____

18. Do you set unrealistic goals for yourself?
Usually/Often _____ Sometimes/Seldom _____

19. Do you focus your attention on completing your tasks to the exclusion of enjoying performing them?
Usually/Often _____ Sometimes/Seldom _____

20. Do you celebrate your accomplishments?
Usually/Often _____ Sometimes/Seldom _____

Chapter V
SHARING: YOUR TIME, WHO YOU ARE, AND WHAT YOU KNOW

21. Do you view your work with your teammates and all associates as what you owe of *yourself* to a community of people?
Usually/Often _____ Sometimes/Seldom _____

22. Do you resent having to attend team meetings called by your boss?
Usually/Often _____ Sometimes/Seldom _____

23. Do you resent having to call team meetings?
Usually/Often _____ Sometimes/Seldom _____

24. Do you withhold information useful to your teammates that will be of competitive advantage to your career?
Usually/Often _____ Sometimes/Seldom _____

25. Do you make sure you're heard on subjects you have strong opinions about?
Usually/Often _____ Sometimes/Seldom _____

Chapter VI
BEING VULNERABLE: AN UNDERRATED STRENGTH

26. Does apologizing to a teammate you've wronged in some way come easily to you?
Usually/Often _____ Sometimes/Seldom _____

27. Do you think you have a firm grasp of which associates in your company should *not* be trusted with your candid thoughts, knowledge of your limitations, and plans for new initiatives?
Usually/Often _____ Sometimes/Seldom _____

28. Are you intimidated by fear of being labeled naive, immature, or idealistic when attempting something with your team that hasn't been tried before?
Usually/Often _____ Sometimes/Seldom _____

29. Are you curious? Do you like to play with ideas?
Usually/Often _____ Sometimes/Seldom _____

Chapter VII
BEING DISCREET: SPEAKING YOUR MIND
WITHOUT LOOSE TALK

30. Are you willing to create a little tension on your team?
Usually/Often _____ Sometimes/Seldom _____

31. Do you speak your mind without timidity to your bosses when corporate action is being considered in an area you care about and in which you have a stake?
    Usually/Often _____ Sometimes/Seldom _____

32. Do you speak your opinions prematurely, long before actual decisions are made, in areas you care about deeply?
    Usually/Often _____ Sometimes/Seldom _____

33. Do you glamorize your role's impact on the total functioning of your corporation?
    Usually/Often _____ Sometimes/Seldom _____

34. Do you pick your battles carefully?
    Usually/Often _____ Sometimes/Seldom _____

Chapter VIII
NURTURING YOURSELF AND OTHERS: MOTHER'S MILK FOR YOUR COMPANY

35. Do you give expression to the child in yourself?
    Usually/Often _____ Sometimes/Seldom _____

36. Do you work actively to foster a feeling of belonging among your subordinates?
    Usually/Often _____ Sometimes/Seldom _____

37. Do you believe your subordinates think of you as a things person rather than a people person?
    Usually/Often _____ Sometimes/Seldom _____

38. Do you actively urge your high-potential subordinates to broaden themselves by leaving your department and moving into another?
    Usually/Often _____ Sometimes/Seldom _____

39. Do you demand growth and contribution from your subordinates to the limits of their abilities?
    Usually/Often _____ Sometimes/Seldom _____

Chapter IX
MAKING DECISIONS:
SITTING AT THE HEAD OF THE TABLE

40. Do you use your decision making as a training and development opportunity for your subordinates? Do you meet with them to explain your reasoning and the trade-offs you faced in making decisions?
Usually/Often _____ Sometimes/Seldom _____

41. Do you put off making decisions because you fear being wrong?
Usually/Often _____ Sometimes/Seldom _____

42. Are you annoyed that your subordinates want decisions from you on their recommendations too quickly?
Usually/Often _____ Sometimes/Seldom _____

43. Have you rebounded quickly from your decisions that hindsight proved wrong?
Usually/Often _____ Sometimes/Seldom _____

44. Do you inflate the importance of your decisions?
Usually/Often _____ Sometimes/Seldom _____

45. Have the big decisions you've made added to your self-esteem?
Usually/Often _____ Sometimes/Seldom _____

Chapter X
RECLAIMING UNIQUE STRENGTHS:
THERE FOR THE TAKING

46. Do you rely too much on your "commodity" or "me-too" strengths for your day-to-day performance?
Usually/Often _____ Sometimes/Seldom _____

47. Do you face your job with a task-force mentality?
Usually/Often _____ Sometimes/Seldom _____

48. Do you plan too much, act too little?
Usually/Often _____ Sometimes/Seldom _____

49. Do you listen to your inner voice to learn what you care about down deep?
Usually/Often _____ Sometimes/Seldom _____

50. Does the urging from your teammates to "do it now!" send chills up and down your spine?
Usually/Often _____ Sometimes/Seldom _____

Chapter XI
EXPLORING VALUES: ORGANIZATIONAL SAVVY AND REAPING THE HUMAN HARVEST

51. Do you look for signs in your corporation to see what form and direction it will take in the future?
Usually/Often _____ Sometimes/Seldom _____

52. Are you and your teammates students of organizations?
Usually/Often _____ Sometimes/Seldom _____

53. Do you think carefully about the "little agenda" that governs your company? Do you support what's best about it?
Usually/Often _____ Sometimes/Seldom _____

54. Do you feel bogged down by the "bureaucracy" in your company?
Usually/Often _____ Sometimes/Seldom _____

55. Do you disagree that your corporation is an appropriate place for the practice of altruism?
Usually/Often _____ Sometimes/Seldom _____

56. Do you place high value on our nation's value shift to teamwork?
Usually/Often _____ Sometimes/Seldom _____

57. Do you believe teamwork is unnatural?
Usually/Often _____ Sometimes/Seldom _____

58. Are you part of a corporate culture that supports team values?
Usually/Often _____ Sometimes/Seldom _____

Chapter XII
SETTING GOALS AND TASKS:
WHAT TO DO AND HOW TO DO IT

59. Do your goals give birth to the will to win?
Usually/Often _____ Sometimes/Seldom _____

60. Do your goals give added meaning to the current time and place?
Usually/Often _____ Sometimes/Seldom _____

61. Do you eliminate "chores" on the job in favor of tasks that support your goals?
Usually/Often _____ Sometimes/Seldom _____

62. Are you a person who takes on tasks nobody else wants?
Usually/Often _____ Sometimes/Seldom _____

63. Do you succeed in conveying concern for details to your subordinates?
Usually/Often _____ Sometimes/Seldom _____

Chapter XIII
BEING TENACIOUS: THE HIGH-OCTANE TEST

64. Are you inclined to feel sorry for yourself?
Usually/Often _____ Sometimes/Seldom _____

65. Do you get bored easily?
Usually/Often _____ Sometimes/Seldom _____

66. Will you risk taking a pounding?
Usually/Often _____ Sometimes/Seldom _____

67. Are you a hare rather than a tortoise?
Usually/Often _____ Sometimes/Seldom _____

68. Do you avoid constructive drudgery in your life and work?
Usually/Often _____ Sometimes/Seldom _____

Chapter XIV
BEING OF GOOD HUMOR: A VERY SERIOUS SUBJECT

69. Do you feel glad more than mad, sad, or afraid?
Usually/Often _____ Sometimes/Seldom _____

70. Do you impose idealized roles on yourself that you have great difficulty living up to?
Usually/Often _____ Sometimes/Seldom _____

71. Do you take humor seriously?
Usually/Often _____ Sometimes/Seldom _____

72. Do you give thought to a wisdom greater than your own?
Usually/Often _____ Sometimes/Seldom _____

Chapter XV
BEING LUCKY: THE COURTSHIP OF DAME FORTUNE

73. Are you a "yes, but" executive?
Usually/Often _____ Sometimes/Seldom _____

74. Do you share an attitude of expectancy with your team?
Usually/Often _____ Sometimes/Seldom _____

75. Do people like to help you out?
Usually/Often _____ Sometimes/Seldom _____

76. Do you reject the notion of can't?
Usually/Often _____ Sometimes/Seldom _____

77. Do you support your teammates with your vitality?
Usually/Often _____ Sometimes/Seldom _____

Chapter XVI
PRACTICING QUALITY:
THE TRUST OTHERS HOLD IN YOU

78. Do you visualize the persons you serve within your corporation as customers to be pleased?
Usually/Often _____ Sometimes/Seldom _____

79. Do you serve systems more than people?
Usually/Often _____ Sometimes/Seldom _____

80. Are you late to meetings and appointments?
Usually/Often _____ Sometimes/Seldom _____

81. Do you count commitments and deadlines you have agreed to as a trust?

Usually/Often _____ Sometimes/Seldom _____

Chapter XVII
BEING PERCEPTIVE: PEERING BEHIND THE FACADE

82. Do you give thought to the ways your corporation's forms are not compatible with its functions?

Usually/Often _____ Sometimes/Seldom _____

83. Do you rely on cause-and-effect thinking on complex issues—believe that the sum of the parts equals the whole?

Usually/Often _____ Sometimes/Seldom _____

84. Do you rely on the parts anticipate the whole thinking on complex issues?

Usually/Often _____ Sometimes/Seldom _____

85. In group discussions with your subordinates, do you actively attempt to anticipate the whole for the team you lead?

Usually/Often _____ Sometimes/Seldom _____

86. Whether team leader or team member, do you allow dissonance in your department by not squarely facing its trade-offs?

Usually/Often _____ Sometimes/Seldom _____

Chapter XVIII
REFINING YOUR GIFTS: NO PAIN, NO GAIN

87. Do you expect the world to be your cheerleader?

Usually/Often _____ Sometimes/Seldom _____

88. Do you find failure devastating? Does failure knock you down and keep you down?

Usually/Often _____ Sometimes/Seldom _____

89. Do you work long hours in areas that encompass your desires?

Usually/Often _____ Sometimes/Seldom _____

90. Do you use your gifts well to reorder your team's expectations—
to make an impact you're proud of?
Usually/Often _____ Sometimes/Seldom _____

Chapter XIX
BEING A FACILITATOR: HELPING OTHERS ACT ON THEIR UNIQUE STRENGTHS AND REFINE THEIR GIFTS

91. Do your associates think of you as a team contributor?
Usually/Often _____ Sometimes/Seldom _____

92. Do you suffer from the "not invented here" syndrome?
Usually/Often _____ Sometimes/Seldom _____

93. Do you hog credit that should go to subordinates and peers?
Usually/Often _____ Sometimes/Seldom _____

94. Are you committed to encouraging your teammates to act on
their unique strengths even when it involves resolving conflict?
Usually/Often _____ Sometimes/Seldom _____

95. Do you pledge your allegiance to the team?
Usually/Often _____ Sometimes/Seldom _____

Chapter XX
VISIONING: A CHINESE PROVERB SAYS IT ALL

96. Do you see your team as an agent of alignment?
Usually/Often _____ Sometimes/Seldom _____

97. Do you associate vision with charismatic people?
Usually/Often _____ Sometimes/Seldom _____

98. Do you associate vision with authentic people?
Usually/Often _____ Sometimes/Seldom _____

99. Do you associate vision with dramatic action?
Usually/Often _____ Sometimes/Seldom _____

100. Does your performance display a mixture of good judgment and
good timing?
Usually/Often _____ Sometimes/Seldom _____

YOUR TEAM-STYLE PROFILE

To determine your team-style profile, check your earlier answers
against the correct ones listed below. Circle each answer here that
corresponds with yours. Then count all your circled answers, and
mark your total team-style profile in the blank provided.

Chapter I—BEING ACCESSIBLE: INVESTING IN OTHERS 3
1. U/O   2. U/O   3. U/O   4. U/O   5. S/S

Chapter II—VISIONING: MORE THAN BEING A BLOTTER
6. U/O   7. U/O   8. U/O   9. U/O   10. S/S   3

Chapter III—ENCOURAGING: THE ART OF
EMPOWERMENT
11. U/O   12. U/O   13. U/O   14. U/O   15. U/O   3

Chapter IV—BEING AFFIRMATIVE: THE DISCOVERY OF
OPTIONS
16. U/O   17. S/S   18. S/S   19. S/S   20. U/O   2

Chapter V—SHARING: YOUR TIME, WHO YOU ARE, AND
WHAT YOU KNOW
21. U/O   22. S/S   23. S/S   24. S/S   25. U/O

Chapter VI—BEING VULNERABLE: AN UNDERRATED
STRENGTH
26. U/O   27. U/O   28. S/S   29. U/O   4

Chapter VII—BEING DISCREET: SPEAKING YOUR MIND
WITHOUT LOOSE TALK
30. U/O   31. U/O   32. S/S   33. S/S   34. U/O   1

Chapter VIII—NURTURING YOURSELF AND OTHERS: MOTHER'S MILK FOR YOUR COMPANY
35. U/O   36. U/O   37. S/S   38. U/O   39. U/O

Chapter IX—MAKING DECISIONS: SITTING AT THE HEAD OF THE TABLE
40. U/O   41. S/S   42. U/O   43. U/O   44. S/S   45. U/O

Chapter X—RECLAIMING UNIQUE STRENGTHS: THERE FOR THE TAKING
46. S/S   47. U/O   48. S/S   49. U/O   50. S/S

Chapter XI—EXPLORING VALUES: ORGANIZATIONAL SAVVY AND REAPING THE HUMAN HARVEST
51. U/O   52. U/O   53. U/O   54. S/S   55. S/S
56. U/O   57. S/S   58. U/O

Chapter XII—SETTING GOALD AND TASKS: WHAT TO DO AND HOW TO DO IT
59. U/O   60. U/O   61. U/O   62. U/O   63. U/O

Chapter XIII—BEING TENACIOUS: THE HIGH-OCTANE TEST
64. S/S   65. S/S   66. U/O   67. S/S   68. S/S

Chapter XIV—BEING OF GOOD HUMOR: A VERY SERIOUS SUBJECT
69. U/O   70. S/S   71. U/O   72. U/O

Chapter XV—BEING LUCKY: THE COURTSHIP OF DAME FORTUNE
73. S/S   74. U/O   75. U/O   76. U/O   77. U/O

Chapter XVI—PRACTICING QUALITY: THE TRUST OTHERS HOLD IN YOU
78. U/O   79. S/S   80. S/S   81. U/O

Chapter XVII—BEING PERCEPTIVE: PEERING BEHIND THE
   FACADE
82. U/O   83. S/S   84. U/O   85. U/O   86. S/S

Chapter XVIII—REFINING YOUR GIFTS: NO PAIN, NO
   GAIN
87. S/S   88. S/S   89. U/O   90. U/O

Chapter XIX—BEING A FACILITATOR: HELPING OTHERS
ACT ON THEIR UNIQUE STRENGTHS AND REFINE THE
GIFTS
91. U/O   92. S/S   93. S/S   94. U/O   95. U/O

Chapter XX—VISIONING: A CHINESE PROVERB SAYS IT
   ALL
96. U/O   97. S/S   98. U/O   99. S/S   100. U/O

Your Team-Style Profile:_____

Superior	92–100
Good	84–91
Satisfactory	68–83
Fair	56–67
Poor	0–55

APPENDIX B

Memo to the CEO: The Power of Team

The chief financial officer of a large and respected corporation recently told me, "I haven't had a performance appraisal in over 20 years."

He went on to clarify that he had been evaluated on his numbers routinely, but as far as his actions and attitudes—his actual behavior on the job—were concerned, he had been left on his own.

I can already hear a few chuckles from some readers. "My God, if this guy's been moved through the chairs over a 20-year period and reached the point where he's been made CFO and elected to the board, how much feedback does he need?"

This CFO and his fellow executives, including the CEO, are embarking on a rigorous feedback discipline that measures their actions and attitudes on the job. This discipline is one facet of a corporate-wide rebirth. It's working: The numbers are up. The fact that top management are spending time and effort on developing themselves is sending the message throughout the company that what matters are actions and attitudes in support of carefully considered, clearly articulated values.

Think Team

One of these key values is the team. The CFO doesn't know how to lead a team. He suspected this, but nobody ever told him—until his boss, peers, and subordinates gave him feedback through questionnaires and other evaluation instruments.

The rigors through which this giant corporation is willing to put itself is an indication that we are in the midst of an organizational wave in worldwide business. Moreover, the team has become the organizational atom. Pure and simple, corporations that won't think team won't make it.

We have been beaten by the Japanese because they have made management-by-teamwork second nature. Yet team building is rightfully viewed by many CEOs as ineffective, because it has often been applied as a new patchwork to old clothing. True to the biblical parable, because it's not woven throughout the entire fabric of an organization, it tears loose and doesn't live up to expectations.

Team building has been practiced in most cases as a special activity and carried out by second- and third-level human resources professionals or consultants. These functionaries are brought in to "do" team building as a freestanding project. When I suggested it to the management committee of one company, its members said, "We have more in mind than that; we did that three years ago. We're looking to do something else."

What these executives didn't understand is that team building is unending. They saw it as an activity that is an end in and of itself rather than a way of managing their entire business. But by using the right kind of processes and guidelines, the development and implementation of their strategic plan could become a magnificent example of team management in action.

So as not to lose the power of the team, we should convert our language from team building to team management to adjust our perspective, and then make two demands on team management.

The first is that it do real work. The second is that it be corporate-wide.

The Organizational Wave

My book *Inside Corporate America* is a study of 13 major corporations from the three segments of business: consumer, service, and industrial. The book is based on a 400-item questionnaire completed by 1,086 managers in the 115 headquarters, subsidiaries, and divisions of these corporations. This group is made up of 515 top and 571 middle-management executives.

One finding was disturbing. The respondents were asked to note the impact on their career success in their companies of being a student of organizations. Two percent of the top executives rated the impact as "very positive." Twenty-six percent rated it as "somewhat positive." The remainder spread their responses between "neutral," "somewhat negative," and "very negative." This is worthy of our attention.

The earliest emphasis in American business was on manufacturing and lasted for almost a century. Then the emphasis was on sales (for a shorter time); then marketing for yet a shorter time. Next came finance, which lasted about 15 years, ending around 1980.

Now we've entered a period that's global, not merely American, and one in which no solitary discipline or swing of the pendulum will serve us well. Some say we're going back to basics on manufacturing, and that's true. But sales and marketing also lay claim to our current rhetoric with the notion of staying in touch with customers. And with the emphasis on shareholder value in running our businesses, finance is as important as ever.

We can call this period the organizational wave and picture it as a subterranean volcano over which business and corporate life teeter. We can't see it, but we sway with its rumblings while signs of internal eruption are everywhere.

Some of these eruptions are structural. The merger, acquisition, and LBO phenomenon is a case in point. This is likely to increase; the stock market may become the greatest futures game of all, since any corporation in the world that draws attention to itself—for reasons good or bad—can have its assets valued and put in play over-night. CEOs must balance the long and short term skillfully and acknowledge that the measure of their worth is shareholder value over time.

Some of the eruptions are behavioral. Loyalty is gone; free agency in professional sports is a good example of talent for hire. But it didn't start in sports: It started in business in the 1940s with the headhunter and has extended to all organizational spheres, including university faculties and hospital staffs. Lifetime employment in the Japanese corporations is already eroding and likely to be increasingly influenced by our style. In this country, Jack Akers presides while IBM lays off employees. Nonetheless, the surveys of Daniel Yankelovich and others show that people from the top to the bottom of the corporate hierarchy still need and want to belong. They covet being productive and being valued for their contribution. Authoritarianism no longer works. Participation is the rule.

We face countless variables, contradictions, and potential break-throughs, while only a fourth of our top executives think being a student of organizational life is important. This is a crisis, and not enough CEOs have grasped what Allen-Bradley president Tracy O'Rourke has: "The competitive environment and the social issues inside a company are changing more rapidly than ever, and management is going to have to stay up with that rate of change. That's causing us all to have to really dedicate ourselves to a productive business life of renewal, reeducating and constantly retraining our-selves. We've never had to do that before and it's going to be hard. You have to apply yourself and take time to do that. All of us convince ourselves that we don't have the time." (Mr. O'Rourke is now chairman and chief executive of Varian Associates, Inc.)

The Organizational Atom

We must mobilize an all-out effort to teach our executives management by teamwork. The team is the organizational atom—the focus of power—and if the CEO is going to take the responsibility for sensitizing the organization to its own resourcefulness, then he or she must start there. What is called a team most often isn't. The "management team" of most companies is usually a case of mistaken identity. Meetings aren't the team either, though a team can't exist without meetings. In its June 21, 1988, issue, the *Wall Street Journal* good-naturedly pointed out the banal quality of most meetings. The article, titled "A Survival Guide to the Office Meeting," stated that executives spend an average of 17 hours a week in meetings and another six in preparation for them.

Given the colossal waste of time and corporate resources, we would be smart to convert this waste to an investment in making meetings work. For example, the CEO of a well-known automotive manufacturer hosts a monthly dinner meeting of his direct reports. The meeting is meant to be informal, but he's made clear he also expects it to be an occasion when issues and matters of concern to the business are brought up by attendees. These meetings have degenerated into small-talk socializing. The CEO complains that when he asks for substantive business issues to be raised, he's met with perfunctory comments, shallow questions, or just plain silence. Frustrated, he threatened the group at a recent meeting by saying that whoever didn't have something significant to offer at the meeting wouldn't be invited back to the next one. He'd keep shrinking the group, he said, until he ended up with someone he could talk to.

How to Harness the Team

If we want to see and feel the power of the team throughout our organizations, we're going to have to measure and reward team behavior. This is simple in concept but requires dedication from the CEO. The good news is that such an initiative is intensely gratifying and the best bet for increasing shareholder value over time.

Management by team is taking the design-oriented idea of quality in products and using it as a guiding light for ensuring the quality of our total management. Through a comprehensive, corporate-wide design of team management—and its measurement—a company can build in total quality performance. Effective team management has to be designed to meet two demands: First, to do real work, and second, to be corporate-wide. As Larry Perlman, president (now CEO as well) of Control Data, tells his people: "We are the competition." Gary Dillon, CEO of the highly successful $1 billion manufacturing business soon to be spun off by Household International, educates his people with a similar message: "We have found the edge and it is us." (This business was indeed spun off as three separate publicly held businesses in the spring of 1989. Dillon runs one of them—Schwitzer, Inc.)

As a CEO, you are best advised to undergo a team-effectiveness workshop. With the aid of a resource person skilled in team methods, you and your officers will be able to evaluate the merits of infusing team management throughout your company. With such a workshop behind you, you may well conclude you're a believer and have the determination to see this through. There are eight action steps you can take.

- *Appoint a task force that will lay the groundwork for the team effectiveness.* "Egad," you protest. "Not another task force. That will consign the project to oblivion right from the start. Just like a blue-ribbon panel in Washington."

  My reply is that it will fail only if you let it. Since the team is to do real work, think of the meaning of task force. It's a team with a real task. Complain all you like, but there's no other way. If you don't begin the effort with your own people (who know the organization best), then this already taxing challenge is doomed to fail for lack of the ideas you'll need. From where else, for example, could team-management measurements come that satisfy most participants?

- *Make the task force interdisciplinary and have it number between five and nine people.* A team is a small group in this range, and a team-management system will set about improving the performance of groups of this size throughout your company. Pick the executive who reports to you who has the best interpersonal skills and put him or her in charge of the task force. Inspire them with your conviction. Make them accountable for conceiving the guidelines for team effectiveness. Then leave and let them get to work. But stay on the case.

- *Draft (or revise) a corporate values statement that reflects the spiritual side of your organization.* (If these values emerge as contradictory to the mission of your strategic plan, you have even more work to do.) To do this, select a second interdisciplinary task force that you will head. Be sure that one member of the team-management task force also sits on this one. Your corporate values statement might include an item that reads something like this: "The manager's first job is to nurture the competence and self-esteem of his or her subordinates."

- *Develop and articulate behavior benchmarks that support team management.* It's one thing to have goals as an expression of your corporation's mission and strategy, but quite another to have "getting there" actions and attitudes that are specified and can be measured. Your company will want to develop its own benchmarks, but you probably can use some guidance on this as well from a number of organizations such as the Center for Creative Leadership in Greensboro, North Carolina, Development Dimensions in Pittsburgh, Pennsylvania, Forum Corporation in Boston, Massachusetts, University Associates in San Diego, California, or our firm.

- *Realize this is a large-scale indoctrination/teaching project, and your entire corporation is the classroom.* What is being taught is small group leadership techniques. The message sent to each manager by the boss is: "You are a team member in this group, but on the next level down you are a team leader. What you are learning and contributing here you must teach and apply there."

- *Keep the two demands of effective team management before you at all times.* First, focus team leadership teaching techniques on real issues to produce joint accomplishment. Second, make team management corporate-wide to achieve the critical mass necessary to bring about steady, lasting improvements in total corporate performance.

- *Reward your achievers.* The achiever's profile is made up of commitment to the team, risk, balance, and results. No values statement or team-management exhortations will be subscribed to or implemented with any verve unless your people are measured against specific behavior benchmarks and rewarded both financially and emotionally for making them part of their job objectives and delivering results.

The required actions and attitudes in support of the achiever's profile need to be made a central feature of your incentive pay and performance appraisal procedures.

• *Make sure your chief human resources officer is enthusiastic about what he or she is supposed to accomplish.* Lack of vitality in organizational thinking is underscored by many corporations placing weak people in charge of human resources. Fortunately, this is changing. Your human resources officer, if not the key point person in the administration of team effectiveness, will nonetheless be an essential player in making it happen. This person has to be proactive. (For more on the need for the human resources officer to be a person of vitality, see appendix C.)

When embarking on the establishment of corporate-wide team management, you're likely to have mixed emotions. Bound up with your anticipation of raising corporate performance a few notches, you may also encounter fears of misdirected effort, poor execution, and outright failure.

But the difference between winners and losers on the corporate playing field is the difference between managing through the team versus doing it poorly or not at all. This demands perseverance, because though the initial stages of team management—well executed—yield immediate benefits, the real payoff is more than a decade away. Remember the Chinese proverb: "A journey of a thousand miles begins with one step." Practice balancing the long and short term in the service of shareholder value, and you'll be a visionary who keeps your eye on today.

APPENDIX C

Memo to the VP–Human Resources: How To Maintain Maximum Impact

Here's a quick quiz for the VP–Human Resources. You'll notice it follows the format of the book and underscores some points made earlier. The emphasis here, however, is how those points pertain specifically to the person placed in charge of organization stewardship.

1. Do you see your role as that of a facilitator?
   Usually/Often _____ Sometimes/Seldom _____

2. Do you coach your company's executives to think "career" instead of "career path"?
   Usually/Often _____ Sometimes/Seldom _____

3. Do you see your associates as customers who are counting on you to deliver the goods?
   Usually/Often _____ Sometimes/Seldom _____

4. Do your views and opinions matter to your CEO?
   Usually/Often _____ Sometimes/Seldom _____

5. Do people confide in you, and do you keep such confidences as a trust?
Usually/Often ——— Sometimes/Seldom ———

6. Do you make yourself vulnerable by confiding in others?
Usually/Often ——— Sometimes/Seldom ———

7. Are you proactive? Are you an advocate? Do your initiatives generate enthusiasm among your associates?
Usually/Often ——— Sometimes/Seldom ———

8. Do you practice an unrelenting commitment to your own personal development as an executive?
Usually/Often ——— Sometimes/Seldom ———

9. Do you exercise vision as *understanding* rather than *clairvoyance*?
Usually/Often ——— Sometimes/Seldom ———

10. Are you committed—and do you prove it by your actions—to team management in your company?
Usually/Often ——— Sometimes/Seldom ———

The right answer to all these questions from this observer's point of view is "Usually/Often." If you answered all ten correctly, you're a superstar in the galaxy of human resource executives. If you missed one, you're still tops. Two wrong, you have some growing to do. Three wrong, you're not as value-added as you should be.

If you missed four or more, you don't understand your job. Let's review the quiz material.

Facilitator

Authoritarianism is a bygone mode. It's appealing but mistaken to think that all top executives should be General Pattons barking out orders. Charisma is overblown, and its value is often short-lived; some of today's most stupid and shallow executives ooze with charisma. On the other hand, we all know the perceptive Steady Eddies— and Edies—are the ones who carry the day, winning respect and a following over time.

To be an effective human resources executive, share yourself, your time, and your information. Encourage your associates to act on their unique strengths and refine their gifts. This attitude, that of a facilitator, serves as a powerful management model on which subordinates and superiors can base their own behavior.

Career

Effective human resources executives are teachers, adopting the entire corporation as a classroom. One of the most important lessons you can teach? It's imperative for people to think about careers, not career paths.

The next decade will test young employees. They may have to work harder and earn less in real terms than their predecessors. Teach these budding executives that performance, rather than advancement, will define the work force's best and brightest.

Your Customers

As an human resources executive, you seldom come in contact with your organization's ultimate customers. Nonetheless, you meet customers at every turn, and your commitment to customer satisfaction needs to be as strong as that of the manufacturing or marketing manager.

Your customer is whoever appears next to you (up, down, or across) on the management organization chart. If you don't satisfy him or her, you fail in your own marketplace.

Opinions That Count

When you meet with your management peers, do people pick lint from their clothes, check their nails, or stare out the window? Does the CEO call you in for frequent counsel when the company faces serious people, organizational, or business decisions? Does it matter that you come to work?

The name of the game isn't absolute power—no one has that—but the power to influence. You need to be able to deliver well-reasoned views at the proper time. To become an effective human resources executive, think hard about the strategic trade-offs the CEO faces. Put yourself in his or her shoes.

Trust

It is one thing to seek trust. It's another to extend it. If your views are respected, and if you wield influence, you will become a sought-after giver of advice on a wide variety of matters. When company executives confide in you, you must keep these confidences as an inviolable trust.

Vulnerability

It is one thing to extend trust. It's another to seek it. Strength sometimes flows from a discreet show of weakness. A fortress invites attack. Play the impenetrable city, and some Joshua will see to it that your walls come tumbling down.

We build linkages with others—and reduce the pressure we put on ourselves—by admitting that we don't have all the answers, that we blew it, that we need help. Seek balanced trust.

Proactive Advocacy

Impressive human resources executives discover and declare what they care about. They get behind an idea and take a stand. Projects get support not because they are always brilliant, but because the human resources will grab an idea and press to make it work.

Don't wait for the CEO to complain that top executives have become complacent. Rather, anticipate the problem and head it off with an executive development program that challenges people. Help top brass put excitement back into their jobs by helping them reclaim strengths they've allowed to go dormant.

Your Own Growth

Too many human resources executives fail to act proactively to develop *themselves*. Rightly concerned about the entire organization's growth, they neglect to ensure their own.

To remain a front-line contributor, you must chart your developmental objectives and eagerly stretch yourself. Otherwise, you'll become an unfortunate example of the Peter principle. Remember, people *drift*, more often than rise, to their level of incompetence.

Vision

By now you know I'm fond of a Chinese proverb that proclaims, "If we do not change our direction, we are likely to end up where we are headed." Organizational vision does not require clairvoyance. It requires an *understanding* of place and direction. To affect the business's long-range quality, you are called on as much as anyone to challenge management to answer two questions: "Where are we now?" and "Where are we headed?" Don't let the company seduce itself with some grand vision based on empty rhetoric or wishful thinking. Instead, help thinking managers forge collective insights about actions taken today that will guide the company to a desirable and realistic destination tomorrow.

Team Zeal

Today's galvanizing concept of corporate effectiveness pertains to teams. Earlier, I refered to the team as the organizational atom; the source of the organization's energy. Effective human resources executives strive with every fiber in their bodies to instill the idea (as presented in appendix B) that every team member on one level is a team leader at another. Therefore, make every meeting a training laboratory that helps people learn how to work, laugh, cry, and accomplish together.

Teamwork is more than just a nice idea. It is a compelling vehicle for executive growth and better quality. It represents the means of survival. Failing the challenge of teamwork (which, by the way, includes *inter*team work) is the guarantor of mediocrity or worse. Because you care about your business, this is not an option.

APPENDIX D

The Cox Team-Achievement Inventory

RATING TEAM-ACHIEVEMENT VALUES

Indicate the extent to which the statements below apply to your management group. Circle one number for each item.

MISSION/GOALS
1. Mission and goals are clear to all and believed in; sense of the "we feeling" prevails.

1 Virtually Never	2 Seldom	3 Some-times	4 Usually	5 Virtually Always

INITIATIVE TAKING
2. Problems are carefully assessed before alternatives are proposed and their consequences considered; initiatives address basic causes rather than treating symptoms.

1 Virtually Never	2 Seldom	3 Some-times	4 Usually	5 Virtually Always

INVOLVEMENT

3. All members participate; their ideas are sought and listened to; no individual or subgroup dominates while others remain silent/inactive.

1 Virtually Never   2 Seldom   3 Sometimes   4 Usually   5 Virtually Always

FEELINGS/EMOTIONAL INVESTMENT

4. Feelings are freely expressed and accepted as legitimate, receive empathic responses.

1 Virtually Never   2 Seldom   3 Sometimes   4 Usually   5 Virtually Always

LEADERSHIP/FACILITATION

5. Leadership functions are spread around; no one person or subgroup tyrannizes; group committed to distinctive performance by acting on its strengths; maintains service orientation.

1 Virtually Never   2 Seldom   3 Sometimes   4 Usually   5 Virtually Always

TRUST/CANDOR

6. Members trust each other; they share self, time, and information in a way they don't with others; give and appreciate constructive feedback and encouragement; humor (not joking or needling) is prevalent.

1 Virtually Never   2 Seldom   3 Sometimes   4 Usually   5 Virtually Always

DECISION MAKING

7. Common ground is sought and evaluated for high standards before a decision is made; however, diverse opinions are invited to frame discussion and improve alternatives; needed decisions not postponed; decisions supported when made.

1 Virtually Never   2 Seldom   3 Sometimes   4 Usually   5 Virtually Always

RESOURCEFULNESS AND GROWTH

8. Timely, effective response to demands placed on group; experimentation urged; rigid roles shunned; yet change for change's sake is avoided; individuals stretch themselves by seeking new tasks.

1 Virtually Never   2 Seldom   3 Sometimes   4 Usually   5 Virtually Always

Inquiries and additional orders for
the *Cox Team-Achievement Inventory*
should be addressed to:

Allan Cox & Associates, Inc.
400 North Michigan Avenue
Chicago, IL 60611
(312) 644-2360

PRICES
1–9 copies	$2.00 each
10–99 copies	1.75 each
100–299 copies	1.50 each
300–499 copies	1.25 each
500+ copies	1.00 each

Prices do not include shipping and handling.

INDEX